Four

Theories

of Rape in

American

Society

LARRY BARON AND

MURRAY A. STRAUS

Four

Theories

of Rape in

American

Society

A STATE-LEVEL ANALYSIS

Yale University Press

New Haven and London

Designed by Sonia L. Scanlon
and set in Ehrhardt type by The Composing Room of Michigan, Inc.
Printed in the United States of America by Book Crafters, Inc., Chelsea, Michigan.

The paper in this book meets the guidelines for permanence and durability of the Committee on Production Guidelines for Book Longevity of the Council on Library Resources.

10 9 8 7 6 5 4 3 2 1

Library of Congress Cataloging-in-Publication Data
Baron, Larry.
    Four theories of rape in American society : a state-level analysis/ Larry Baron and Murray A. Straus.
        p. cm.
    Bibliography: p.
    Includes index.
    ISBN 0-300-04519-0 (alk. paper)
    1. Rape—United States—States.   2. Rape—Research—United States—Statistical methods.   3. Criminal behavior, Prediction of—   Statistical methods.   I. Straus, Murray Arnold, 1926–.   II. Title.   III. Title: 4 theories of rape in American society.
HV6561.B34   1989
364.1′532—dc20   89-5716
                                                                          CIP

To Sandra

With love, now and forever

    Larry Baron

To William H. Sewell

Whose many contributions included

teaching me the critical importance of valid

and reliable measures and how to construct them.

    Murray A. Straus

CONTENTS

List of Figures / ix

List of Tables / x

Acknowledgments / xiii

PART I   **ISSUES, METHODS, AND DATA**

1. The Cultural and Social Organizational
   Basis of Rape / 3
2. Methods and Measures / 17
3. Rape in American States and Regions / 40

PART II   **FOUR THEORIES OF RAPE**

4. Gender Inequality / 61
5. Pornography / 95
6. Social Disorganization / 125
7. Legitimate Violence / 146

PART III   **AN INTEGRATED THEORY AND
ITS IMPLICATIONS**

8. Toward an Integrated Theory of Rape / 173

APPENDIXES

A. Methods Used to Compute and
Standardize Indexes / 197
B. Correlation Matrix / 199
C. Methodological Analyses / 200
D. References to Data Sources / 208

References / 223
Index / 245

FIGURES

3.1   Rape Rates by Division and Region, 1980 and 1970 / 44

4.1   Gender Equality Index by Division and Region / 87

5.1   Mean of Sex Magazine Circulation Index by Division and
        Region / 122

6.1   Causal Model of Social Disorganization Theory / 138

6.2   Mean of Social Disorganization Index by Division and
        Region / 144

7.1   Legitimate Violence Index by Division and Region / 164

8.1   Theoretical Model of Variables Antecedent to
        Rape / 174

8.2   Reduced Model of Variables Antecedent to Rape / 182

TABLES

2.1   Comparison of Percent Black in Each Census Division Obtained by Aggregating Individuals and Averaging States, 1980 / 34

3.1   UCR Rape Rate per 100,000 Population, Arrayed in Rank Order by State, 1960, 1970, 1980 / 42

3.2   Temporal Consistency of UCR Rape Rates, 1960, 1970, and 1980 / 43

3.3   UCR Rape Rate per 100,000 Population for SMSAs, Other Cities, and Rural Areas, 1980 / 46

3.4   Correlation of Rape Rates for SMSAs, Other Cities, Rural Areas, and States, 1980 / 47

3.5a,b   Ranking of the States on Social Organizational Variables / 49

3.6   Regional Differences in Social Organization / 51

3.7   UCR Rape Rate per 100,000 Population, 1980–1982 / 52

4.1   Initial Pool of Economic Gender Equality Indicators / 66

4.2a,b   Rank Order of the States on Economic Gender Equality Indicators / 67

4.3   Regional Differences in Economic Gender Equality Indicators / 70

4.4   Reliability Analysis of Economic Gender Equality Index / 72

4.5   Initial Pool of Political Gender Equality Indicators / 74

4.6a,b   Rank Order of the States on Political Gender Equality
               Indicators / 75

4.7   Regional Differences on Political Gender Equality
               Indicators / 77

4.8   Reliability Analysis of Political Gender Equality
               Index / 78

4.9   Initial Pool of Legal Gender Equality Indicators,
               1980 / 80

4.10   States Enacting 15 Legal Equality Measures, 1980 / 82

4.11   Regional Differences in Legal Gender Indicators / 84

4.12   Reliability Analysis of Legal Gender Equality Index / 85

4.13   Rank Order of the States on Gender Equality
               Indexes / 86

4.14   Reliability Analysis of the Composite Gender Equality
               Index / 89

4.15   Correlation of Selected Characteristics of the States with
               Gender Equality Indexes / 89

5.1   Nominal Definitions of Pornography / 104

5.2   Correlation Matrix of Sex Magazines / 116

5.3   Reliability Analysis of the Sex Magazine Circulation
               Index / 117

5.4a,b   Ranking of the States in Sex Magazine Circulation / 118

5.5   Regional Differences in Sex Magazine Circulation / 120

5.6   Rank Order of the States in Sex Magazine
             Circulation / 121

6.1   Correlation Matrix of the Social Disorganization
             Indicators / 130

6.2   Reliability Analysis of the Social Disorganization
             Index / 130

6.3a,b   Ranking of the States on the Social Disorganization
             Indicators / 140

6.4   Regional Differences on Social Disorganization
             Indicators / 142

6.5   Rank Order of the States on the Social Disorganization
             Index / 143

7.1a–c   Ranking of the States on the Legitimate Violence
             Indicators / 152

7.2   Regional Differences on Legitimate Violence
             Indicators / 155

7.3   Reliability Analysis of the Legitimate Violence
             Index / 161

7.4   Correlation Matrix of the Legitimate Violence
             Indicators / 162

7.5   Ranking of the States on the Legitimate Violence
             Index / 163

8.1   Unstandardized Regression Coefficients and Standard
             Errors / 179

ACKNOWLEDGMENTS

This book is a publication of the Family Violence Research Program (FVRP) and the State and Regional Indicators Archive (SRIA), University of New Hampshire, Durham, New Hampshire. The work of the first author was supported by grants from the National Institute of Mental Health (T32MH15161 to the University of New Hampshire and 5T32MH15123 to Yale University) for postdoctoral research fellowships. A number of other grants, although not directly supporting this research, contributed importantly by enabling the Family Research Laboratory to create a true community of scholars whose support and suggestions have helped to produce not only the research described in this book, but also a number of other books and articles. These include grants from the National Science Foundation (grant SES8520232), National Institute of Justice (grant 85IJCX0030), National Center of Child Abuse and Neglect, Centers for Disease Control, Conrad Hilton Foundation, Eden Hall Foundation, and the University of New Hampshire.

This project could not have been completed without the indispensable contributions of the support staff of the FVRP and the SRIA. Sieglinde Fizz, computer specialist and program assistant for the FVRP, kept the project running smoothly from beginning to end with her word-processing skills, knack for organization, and creative resolution to innumerable problems. We are grateful to Charlene Hodgdon and Donna Wilson for typing the manuscript and providing a cheerful atmosphere in which to work. Special thanks goes to Susan Frankel and Kimberly Vogt, the archivists of the SRIA during the period of time that the data for this book were being analyzed. Without their diligent efforts at locating data and performing certain statistical analyses, this project would have been delayed indefinitely.

We are indebted to the many colleagues listed below who provided important suggestions and criticisms, even though we were not always able to follow their advice. These include Lawrence Hamilton, Arnold S. Linsky, Colin Loftin, James D. Orcutt, James Parker, Libby Piper, Albert J. Reiss, Sally K. Ward, Kirk R. Williams, Stuart Wright, Kersti Yllo, and the following members of the members of the Family Violence Research Program seminar over several years: Sharon Araji, Angela Browne, David Finkelor, Jean Giles-Simms, Gerald T. Hotaling, Valerie Hurst, Candice Leonard, David Jaffee,

Dean Knudsen, Alan Lincoln, Judy Meyers, Pat Murphy, Jim Ptacek, Dan Saunders, Richard Sebastian, and David B. Sugarman.

Development of the Legitimate Violence Index was greatly aided by discussions with Steven F. Messner during a semester when Murray Straus was at Columbia University. Dr. Messner obtained the data on television viewing rates for programs with a violent content from the A. C. Nielson Company. We appreciate their permitting us to use these data. We are particularly indebted to David Jaffee and David Sugarman, the coauthors of articles which formed the basis of two chapters. Sections of these articles, as well as parts of another previously published article, are reprinted with permission of the journals indicated.

> Chapter 4: Sugarman, David, and Murray A. Straus. 1988. "Indicators of gender equality for American states and regions." *Social Indicators Research* 20:229–270.

> Chapter 7: Baron, Larry, Murray A. Straus, and David Jaffee. 1988. "Legitimate violence, violent attitudes, and rape: A test of the cultural spillover theory." Pp. 79–110 in *Human Sexual Aggression: Current Perspectives,* edited by Robert A. Prentky and Vernon L. Quinsey. New York: New York Academy of Sciences.

> Chapter 8: Baron, Larry, and Murray A. Straus. 1987. "Four theories of rape: A macrosociological analysis." *Social Problems* 34:467–488.

Finally, we would like to express our thanks to the senior editor at Yale University Press Gladys Topkis for her enthusiastic support of this book, and Alexander Metro for his meticulous and skillful editorial work.

Part I

ISSUES, METHODS, AND DATA

THE CULTURAL AND SOCIAL ORGANIZATIONAL BASIS OF RAPE

Rape is a persistent social problem that has lately become the focus of renewed concern by both the general public and social scientists. One reason is the dramatic rise in the incidence of rape as reported in official statistics. Between the years 1960 and 1987, the number of rapes known to the police in the United States escalated from 16,860 to 91,111 (Federal Bureau of Investigation, 1968, 1988). This represents an increase of approximately 440% over twenty-eight years. Reported rapes increased at a faster pace than any other major violent crime (that is, murder, aggravated assault, and robbery) in this time period. Perhaps an even more important reason for the current concern with rape is the fact that women are the predominant victims; thus, rape has become a focal point for feminist scholarship and feminist action.

Our interest in doing research on rape was influenced by two additional factors. One is the theoretical assumption that has guided much of our work in the Family Violence Research Program[1] at the University of New Hampshire: various forms of violence are related to one another and to characteristics of society, including historical circumstances, cultural norms and values, and aspects of social organization such as the age structure, the distribution of wealth, and sexual inequality.[2]

1. The Family Violence Research Program at the University of New Hampshire began about 1970 and has become a leading center for research on this issue. Twenty-four books and over 150 articles have been published during this period. More than 40 scholars have contributed to the program in the form of authorship or coauthorship of one or more of these works. A program bibliography and list of reprints available for distribution may be obtained from the Family Research Laboratory, University of New Hampshire, Durham, N.H. 03824.

2. A word needs to be said about some of the main concepts employed in our *structural analysis* of rape in the United States. Our conception of structural analysis and the terminology for that analysis is based on the work of Robin Williams (1970:21–46) and is also roughly consistent with the usage followed by Wallace (1983:13–49). Specifically, *social structure* is used as a general term which encompasses two main types of social structure. The first type, *social organization*, refers to the interactional patterns and organizational structure of a social unit, such as the age, sex, and racial composition of a university or a nation, the regularity with which students attend lectures,

A further factor leading to the present study is our affiliation with the State and Regional Indicators Archive at the University of New Hampshire. This led us to examine criminal violence in American states and regions and to compare the rates of rape in those areas. We found that the states with high rape rates have several times more rapes per capita than the states with the lowest incidence of rape. And this has been the case for many years. In 1982, for example, the number of rapes known to the police in Alaska was 85.4 per 100,000 population, compared to 12.5 per 100,000 population in Iowa (Federal Bureau of Investigation, 1985).

The reasons for differences of this magnitude need to be understood. They could simply reflect the fact that these counts represent rapes reported to the police rather than all rapes. It is possible, for example, that Nevada, Alaska, and California do not have higher rates of rape than North Dakota, Maine, and Iowa but have a larger proportion of women who are willing to report sexual assault to the police. But there is no firm evidence that more complete reporting exists in high rape-rate states like Nevada and Alaska than in low rape-rate states like North Dakota and Iowa. For the most part our analyses suggest that the differences in rapes reported to the police reflect real differences among the states. This issue is examined in greater detail in chapters 2 and 8.

If we assume that the wide variation among the states in rapes reported to the police does reflect actual differences in the incidence of rape, it is important to understand what could account for these large differences. This is a critical question for sociology as a disciple since the answer can provide insights into the nature of human society. Consequently, the present study uses a *macrosociological* approach and empirically assesses theories that might explain the wide variation among states in the incidence of rape.[3]

---

and the degree of social differentiation including hierarchical stratification. A possible source of confusion stems from the fact that many authors use the term *social structure* to refer to the specific type of structure we call social organization. The second type of social structure is the culture or *cultural structure* of a social unit. Following Williams' conceptualization, we are mainly concerned with cultural norms and values. These provide a blueprint that guides the social organization of society but does not determine it. Finally, it is assumed that social structures are in a constant state of change, as is true of all *social systems*. In the actual operation of a social system, new norms and values tend to emerge as codifications of the actual organizational structure, and new organizational and interactional structures are created in accordance with preexisting norms and values.

3. Theodorson and Theodorson (1969) define macrosociology thus: "The study of large-scale social systems and patterns of interrelationships within and between these systems, including, for example, national and international forms of social organization." A macrosociological analysis entails gathering data and testing hypotheses on large-scale systems such as cities, states, and nations, as compared to microsociology, which uses individuals or small scale systems (e.g., families) as the unit of analysis.

The theoretical perspectives guiding this work reflect long-standing sociological approaches to explaining crimes of violence, such as *impoverishment* and *economic inequality* (Bailey, 1984; Blau and Blau, 1982; Loftin and Hill, 1974; Schwendinger and Schwendinger, 1983; Smith and Bennett, 1985; K. R. Williams, 1984), *cultural support for violence* (Amir, 1971; Baron and Straus, 1988, Curtis, 1975; Messner, 1983; Wolfgang and Ferracuti, 1967), and *social disorganization* (Blau and Blau, 1982; Bursik, 1988; Crutchfield, Geerken, and Gove, 1982; Shaw and McKay, 1931; M. D. Smith and Bennett, 1985; Thomas and Znaniecki, 1927). We have also drawn upon the ideas of feminist writers, especially those pertaining to the relationship between *sexual inequality, pornography,* and rape (Brownmiller, 1975; Clark and Lewis, 1977; Greer, 1973; Griffin, 1971; Medea and Thompson, 1974; Russell, 1975, 1984).

Although we think of this study as "basic research" in the sense that it is focused mainly on theories that purport to explain why women are at greater risk of being raped in some states than in others, the research was also prompted by the belief that the findings might be useful in reducing or mitigating the high incidence of rape in American society. Ironically, the fact that some states have more than five times the per capita numbers of rapes than other states is a source of hope. Perhaps an understanding of why rape occurs so much more often in some states can suggest ways of reducing the national average rape rate to a figure even lower than that found in the Dakotas.

THEORIES OF RAPE

The primary objective of this research is to provide empirical data on theories which have been put forward as explanations for rape. Following the suggestions of several feminist writers, we will investigate the argument that rape is a function of such factors as the patriarchal domination of women and the prevalence of pornography. We also analyze several other theories which have been suggested as accounting for the differences among social groups in the incidence of rape. They include the age structure of the population, economic inequality, the sex ratio, social disorganization, and implicit norms approving of violence.

Feminist Theories

PATRIARCHY AND RAPE. Fundamental to the feminist view of rape is that violence against women, both sexual and nonsexual, is an expression of a patriarchal (male dominant) social system (Brownmiller, 1975; Clark and

Lewis, 1977; Russell, 1975, 1982; Sanday, 1981). The subjugation of women by men is seen as built into the organization of society—in the opportunity and reward structure—so that women are systematically disadvantaged in respect to attaining valued socioeconomic resources on which the perpetuation of male power depends. Thus, rape is construed as integral to the historic powerlessness of women in male-dominated societies.

Cross-cultural evidence for this view has been offered by Sanday (1981), who hypothesized that the incidence of rape would vary according to the degree of power and status attributed to women in tribal societies. She found a high incidence of rape in societies where women are excluded from positions of power and their contributions to the functioning of society are assigned little significance. By contrast, in societies based on the relatively equal distribution of power, mutual respect, and appreciation for the contribution that women make to society, rape is infrequent or almost nonexistent.

Others have suggested that rape is a manifestation of the asymmetrical pattern of male-female sex-role socialization in which males are taught to be aggressive and dominant while females are taught to be passive and submissive (Cherry, 1983; Greer, 1973; Griffin, 1971; Russell, 1975; K. Weis and Borges, 1977). The argument is that normal sex-role socialization is responsible for shaping men into assailants and women into victims. As Weis and Borges (1977:44) point out: "Rooted in a social structure which is characterized by male domination, the socialization processes of the male and female act to mold women into victims and provide the procedure for legitimizing them in this role."

Research indicates that the belief in traditional sex roles is correlated with attitudes endorsing violence toward women as well as aggression against women. In one study, McConahay and McConahay (1977) examined seventeen primitive cultures from the Human Relations Area Files and found a higher degree of violence in cultures marked by an inflexible sex-role system. In another study, Burt (1980) interviewed a representative sample of 598 Minnesota adults and found that the belief in sex-role stereotypes is positively correlated with the endorsement of rape myths, attitudinal support for violence against women, and the belief that sexual relationships are necessarily deceptive, manipulative, and exploitative. Burt's findings have been corroborated by Check and Malamuth (1983), who found that college students who scored high on Burt's Sex Role Stereotype Scale were more likely to become sexually aroused by rape depictions and to report a greater likelihood of raping than were those who did not hold stereotypical beliefs.

Early feminist writing on rape emphasized that rape functions as an instrument of social control whereby "all men keep all women in a state of fear"

(Brownmiller, 1975:15; see Griffin, 1971, for several parallel statements). While Brownmiller has been amply criticized for her hyperbolic indictment of *all* men (Curtis, 1976; Elshtain, 1976–77; Geis, 1977; Schwendinger and Schwendinger, 1983), there is evidence that rape and the fear of rape act to restrict the behavioral options of women and prevent their full participation in society (Gordon and Riger, 1989; Riger and Gordon, 1981; Warr, 1985).

The feminist literature suggests, then, that rape and the fear of rape are a reflection of a sexual-stratification system in which women are subordinate members. Although feminist writers agree that rape is an effort to keep women subordinate, there might be disagreement about whether rape will be positively or negatively related to the status of women. Russell (1975) maintains that some men rape because they feel threatened by the women's movement and the prospect of women's obtaining equality. Thus, the desire of feminist women to break out of traditional sex roles may anger men and increase the number of rapes. In Russell's (1975:14) words: "Rape is the way some men express their hostility to women. More threatened male egos may mean more rapes."

The empirical measure that was developed to gauge the degree of patriarchal domination in society is called the Gender Equality Index. This index measures the extent to which women have parity with men in three spheres of life: economic, political, and legal. The Gender Equality Index makes it possible to examine the extent to which male-dominant social structures increase the risk of rape.

PORNOGRAPHY AND RAPE. A central assumption of the feminist antipornography movement is that pornography inspires violence against women. Antipornography feminists contend that pornography sexually objectifies women, eroticizes violence, and fosters male dominance (Barry, 1979; Dworkin, 1979; MacKinnon, 1984; Ratterman, 1982). It is further claimed that depictions of sexual violence are now standard pornographic fare and that men exposed to such images are likely to model the behavior portrayed (Dworkin, 1979; Longino, 1980; Morgan, 1980).

The feminist contention that pornography causes rape is at odds with the 1970 Report of the Commission on Obscenity and Pornography. The findings of the various researchers, who used a variety of methodologies, research designs, and samples in their studies, are startling in their similarity. The commission felt that the weight of evidence indicated that there is no relationship between exposure to pornography and the incidence of sex crimes.

Since the publication of the 1970 commission report, three more government commissions have investigated the linkage between pornography and rape (see Einsiedel, 1988). In 1979 the British Committee on Obscenity and Film Censorship came to the conclusion that "there does not appear to be any strong evidence that exposure to sexually explicit material triggers off anti-social behavior" (B. Williams, 1979:60). The Frazer Committee on Pornography and Prostitution in Canada published its final report in 1985 and concluded that pornography is not causally related to the incidence of sex crimes (Report of the Special Committee on Pornography and Prostitution, 1985:99). The most recent government study was conducted in the United States and is known as the Meese Commission Report on Pornography (Attorney General's Commission on Pornography, 1986). The Meese Commission departed from all previous commissions in concluding that most pornography leads to sexual violence. This conclusion was reached despite the fact that the research is inconsistent with the commission's allegations of harm (for criticism of the Meese Commission Report see Baron, 1987; Lab, 1987; Linz, Donnerstein, and Penrod, 1987; Lynn, 1986a; Nobile and Nadler, 1986; T. W. Smith, 1987; Vance, 1986; West, 1987).

For obvious ethical reasons there is no research that directly examines the relationship between exposure to pornography and rape. In the last ten years, though, there has been a substantial amount of laboratory research on the effects of pornography on aggressive behavior (Donnerstein, Linz, and Penrod, 1987; Malamuth and Donnerstein, 1982). In what has become a standard design in most of these experiments, previously angered male subjects are exposed to either neutral stimuli (for example films that are nonsexual and nonviolent) or stimuli with varying degrees of sexual (for example, a couple having intercourse) and/or violent content (for example, a rape), and later given the opportunity to act aggressively toward a female associate of the experimenter. Aggression has been tested in a number of ways, among them the Buss shock apparatus, which gives the subjects the illusion that they are actually inflicting painful shocks. The experimenter then compares the level, duration, or number of shocks delivered by the subjects according to the type of stimuli that they were exposed to. The results of this body of research indicate that *pornography without violent content diminishes aggression, whereas pornography with violent content increases aggressive behavior* (for a detailed review of this literature see Donnerstein, Linz, and Penrod, 1987). It seems reasonable to conclude, then, that it is the violent content rather than the sexual content that facilitates aggression.

The issue, however, is far from settled. Almost all the new research on pornography and rape consists of laboratory experimental studies (for three exceptions see Court, 1984; Kutchinsky, 1988; and Scott, 1985). As excellent as these experimental studies are, the external validity of the findings is unknown. Furthermore, none of these studies addresses the social structural conditions which are at the heart of the feminist theory of rape. That is to say, the theories and conclusions of feminist analysis are about the characteristics of societies (such as sexist norms and sexual stratification), but most of the available research is based on data describing the characteristics of individual persons rather than data on social units. It follows that an adequate test of feminist propositions demands the use of societal level data and the measurement of theoretically relevant variables. The present study is intended to provide such an analysis. This will be done by investigating data on rape, pornography, and sexual inequality in each of the fifty states.

In order to study the affects of pornography at the societal level, we constructed a Sex Magazine Circulation Index, which summarizes the circulation rates of eight of the most widely read sexually explicit magazines (for example, *Playboy, Penthouse,* and *Hustler*). The Sex Magazine Circulation Index was designed especially for the present study and allows us to examine the relationship between state-to-state differences in the amount of mass-circulation pornography and state-to-state differences in the rape rate.

Cultural Support for Violence

Although feminist theories have been the most important recent contributions to explaining group differences in the incidence of rape, there are many other explanations which need to be investigated. A distinctive feature of this study is what we call *cultural spillover* theory. This theory is based on the idea that rape may be influenced by the implicit or explicit approval of violence in various areas of life such as education, the mass media, or sports. Cultural spillover theory predicts a carryover or diffusion from social contexts in which the use of violence is socially approved to social contexts in which the use of violence is considered illegitimate or criminal.

An illustration of cultural spillover theory comes from LeVine's (1977) analysis of rape among the Gusii of southwestern Kenya. According to LeVine, male sexual aggression is a normatively approved aspect of marital sexuality in Gusiiland. Gusii men are encouraged to be sexually violent toward their wives and to inflict pain during intercourse as a sign of sexual prowess. Since the rape rate in Gusiiland is comparatively high, LeVine surmises that the marital sexual script, which encourages men to force sex on their wives, is carried over into premarital relationships, where it is considered illegitimate. LeVine (1977:221) concludes: "Rape committed by Gusii men can be seen as an extension of this legitimate pattern to illegitimate contexts under the pressure of sexual frustration."

One of the contributions of the present study is that we developed a Legitimate Violence Index to measure state-to-state variations in culturally approved forms of violence. The Legitimate Violence Index is composed of indicators of noncriminal and vicarious violence and allows us to estimate the extent to which such cultural support for violence is associated with rape.

Social Disorganization

The concept of social disorganization is part of a tradition going back to the work of the Chicago school of sociology, which focused on the disruptive influences of immigration, urbanization, and industrialization (Ogburn, 1922; Park, Burgess, and McKenzie, 1967; Thomas and Znaniecki, 1927). Proponents of social disorganization theory argue that crime and deviance reflect conditions that disrupt the integrity of communities and weaken the regulatory power of social norms. Such disorganizing factors as migration, marital disruption, and cultural heterogeneity have been linked to criminal activities (Blau and Blau, 1982; Crutchfield, Geerken, and Gove, 1982; Shaw and McKay, 1942; D. A. Smith and Jarjoura, 1988; Stark, Doyle, and Kent, 1980). Moreover, studies show that rape rates are higher in areas where a disproportionate number of divorced and separated persons reside (Baron, Straus, and Jaffee, 1988; Blau and Blau, 1982; M. D. Smith and Bennett, 1985). Other research shows that geographical mobility is associated with rape (Crutchfield, Geerken, and Gove, 1982). To the extent that marital disruption and migration are disorganizing factors, such conditions may reduce social constraints against rape.

A Social Disorganization Index was created to gauge the level of instability in society. This measure has the advantage of combining several indicators of social disruption into a composite index. The Social Disorganization Index was constructed to test the idea that poorly integrated and unstable societies are characterized by a high rate of violent crime, including rape.

Other Sociological Explanations of Rape

In addition to the aforementioned factors, we will examine the effects on rape of other aspects of the structure of society, such as the age and racial structures of the population, the degree of urbanization, economic inequality, unemployment, and the sex ratio of the population. The inclusion of these variables in the analysis allows us to control for spuriousness when examining the relationship between the rape rate and the variables of central theoretical interest such as gender inequality, social disorganization, and the circulation of pornography.

We will seek answers to such questions as: Are state-to-state differences in rape related to differences in the age and racial structures of the population, or the ratio of men to women? Does economic inequality increase the likelihood of rape? Is there a relationship between rape and the level of social disorganization and urbanity of the states? Answers to these questions will help to identify the social organizational components of the states that alone, or in combination with other factors, may help us to understand the extent to which rape, rather than being only a form of individual deviance and criminality, grows out of the very structure of society.

MACROLEVEL RESEARCH AND EXPLANATIONS OF RAPE

It is important to emphasize that the research reported in this book uses states rather than individual persons as the unit of analysis. Our objective is to provide information which will help us to understand why the incidence of rape is so much higher in some states than in other states. Indirectly, that may suggest why some individuals rape and others do not, but such microlevel explanations are not the objective of this macrolevel study. In the following section, we will try to clarify the difference between individual and societal level research.

Individual-level Research Findings Are Not a Substitute for Macrolevel Analyses

Since many of the issues that we are investigating at the state level can also be investigated at the individual level, what is the advantage of a macrosociological study using data on states rather than data on actual rapists and their victims? The fundamental answer is that one is not a substitute for the other. The type of person who is most likely to commit rape may be quite similar in California, New York, or North Carolina. However, that does not explain why there are such large differences among these three states in *rates* of rape. As Robinson (1950) convincingly argued, the results of the two modes of investigation are not necessarily the same. Moreover, when the two types of analysis produce different results, it is not because one is correct and the other incorrect; each taps a different part of the social world. Many sociologists agree with Menzel's (1950) rejoinder to Robinson, in which he asserted that the "group or social system level" is actually more meaningful for analysis of social phenomena.

The causal processes that may be uncovered by analysis of social units (such as nations, states, and cities) are not simply a reflection of grouped individual effects. For instance, a 10% rate of unemployment affects not only the one in ten persons who may be out of work but also their families and local businesses. And it may additionally have a socially and economically depressing effect on communities throughout a state.

The example of unemployment is a particularly good one for illustrating the perils of generalizing from one level of analysis to another. Suppose that a researcher investigates the relationship between unemployment and homicide using city data. Let us further assume the results show that the higher the unemployment rate, the higher the homicide rate. Does this finding permit us to conclude that unemployed *individuals* are more likely to commit homicide? This might appear to be a plausible inference to make, but data on the characteristics of cities do not necessarily tell us anything about the social characteristics of individual murderers. We could find out if unemployed individuals are more inclined to commit homicide by interviewing a sample of convicted murders and comparing their record of employment to a group of randomly selected adults, but it would be improper to make such an inference on the basis of city-level data alone.

Perhaps a more germane example is the controversial argument that pornography causes rape. In the present study we examine the relationship between the circulation rates of soft-core pornographic magazines and the incidence of rape. If we were to find a positive association between the readership of pornography and the rape rate, would this demonstrate that the men who read pornographic magazines are more likely to rape? Again, the answer is no. A correlation between sex magazine circulation and rape does not allow us to conclude that the men who read *Hustler* or other sexually explicit magazines are the ones who rape. This relationship *might* hold on the individual level, but without collecting data on individuals it is not possible to know. Such unwarranted inferences from social units to individuals is what Robinson (1950) referred to as the ecological fallacy.

It cannot be emphasized too strongly that the focus of this research is the characteristics of states as social entities, not the characteristics of individual criminals or victims. We undertook this study in the hope that it would reveal important ways in which the states differ (or in some cases, important similarities) with respect to rape, and offer clues as to why they differ. The main focus of the study is to identify factors that might be helpful in understanding why the incidence of rape is so much greater in some states than in others.

THE PLAN OF THE BOOK

Theory and Research

SINGLE-CAUSE MODELS. One of the key theoretical and methodological problems of social science is a tendency to concentrate on theories and research which assert or imply a single factor as the cause of the phenomenon being studied. Previous research on the precursors of rape, including the variables identified in this chapter such as pornography, cultural support for violence, and the male dominant power structure, has for the most part treated these presumed antecedents in isolation from one another.

In some cases the concentration on one explanation is deliberate. This is likely to occur when the research is confounded with a social movement which has a vested interest in one particular explanation, such as the Marxist approach taken by Schwendinger and Schwendinger (1983) or the cultural feminist approach taken by Dworkin (1979). Even when the research agenda is not confounded with the agenda of a social movement, scholars can be caught up in their own theoretical position to the point where they lose sight of the true complexity of the world. Up to a certain point the narrow focus engendered by a social movement, or by a scholar with an exclusive focus on one theory, is desirable. It often takes such a commitment to persevere and develop a new perspective in sufficient depth. However, such an approach runs the risk of suggesting that there is a single causal factor at the root of the issue being investigated.

The research described in this book, although far from perfect, at least avoids the single causal factor approach. It examines the separate and combined effects of variables which are involved in some of the most widely discussed theories concerning the causes of rape. It takes up each of these variables to determine the extent to which they are related to one another, as well as to rape, and concludes with a carefully specified and empirically tested theoretical model. Each chapter develops a part of that model, and the final chapter puts the parts together and examines their relationship in a multivariate analysis.

Theory and Measurement

Chapters 4–7 have both theoretical and methodological dimensions. As will be indicated in the chapter summaries in part II, each is a theoretical analysis intended to clarify a theory and, if necessary, to reformulate the theory in a way which makes an empirical test possible. Second, as part of the process of linking theory and research, each chapter describes the methods we used to measure the central concept of the theory as a societal characteristic and, specifically, the extent to which the 50 states differ from one another in gender equality, pornography, social disorganization, and culturally legitimate violence.

We regard the measures that we developed for this study as important contributions to sociology, although some readers may find that more space is devoted to these measures than suits their taste. If this is the case, we think it reflects the fact that sociologists do not devote enough effort to developing indexes and scales and reporting them in a form that is useful to other scholars. Evidence of this is reported in Straus's analysis of measures used in research on the family (Straus, 1964; Straus and Brown, 1978). Straus found that the typical instrument in sociology of the family is based on two or three indicators (often a single indicator), and that the authors almost never report evidence of validity and seldom report reliability coefficients. That situation continues to this day, as is illustrated by our discussion of previous measures of social disorganization in chapter 6.

In his presidential address to the American Sociological Association, Blalock (1979) argued that sociology pays a heavy price for failing to invest in developing valid and reliable instruments to measure concepts that are central to its theories. Specifically, he suggested that, although sociological theories may be correct, those theories may not be confirmed by empirical studies because the measures used to test the theories are inadequate. We see our work as a contribution to overcoming that problem.

Chapter Outline

Chapter 2, Methods and Measures, is mainly of interest to those concerned with methodological issues. It describes our reasons for choosing states as the unit of analysis and discusses the methodological criticisms that have been made against state-level research. Since our data on rape are taken from the *Uniform Crime Reports* (UCR), we also examine the strengths and weaknesses of official statistics. The chapter ends with a discussion of causal inference and the potential pitfalls of using ratio variables.

Chapter 3, Rape in American States and Regions, presents information on the large differences among states and regions in the incidence of rape and the consistency of these geographic differences since 1960. The theoretical part of chapter 3 focuses on explanations which hold that rape reflects certain aspects of the way society is organized, such as the racial and economic structures, or the age and sex compositions of society. This chapter also presents information on how much of the state-to-state differences in rape are explained by these aspects of the social organization of society.

Chapter 4, Gender Inequality, develops the distinction between what we call "gender attainment" and "gender equality." The former is the *absolute* degree to which women have attained valued social characteristics, such as education, income, and health, and the latter is the *relative* degree to which women have attained these characteristics as compared to men. Thus, women in a rich state might have a high income, but an income which is nonetheless considerably lower than the income of men in their state (a high level of gender attainment but a low level of gender equality). The reverse is also possible, as in states where *both* men and women are poorly paid. The chapter also describes the methods used to construct a Gender Equality Index to measure state-to-state differences in the degree to which women have achieved equality with men. This unique index is a valuable social indicator which can be used to track changes over time as well as to test theories concerning the extent to which women approach equality with men in the key areas of political power, economic resources, and legal rights. The Gender Equality Index permits empirical research on a number of issues concerning sexual stratification, including certain components of feminist theories of rape. In addition to describing how the index was constructed, rank-order distributions, regional breakdowns, and the correlation between gender inequality and rape are reported.

Chapter 5, Pornography, focuses on the argument of antipornography feminists and presents an overview of the controversy surrounding the civil rights antipornography legislation sponsored by Catharine MacKinnon and Andrea Dworkin. The chapter includes a careful review of the long and confusing history of attempts to define pornography and provides what some have given up as hopeless—a definition. We hope that our conceptual analysis and definition will serve as a basis for future theoretical and empirical research. On the operational side, the chapter describes the Sex Magazine Circulation Index, which we used to measure state-to-state differences in the readership of pornography. State and regional differences in sex magazine circulation are reported for each of the eight sexually explicit magazines that comprise the index as well as for the overall index. This index is used to test the feminist theory that pornography contributes to a social atmosphere conducive to rape. The chapter concludes with the correlation between the circulation rate of sex magazines and the rape rate.

Chapter 6, Social Disorganization, presents one of the earliest sociological explanations of crime and deviance: the theory that social instability weakens institutional controls, thereby releasing individuals to engage in illegal activities. Over the years, several criticisms have been leveled against social disorganization theory, among them that the theory is essentially circular. We evaluate the cogency of these criticisms and attempt to elucidate the causal structure informing social disorganization theory. Unlike earlier researchers who relied on only one or two indictors to measure social disorganization, we introduce a six-item index. Perhaps the conceptual and methodological clarification that is contributed by both the causal model of social disorganization theory and the Social Disorganization Index will revive interest in a concept which may have prematurely gone out of fashion in sociology. The chapter concludes by showing the large differences among states and among regions in scores on the Social Disorganization Index, and by presenting the correlation between social disorganization and rape.

Chapter 7, Legitimate Violence, introduces cultural spillover theory, which is based on the idea that high rates of rape and other violent crimes reflect a cultural milieu that tolerates and approves of violence. Cultural support for violence is measured with two multi-indicator indexes. The first is called the Legitimate Violence Index, which consists of 12 indicators of noncriminal violence. The other is called the Violence Approval Index and is composed of 14 indicators of the social approval of violence. These two indexes enable us to examine the relationship between cultural support for violence and the incidence of rape.

Chapter 8, Toward an Integrated Theory of Rape, brings together each of the key theories for which we have empirical data in the form of a theoretical model. Multiple regression is used to estimate the relative effects of each variable in explaining state-to-state differences in the incidence of rape. The theoretical model also takes into account indirect as well as direct influences, interactions among the independent variables, and provides for an overall estimate of how much of the state-to-state variation in rape is accounted for by a linear combination of the variables tested. The chapter concludes with a discussion of the policy implications of the findings, with particular attention to the much debated question of whether restricting pornography will reduce the rape rate, and the implications of the findings for primary prevention.

2

METHODS AND MEASURES

Several aspects of the methods used in this study are controversial, especially the question of whether the states of the United States are appropriate units for sociological research, and the question of whether the Uniform Crime Reports can provide data on rape which are worth analyzing. Consequently, the first section of this chapter discusses the pros and cons of research in which states are the societal units, and the second section evaluates the Uniform Crime Reports. The third section explains the method used to compute statistics for the different regions of the United States. The fourth section, the final one of the chapter, covers a variety of methodological issues including the statistical analysis, definition of terms, and the issue of whether causal inferences can be derived from nonexperimental data.

STATES AS UNITS FOR MACROSOCIOLOGICAL ANALYSIS

Why did we choose to use states rather than cities, counties, regions or nations? Every research decision has its advantages and disadvantages, and the decision to use the 50 American states as the units for a study of the social origins of rape is no exception. The first part of this section explains the reasons for that decision. The second section is intended to inform readers about the limitations and problems of using states for research of this type and to present our evaluation of these problems.

Reasons for Research Using States

The reasons for our decision to use the American states for this research are interrelated, but they can be grouped under the following eight categories.

LARGE STATE-TO-STATE DIFFERENCES. A first consideration is whether there is enough variation among the states to make the research practical. There is little doubt that American society is becoming more uniform. One sees the same Avis and the same Holiday Inn when stepping off a plane in any part of the country. Statistical evidence for the homogenization of the United States is documented in declining coefficients of variation among states and regions for a number of variables extending back to the mid-nineteenth century (Sharkansky, 1970; Williamson, 1965).

Given this trend, is there sufficient state-to-state variance to make an explanatory effort worthwhile? Before we began this study, our preliminary investigations suggested that, despite the homogenization of America, very large differences continue to exist among the states. Furthermore, these differences occur in characteristics that are central to understanding American society and that are also of great practical importance. The statistics on state-to-state differences in rape in chapter 3 show that this is certainly the case for the central focus of this book. For example, Nevada led the rest of the country with 67.2 rapes per 100,000 population in 1980. The rate for Nevada was seven times higher than for North Dakota, the lowest ranking state, and two times higher than the national average rape rate. The other chapters of the book also contain tables which array the states in rank order with respect to a variety of factors. Almost every one of these rank-order listings illustrates the large differences which continue to characterize the states.

STATES ARE THE BASIC UNITS OF GOVERNMENT AND LAW ENFORCEMENT. The states have primary or exclusive responsibility in all spheres not allocated by the Constitution to the federal government. This includes many vital functions and institutions such as education, police, family, business, and welfare. As a practical matter, criminal law and its enforcement, and legislation regarding sexual assault in particular, are overwhelmingly a state responsibility. Although the role of the federal government has grown in respect to many state functions, states are still extremely important. Even under the system of "categorical" grants from the federal government to the states, large areas of state discretion exist and are exercised. This could well increase if the block grant system becomes more prominent.[1]

STATES ARE AN IMPORTANT BASIS OF NONGOVERNMENT SOCIAL ORGANIZATION. Many nongovernment activities are carried out on a state-by-state basis. The medical profession is, to a considerable extent, organized around state medical societies. Another example of differences among states in nongovernmental social organization is services for battered women such as shelters or safe houses. These are largely private nonprofit organizations. Yet, Kalmuss and Strauss (1983) found that the level of services per 100,000 women in some

1. Categorical grants provide funds for a specific program such as AFDC (Aid to Families with Dependent Children). Both categorical and block grants are funds which a state can use for any purpose within broad specifications such as welfare or education.

states (for example, North Dakota and Alaska) is 30 times greater than in others (for example, Arkansas and Mississippi).

STATES ARE A SOURCE OF IDENTITY AND PRIDE. Although it is difficult to document, a strong sense of identification with one's state seems to be widespread. Research is needed on how closely identified people feel with their states and how this compares with identification with one's city or region. In the absence of such data, informal evidence abounds, as illustrated by a *New York Times* article, "Colorado Feud Pits 'Native' versus 'Alien'" (August 12, 1981, p. A10). The "aliens" in this story are not Vietnamese or Mexican but migrants from other states. The article reports that "thousands of . . . Coloradoans have placed bumper stickers on their cars that bear the boastful legend 'Native.'" To the extent that there is identification with and pride in one's state of residence, states are appropriate units for macrosociological research because they are important in the social-psychological lives of their residents.

AVAILABILITY OF DATA. Even if the above were not true, states are the optimum units for this research because the data for many of the variables critical for this research are not available for units smaller than states. In some cases, such as the data on the legal status of women, jurisdiction is given to the states by the United States Constitution. Also, data on the circulation rates of the magazines used in the Sex Magazine Circulation Index are available only on the state level, and many of the indicators used in the Legitimate Violence Index and Social Disorganization Index are reported for states only. Thus, using states as the unit of analysis permits us to test theories of rape that would not be possible if we were to use data at a lower level of aggregation.

UNIFORM CRIME REPORT DATA FOR STATES ARE MORE DEPENDABLE. One of the problems with rates based on the Uniform Crime Reports (UCR) is that, despite the uniformity in definitions of crime, the UCR lacks uniformity in certain other respects. In particular, UCR data depend on the willingness of the public to report a crime, on police policy and procedures in respect to recording reports, and on the accuracy of the clerical and tabulating process used by each police department. These variables are likely to vary somewhat from city to city. In one city, various circumstances may have led to establishing a special task force on rape, and rape reports may therefore be a greater proportion of the actual number than in other cities. In another city, there may be a crackdown on residential burglaries or drunk driving, and rape may tend to be neglected. This might lead to a smaller proportion of rapes being reported than in most other cities. However, because the number of rapes reported for a state is an average of all the police departments, the state rates are less likely to be biased by a unique local circumstance than is the rape rate for a specific city or county. Thus, research on crime using UCR data on states may avoid some of the problems of UCR data when the units of study are cities.

USEFULNESS DEMONSTRATED BY PREVIOUS RESEARCH. Research using state-level data has many precedents. Although the largest part of this work has been in political science, much work has also been done in economics, sociology, and criminology. In our own discipline of sociology, a number of studies using state-level data have been published in each of the major sociological journals. Examples of this research include the study by Hicks, Friedland, and Johnson (1978) showing that the presence in a state of the headquarters of large business and labor organizations influences the extent to which a state uses its taxing and spending powers to redistribute income. A study by Jacobs and Britt (1979) showed that the greater the degree of inequality within a state, the higher the rate of violence by the police. Finally, a study by Stack (1980) revealed that the incidence of divorce was highly associated with the suicide rate. Each of these studies avoided such common methodological errors as failing to control for confounding variables or committing the ecological fallacy. All of this suggests that there is a well-established and continuing tradition of high quality research using data on American states. This is particularly true in criminology, as illustrated by the cumulative nature of research on deterrence, beginning with the pioneering study by Gibbs (1968) and continuing through progressive refinements of the model in the work of Parker and Smith (1979) and Loftin (1980).

THEORETICAL CONTRIBUTIONS. The large differences among states is a basic aspect of American society that requires explanation. Research that demonstrates correlates of the social characteristics of the states will increase our understanding of American society. Such findings can also contribute to sociology as a discipline. For instance, the material on sex magazines, status of women, and legitimate violence is intended not only to describe these much debated aspects of American society but also to contribute to theories on the social conditions that are associated with these variables.

Arguments against Using State-Level Data

As indicated earlier, there are also disadvantages to using states as the units of study. Loftin and Hill (1974) and Messner (1980, 1982, 1983), for example, have been highly critical of state-level analysis. However, the problems they point out are matters of *possible* error rather than proved sources of error; and they are also problems encountered using the units favored by Loftin and Hill, and Messner—cities, counties, and SMSAs.[2] Their criticisms focus on the following four points.

ARBITRARY BOUNDARIES. State boundaries are held to be "artificial" because in many instances they were determined when the states were largely unin-habited territories. They are also artificial in the sense that many states have cultural, political, and economic similarities with adjacent states. However, these same points are also true of cities and SMSAs. A good case could be made that the boundaries of SMSAs are even more arbitrary, since they are set by the census on the basis of criteria that include the opinions and prefer-ences of residents, city councils, or state legislatures, and in some instances go back to a time when each was a sovereign unit.

CITIES REPRESENT A MORE COHESIVE UNIT THAN STATES. The belief that cities represent a more cohesive unit than states is based on three interrelated points. First is the greater heterogeneity of states than cities; second, the greater physical size of states. For example, since it can take 8 hours to drive from one side of many states to another, people in a city have a greater opportunity to interact with one another, even though not all do. Third is the belief that cities share more symbolic elements and services than do states. For instance, it could be argued that the focus of most newspapers is the city, even though some try to serve also a part of the state, and television stations may also be primarily oriented to cities.

Although these are plausible arguments, the proponents do not provide empirical evidence in support of them, and plausible counterarguments can be made for the idea that states constitute a more legitimate social unit than cities. This is most clearly the case with regard to governmental activities. Cities, for example, exist at the sufferance of the states; that is what is meant by a city charter. Moreover, cities can levy only taxes that the state authorizes and must comply with state regulations in regard to a wide variety of functions such as education and law.

INTERNAL HETEROGENEITY. Loftin and Hill (1974) suggest that the use of a single statistic to represent a state disguises the immense variation within states. While this is certainly true, it is also true of a single statistic to represent Catholics or Jews, or working class and middle class, or any city or metro-politan area. Compared to the entire United States, states are clearly more

2. Standard Metropolitan Statistical Area (SMSA) is a concept used by the United States Census to designate a city of at least 50,000 population and the surrounding urbanized areas.

homogeneous. Yet this has not deterred work on compiling and using national statistics such as those reported in Social Indicators III (U.S. Bureau of the Census, 1980), nor has it prevented the development of cross-national comparative research, such as the highly regarded study of homicide by Archer and Gartner (1984). If researchers are willing to accept, at least for certain purposes, a single statistic to represent the entire United States and each of about 70 nations (some as heterogeneous as India), the same logic should apply to data on individual states. Thus, the question is not whether there is heterogeneity but whether the units—aggregations of individuals, such as Catholics and Jews, or social units such as nations, states, counties, and cities—are theoretically meaningful for the issue under investigation. We believe that states are meaningful units for the study of a number of issues, including rape.

It can, however, be argued that cities or SMSAs are better statistically because, being smaller units, they have less internal heterogeneity. If internal heterogeneity were the only criterion, that might be an appropriate conclusion. But since there are many criteria, such as the legal system, citizen identification, and availability of data, it does not necessarily follow that SMSAs are better than states just because they are smaller units, or that counties are better than SMSAs, cities are better than counties, precincts are better than cities, or that individuals are better than precincts because they are the smallest unit of all. If one were to follow this logic, it would rule out investigation of most societal level phenomena.

To make a claim for a particular type of unit it is necessary to demonstrate, not just assert, that the unit being advocated has characteristics which make it better suited to the issue under study than other alternatives. That is rather hard to do and is not likely to be a worthwhile exercise because one type of societal unit is not a substitute for another. When states are the units being studied, a different "reality" is being examined than when one studies individuals, cities, SMSAs, or nations. It should be clear, then, that we do not see state-level analysis as a substitute for research at other levels of analysis. Rather, replication at various levels is needed in order to achieve a more complete understanding of the causes of rape.

THE REAL SOURCE OF VARIATION IS AT A LOWER LEVEL OF AGGREGATION. A final objection to studying states is that differences among states come about because of differences among specific parts of the states being compared. For example, the high incidence of rape for Alaska might occur because the city of Fairbanks has a high rape rate, whereas the rate for the rest of the state may not be particularly high. This, however, is an unsubstantiated assertion. In fact, what research we have done on this issue suggests that this is not likely to be correct. In chapter 3 we show that the high incidence of rape in certain states tends to be characteristic of the rural areas, small cities, and also the SMSAs of those states. This is also true for other characteristics of states such as the distribution of poverty. The median income of Mississippi, for example, is low relative to other states, irrespective of whether one is comparing the rural parts of Mississippi with rural areas in other states, small cities in Mississippi with those in other states, or the SMSAs in Mississippi with those in other states.

EMPIRICAL DATA ON STATES AS UNITS FOR MACROSOCIOLOGICAL RESEARCH. A paper by Straus (1985) extended the type of analysis just mentioned in order to provide more comprehensive empirical data on the extent to which the 50 states are meaningful units for macrosociological research. Three sets of analyses were carried out.

1. All variables in the *County and City Data Book* were used to compute correlations across states between variables describing characteristics of the Standard Metropolitan Statistical Areas of each state with the identical variables describing the nonmetropolitan parts of the states. Of the 90 correlations, 85 were statistically significant, 41% had coefficients in the .50 to .79 range, and 36% were .80 or higher. The consistency and size of these correlations indicate that the metropolitan and nonmetropolitan areas within each state tend to share similar sociocultural characteristics.

2. Three analyses were carried out to provide information on the extent to which tests of hypotheses produce different results when the units are the entire state, the SMSA areas, or the non-SMSA areas; or rural versus urban areas of the states. In each case, the conclusions which one would reach from testing the hypothesis with state-level data were close to those which would be reached on the basis of the more homogeneous aggregations. For example, the hypothesis that there is little or no relationship between educational achievement and the median income of the black population was supported, irrespective of whether the hypothesis was tested with rural data, urban data, or data on the state as a whole.

3. Published research on the macrostructural correlates of homicide and rape has revealed parallel results using states, metropolitan areas, and cities. For example, both state-level and city-level studies show that poverty, income inequality, divorce, and percentage of blacks are correlated with homicide. These findings suggest that there is a "state effect" despite the internal heterogeneity and that American states are appropriate units for macrosociological research.

UNDERESTIMATION OF THE IMPORTANCE OF STATES. If, as we have tried to show, the problems and limitations of doing research on states are not significantly different from the problems and limitations of doing research on SMSAs, nations, or other social units, what could account for the fact that many researchers doubt the value of doing research using states? We suggest that the doubts arise from a belief that states are no longer important units of American society. However, since much of the chapter up to this point has focused on providing a convincing argument that the states are important units of American society, and especially important in relation to crime and criminal justice, we must ask a second question: Why, despite this, do a number of social scientists think that states are unimportant? There seem to be at least three factors at work.

1. The tremendous growth of the federal government since the 1930s has resulted in a drift of power away from the states. Federal laws and regulations have superseded many state laws, and the growth of federal administration control and financial support tends to give the impression that states are no longer important units of American society. However, despite this, states continue to exercise enormous power, especially with respect to all aspects of the legal and criminal justice system. Moreover, states are now gaining power relative to cities and other local units. This is partly due to changes in the fiscal plight of some cities. These financial difficulties have led to an increase in financial dependency on the states and an increase in the power of the states over the cities—a process that was most dramatic in New York City but is occurring nationwide (*New York Times*, 27 September 1978:1).

2. A second factor is the concentration of the population in metropolitan areas. The fact that more than two-thirds of the United States population now live in SMSAs has led to an implicit assumption that differences among SMSAs overshadow differences among states. Nevertheless, to our knowledge, no one has shown that there are greater differences among SMSAs than there are among states. Differences among SMSAs may or may not be as great as those shown for states. This is an empirical question that needs to be investigated. But even if it is true, it is not a matter of common knowledge among sociologists. Consequently, as in the case of the drift of power thesis, the idea that cities or SMSAs differ more than states cannot by itself explain the neglect of the states.

3. Finally, the detailed statistics for metropolitan and local areas from recent census reports may have preempted the attention of social scientists. However, research on states is also needed. The existence of valuable data on cities and SMSAs should not obscure the fact that the census and other public and private sources publish more information on states than any other social

unit. Research using this tremendous data resource can make a valuable contribution to understanding American society.

SUMMARY. There are clearly identifiable problems and limitations encountered in research using states as societal units. However, as indicated above, every methodology and every unit of analysis has both advantages and limitations. Considering the pros and cons summarized up to this point, we believe that the advantages of using states outweigh the disadvantages. Our view is that analysis of the states is one of several appropriate approaches to research on the social sources of rape in American society. It will clearly not provide definitive answers to the complicated issues which are involved, but neither will any other method of study. Definitive answers will come, if they come at all, from multimethod triangulation,[3] and we view this research as one leg of the triangle.

Should the District of Columbia Be Included in the Analysis?

Another issue that must be addressed is whether or not Washington, D.C., should be treated as a state and included in the analysis. Data on the District of Columbia are reported in almost all census tables and in many other governmental and private statistics as though it were a state.

There are reasons for including the District of Columbia:

1. The population is sizable; greater, in fact, than that of the seven smallest states.
2. The District of Columbia may more clearly represent a low or high level of a variable than do other states. If an important issue is the relationship between degree of urbanization and some other variable, the District of Columbia is certainly a case at the high end of the urbanization continuum.
3. Given the relatively small sample size for studies using states as the units of analysis, the loss of even one case is not to be taken lightly.

On the other hand, there are reasons for excluding the District of Columbia.

1. It lacks many of the legal, political, and social characteristics of states.
2. Although there is considerable agitation in the District to secure admission as the fifty-first state, that does not seem too likely in the near future. Even if the District of Columbia does become a state, it would

3. Multimethod triangulation refers to the confirmation of a proposition by two or more measurement processes (Webb et al., 1981).

differ from all other states in a number of ways which question whether it is a similar type of social unit. For example, it would be the only state that is also a city, the only state that has almost all black and poor citizens but at the same time contains a significant number of people with above-average education and income. It would also be the only state that is at the same time the national capital and, to a substantial extent, an international center. These characteristics exacerbate the problem of internal heterogeneity and raise even more serious questions about the utility of measures of central tendency to characterize such a bimodal population.

In view of the above, it was decided not to include the District of Columbia. This decision was also based on the absence of data for some of the items used in the indexes of key theoretical interest. In addition, the results of certain empirical analyses contributed to our decision to exclude Washington, D.C. We replicated multiple regressions of the state-level determinants of rape with and without the District of Columbia and found that including or excluding the district does not importantly effect the findings (Baron and Straus, 1984).

THE UNIFORM CRIME REPORTS DATA ON RAPE

Since the very beginning of the Uniform Crime Reporting (UCR) system in the 1930s, social scientists have had an ambivalent relationship to UCR data. The references in Hindelang's article "The Uniform Crime Reports Revisited" (1974) show that questions about validity appeared not long after the publication of the first report. Another example is O'Brien's (1983) critique of UCR data. Indeed, it is probably not an exaggeration to say that the UCR is the most frequently and strongly criticized set of criminological data. Despite the warnings about the dire consequences of using UCR data, it is probably the single most widely used source of data on crime in the United States.

The contradiction between the many criticisms and the continued use of UCR data needs to be resolved. Why does so much criminological research, including this study, rely on data which are so heavily criticized? There is no definitive answer to that question, but this section provides information intended to help readers to understand the basis for our decision to measure the incidence of rape by means of UCR data. Specifically, this section is intended to alert readers to some of the major criticisms of the UCR data and to evaluate each of these criticisms.

Problems with UCR Data

UNDERREPORTING. The most frequently cited limitation of the UCR data is that many crimes are not reported to the police and the UCR therefore presents an incomplete picture of crime in the United States (Hindelang, 1974; Savitz, 1978; J. G. Weis, 1983). Further, it is widely believed that rape is the most seriously underreported of the seven major crimes (Federal Bureau of Investigation, 1988). The fact that half or fewer of the total number of rapes committed in the United States are known to the police would not be a problem for theory-testing research if the same degree of underreporting prevailed in all states. This is because an even distribution of underreporting would not alter the relative ranking of the states in the incidence of rape. However, as explained below, a uniform degree of underreporting may not exist.

CLERICAL AND TABULATING ERRORS AND RECORDING EFFORT. Although major improvements have been made in the 50 years since the founding of the Uniform Crime Reporting system, the extent of clerical error remains a point of concern. A similar source of error is failure or refusal on the part of the police to record a crime due to either political exigencies or badly trained personnel. Differences among states in either clerical errors or in reporting procedures and effort could produce spurious findings. States that have more accurate procedures, or whose policies lead to recording a larger proportion of rapes, could artificially inflate rates of rape relative to other states. Moreover, if differences are correlated with the social characteristics of the states, completely erroneous findings could occur. For instance, if states with more accurate reporting are the more urban states, this correlated error could account for part of the higher rates of rape in urban states.

Fortunately, the use of data on states mitigates this problem since the UCR is a collation of *local* reports. Therefore, the figures for each state do not reflect a single state-reporting system. Rather, within each state, crime reporting is the responsibility of municipal and county police departments. Although many states have assumed the responsibility for collating these statistics and forwarding them to the FBI, the state per se is not the unit of primary reporting, and differences in reporting procedure and effort occur at the local level instead of at the state level. Thus, although a city or a county can have a crackdown on crime that raises the rates over what they were previously (even though there may be no increase in the true incidence rate), or can become lax in reporting, such changes are not likely to occur in many of the cities and counties of a state during the same year. In fact, while one police department is cracking down, another may (for a variety of reasons) become lax. It is therefore unlikely that state-to-state differences in rape rates reflect

differences in reporting procedures or reporting effort because local governments, not state governments, are the units for which reporting varies. Nevertheless, the possibility that there might be state-to-state differences in the
general climate of crime reporting cannot be ruled out.

LACK OF AGE STANDARDIZATION. Another methodological problem with the
UCR rape rates is that they are not standardized for state-to-state differences
in the number of men in the high rape ages of 18–24. The lack of age
standardization, like underreporting, is probably a greater problem for descriptive analyses of rape than it is for the theoretical analyses on which this
book is based. This is because there is no way to compute age-standardized or
age-specific rates from the UCR data. However, for purposes of theory testing, an alternative to age standardization is possible. This entails the use of age
as a control variable in multiple regression. We therefore include the percent
of each state's population that is between the ages of 18 and 24 (the peak ages
for both rapists and rape victims) in the regression analyses reported in chapter 8. The inclusion of this variable should deal with the threat to validity that
comes from using unstandardized crime rates.

VARIATION IN CITIZEN WILLINGNESS TO REPORT. A large percentage of rapes
are not reported to the police. Consequently, even if there were no differences
in police efficiency, erroneous state-to-state differences could arise because
of differences in the extent to which women are willing to report rape to the
police. This is a particularly critical problem for the present study because
willingness to report rape may be correlated with the independent variables of
this study as well as the dependent variable. It is not at all unreasonable to
suppose that women in states where the status of women is high will be likelier
to report a rape than in states where women have comparatively low status.
Similarly, a social climate that contributes to a high readership of sex magazines (for example, a sexually liberal milieu) might also lead a larger percentage of sexually assaulted women to report their victimization to the police than
in more sexually conservative states.

Since there are grounds for believing that some of the variation among
states may be due to such factors as coverage of the UCR system, expenditures for law enforcement, and the willingness of women to report rather than
actual differences among the states, we conducted several methodological
analyses of the UCR data. Appendix C reports our research on the extent to
which the use of UCR data threatens the validity of the findings reported in
this book.

Reporting Effects: Comparison of UCR and NCS Rates

The National Crime Survey (NCS) data on rape victimization can be compared with UCR data on rapes known to the police to help evaluate whether the results reported in this book are a function of error in the UCR crime rates. The NCS is an annual household survey that began in 1972. It uses a national probability sample of roughly 60,000 private residences as its data base. The purpose of the NCS is to reveal the hidden volume of crime that escapes the attention of law enforcement agencies and to provide a more accurate estimate of victimization (for details see Garofalo and Hindelang, 1977; J. G. Weis, 1983). Since the NCS data are gathered by uniform methods in each state and are more complete than the UCR (the rates for rape are about double those found in the UCR), it may be less subject to state-to-state differences in reporting error.

On the other hand, the NCS is far from a perfect measure of the extent of rape. There are in fact numerous problems with the NCS data (see the discussion and references in O'Brien, 1983; Russell, 1983). For example, record check studies reveal many crimes reported to the police which are not reported to the NCS interviewers (about one-third in the case of rape). Consequently, one cannot take state-to-state differences in NCS rates as necessarily more valid than state-to-state differences in UCR rates. Specifically, one cannot interpret a correlation of less than 1.0 between the UCR and NCS rape rates as a measure of error in the UCR. It could reflect error in the UCR, error in the NCS, or more likely error in both. Paradoxically, a perfect correlation (or near-perfect correlation such as .95) could indicate that the UCR has the same bias as the NCS and that the objectives of the NCS were not being achieved. Nevertheless, because both are intended to be measures of roughly the same phenomenon, the validity of the findings in this book would be questioned if there is not at least a moderate correspondence between the two.

NCS data for states are available only for the ten largest states. Although this is too small a number for some analyses, the simple correlations are informative. We found a correlation of .49 between the NCS rape rate and the 1980 UCR rape rate for all rape victimizations (Baron and Straus, 1984). Given the fact that the NCS measures rape as a residual category, we suggest that a correlation of .49 is about as high as can be expected. Consequently, state variations in the UCR rates are not just a function of differences in the willingness of rape victims to get involved in the criminal justice system, or state-to-state differences in police reporting policies and procedure. Rather, states with high UCR rape rates probably do have a higher incidence of rape than states with a low UCR rape rate.

Evaluation of the Criticisms of UCR Data

UNDERREPORTING. The effect of underreporting depends on the purpose for which the data are used. We will distinguish between two broad types of uses: (1) administrative or policy decisions based on the volume of crime, and (2) theory testing based on the relationship among several variables.

When UCR data are used by police and other public officials as one of the bases for allocating resources for prevention and control measures or for victim assistance programs, any underreporting is a serious problem. If public officials were to rely only on UCR data there would be an underallocation of resources corresponding to the degree of underreporting. This problem could be especially serious in the case of rape because underreporting is thought to be greater for rape than other serious crime. However, Archer and Gartner's (1984:39) comparison of UCR data with NCS data reveals that the under-reporting of rape is about the same as for robbery and aggravated assault. In fact, the most underreported crimes are minor assaults and property crimes, not rape.

Even if the underreporting is not greater for rape than other major crimes, there can be no doubt that there is serious underreporting for all crimes, with the exception of murder (Cantor and Cohen, 1980; Hindelang, 1974). What are the implications of this for a study of the correlates of crime? The critical issue is not the amount of underreporting but differential underreporting; that is, whether the degree of underreporting is the same from state to state. If only one-quarter of the actual number of rapes were reported in all states, the correlation coefficients would be the same as if all rapes were reported to the police. If there are differences among the states in the extent to which rapes are reported to the police, the states with a high rape rate might not have more rapes than states with low UCR rape rates, only more reported rapes. Conse-quently, as previously indicated, underreporting poses the most serious threat to the validity of research using UCR data because of the possibility that the degree of underreporting is correlated with the independent variables of the study.

A study of Hindelang (1974) provides relevant information on this issue. Hindelang compared 1965 UCR data with comparable data from a National Opinion Research Center (NORC) victimization survey of 10,000 house-holds. Although the NORC data did not include enough cases to compute rates for each state, Hindelang was able to perform regional comparisons and comparisons for cities and rural areas, and to compute the percentage of crimes that were rapes. The results showed similar regional distributions and comparable rural and urban distributions for rape and other crimes of violence. Hindelang also found that rapes occupied the same position relative to other crimes in both the UCR and the victimization survey. The Hindelang study gives us no reason to doubt the accuracy of the UCR data with respect to the relative ranking of the states in rates of rape. This finding is most important for the present study because our concern is to explain the variation among states in the incidence of rape, not to ascertain the absolute number of rapes.

In another methodological study, Gove et al. (1985) conducted a comprehensive empirical and theoretical analysis of the validity of official crime statistics. They found that the perceived seriousness of a crime is the major factor in explaining whether victims report to the police and the police officially record the crime. This suggests that the UCR represents an accurate measure of those crimes that victims and the police view as the most serious violations of the law. Gove et al. do not present any evidence that would undermine our confidence in the UCR data. In fact, their conclusion bolsters our confidence: "It is clear that the UCR provide a valid indicator of the index crimes and can be used in studies of the relationship between crime and social structural characteristics and in etiological studies"(Gove et al. 1985:490-491).

ADDITIONAL EVIDENCE THAT THE UCR DATA ARE USEFUL FOR THEORY TESTING. None of the studies cited up to this point has uncovered evidence of differential underreporting or other correlated errors that could affect the results of this study. In addition, there are two more types of evidence which encouraged us to proceed using UCR data.

REGIONAL SIMILARITY. The similarity of rape rates within each of the nine regional census divisions suggests that, whatever factors are responsible for the variation among states in rape, the differences are not solely attributable to the reporting systems of individual states (see chapter 3 for regional and divisional breakdowns of the rape rate). Because the states have separate reporting systems, as do the police departments within each state, they are not subject to any one governor or other state official who might have sufficient influence to exert an upward or downward pull on the rape rate. Thus, the fact that all states in the Pacific division tend to have a high incidence of rape suggests that their high rates reflect something in the social organization or culture of these states rather than something in their method of reporting crime.

CORRELATION WITH HOMICIDE. Those who have analyzed the validity of UCR crime data are virtually unanimous that homicide is the crime which is least subject to error (Cantor and Cohen, 1980; Hindelang, 1974). Practically all homicides come to the attention of the police. State-to-state differences in homicide therefore represent real differences instead of artifacts of the reporting system. This fact enables a test of the idea that state-to-state differences in the UCR rates for other violent crimes also reflect real differences. If that is the case and if there are similarities in the social process which produce violent crime, there should be a correlation between the UCR homicide rate and the UCR rates for other violent crimes. This is exactly what we found (Baron and Straus, 1984). Specifically, there are substantial correlations among the rates of homicide, rape, and aggravated assault. This, combined with the findings that the societal characteristics found to be associated with homicide are virtually identical to those found to be associated with rape, strongly suggests that state-to-state variation in the UCR rape rate reflects whatever factors produce the state-to-state variation in homicide, and not the operation of the reporting system.

STATISTICS ON REGIONS

There are several ways of grouping the states into regions (Sharkansky, 1970). Each has its advantages and disadvantages. We chose the Bureau of the Census categories because their wide use makes for greater comparability. Actually, the Census Bureau has two classifications: (1) states are divided into four regions, and (2) within each region there are two or three divisions. The states in each region and division are:

NORTHEAST
>   *New England:* Maine, New Hampshire, Vermont, Massachusetts, Rhode Island, Connecticut.
>   *Middle Atlantic:* New York, New Jersey, Pennsylvania.

NORTH CENTRAL
>   *East North Central:* Ohio, Indiana, Illinois, Michigan, Wisconsin.
>   *West North Central:* Minnesota, Iowa, Missouri, North Dakota, South Dakota, Nebraska, Kansas.

SOUTH
>   *South Atlantic:* Delaware, Maryland, Virginia, West Virginia, North Carolina, South Carolina, Georgia, Florida.

East South Central: Kentucky, Tennessee, Alabama, Mississippi
West South Central: Arkansas, Louisiana, Oklahoma, Texas.
WEST
Mountain: Montana, Idaho, Wyoming, Colorado, New Mexico, Arizona,
Utah, Nevada.
Pacific: Washington, Oregon, California, Alaska, Hawaii.

Alternative Methods of Computing Regional Statistics

Although we use the census groupings of states into regions and divisions, the data for regions and divisions reported in this book differ from the census data because our figures are the *mean of the states* in each region or division, irrespective of the fact that some states are much larger than others. We followed this procedure because the basic conceptual framework of the study is the states as units of American society. By contrast, the basic focus of the census is on individual people, families, and households. Consequently, the census data on regions weight each state according to the number of people, families, and households in each state. Sometimes the results are almost identical. Sometimes they are quite different. This is illustrated by table 2.1, which shows the percentage of the population who are black in each census division using the population of each division as the denominator, compared to the percentage of blacks for the states in the division divided by the number of states in the division.

The different meaning of the two methods of calculating each region can be seen by looking at the figures for the Pacific region. The difference between the census figures and our figures occurs because California has 74.4% of the population in the Pacific region. Thus, the census figures on the Pacific region are largely figures for California. The Census Bureau's method is acceptable as long as it is desirable to make the population the center of interest. Approximately 6.3% of the residents in this region were black in 1980. However, if we want to get a picture of the states in this region, this is far too high a number. On the average, these states had only half that percentage of blacks (3.4%).

What may be concluded from this is that each method of computing figures for a region has both advantages and disadvantages; there is no one preferred method. The method of choice depends on one's purpose. Since the conceptual focus of this research is the states as societal units, we believe that the best method is to use the states, rather than individual persons, as the units for the regional figures.

Table 2.1

Comparison of Percent Black in Each Census Division Obtained
by Aggregating Individuals and Averaging States, 1980

	Data Aggregation	
Division	Individuals	Mean of States
New England	3.8	2.5
Middle Atlantic	11.9	11.7
East North Central	10.9	9.8
West North Central	4.6	3.2
South Atlantic	20.7	19.3
East South Central	19.6	20.9
West South Central	14.9	16.1
Mountain	2.4	2.0
Pacific	6.3	3.4

THEORETICAL MODELS AND MULTIPLE REGRESSION

A considerable portion of this book is devoted to showing rank-order distributions, regional breakdowns, and correlation coefficients. No special explanation is needed for these statistics. However, the key theoretical and empirical
section of the study, presented in chapter 8, relies on multiple regression.
This raises the perennially difficult question concerning the extent to which
one can make causal inferences from cross-sectional data, and the sense in
which the term "test" and other related terms are used.

Causal Inference

Davis (1985) and Hirschi and Selvin (1967) identify three basic requirements
necessary for making inferences about cause and effect from nonexperimental
data. First, there must be a statistically reliable association between the independent and dependent variable. Second, the independent variable must
occur prior in time to the dependent variable. Third, the relationship must not
be the result of confounding with some other variable. If these three criteria
apply, it does not prove a causal relationship, but it does indicate that the study
has resulted in findings which are consistent with a causal relationship.

STATISTICAL SIGNIFICANCE. Since this research uses the entire universe of American states, it can be argued that there is no need to compute tests of significance. Strictly speaking, that is correct. However, tests of significance are appropriate if one regards the data as representing a hypothetical universe of events over time and of similar societal conditions (Hagood and Price, 1952:293). We also computed tests of significance because it provides a convenient and meaningful standard against which to judge the findings as a deviation from purely random events. Tests of significance compare the findings to those which could occur if random data rather than real data were entered into the equations. We will regard a result as statistically reliable only if the statistic could occur by chance fewer than 5 times out of 100 tests. Tests of significance will vary according to what is appropriate for each type of analysis. For instance, analysis of variance (ANOVA) is used to test the significance of the difference among regions, whereas t tests are used for regression coefficients.

CAUSAL ORDER. Causal order is the most problematic aspect of the statistical analysis used in this research. What complicates the choice of a particular causal model is that the sequence of variables cannot be decided simply on the basis of the year in which the data were gathered. Even when the data for an independent variable refer to a period prior to the year for the dependent variable, the causal order requirement is not necessarily met because the variables may refer to ongoing characteristics of society which preceded the year in which the data were gathered. For example, the high 1980 rape rate in Alaska is not something which suddenly occurred. As will be shown in chapter 3, Alaska and other states with a high incidence of rape have been at the top of the distribution at least since 1960. Similarly, in 1979 Alaska had the highest circulation rate in the nation of sexually explicit magazines. Certainly, men in Alaska did not suddenly discover *Hustler* in 1979. Consequently, one cannot unequivocally assert that the necessary temporal sequence exists just because we are using 1979 data on sex magazine circulation and data on the average number of rapes for a subsequent year or years.[4] Thus, a positive correlation between the circulation of sex magazines and rape does not provide evidence that reading sex magazines necessarily influences the rape rate. Such a correlation could just as logically indicate that a high incidence of rape contributes to a high readership of sex magazines.

Similarly, the referent years for the independent and dependent variables

4. As will be explained in chapter 3, we decided to use the three-year average rape rate for 1980–82 in the computation of correlations and regression coefficients. In cases where different rape rates were used, we make note of it in the body of the text.

can be identical, but this does not automatically violate the causal order requirement. If 1980 census data on the percent of the population with income below the poverty level is correlated with 1980 data on rape, one can be reasonably sure that the proportion of poor families predated 1980. On the other hand, it is just as likely that the magnitude of rape in a state also predated 1980.

One further example will illustrate how ambiguous the causal order situation can be for research of this type. Suppose this study had used 1975 data on poverty or sex magazine circulation and 1980 data on rape. Would that meet the causal order requirement? Not necessarily because, as the previous examples show, these are variables which for the most part represent ongoing characteristics of society which preceded the referent year. Given these characteristics of the data, there is no way of being sure that the independent variables actually preceded the dependent variables. The most one can say is that the data used in this research do not violate the causal order requirement in any obvious way.

NONSPURIOUS RELATIONSHIPS. It is widely believed that state-to-state variation in the types of phenomena which form the focus of this research, such as rape, pornography, and the status of women, does not reflect real differences in the unique characteristics of the states. Rather the differences are held to be a function of other social characteristics, such as the degree of urbanization, economic inequality, or the racial composition of the states. This research gives us an opportunity to test these possibilities.

If the results show that such factors as sexual inequality, readership of pornography, and cultural support for violence explain a significant portion of the large state-to-state variation in rape, it is important evidence supporting the view that rape is rooted in the social organization of society, as opposed to the view that rape is only the personal aberration of individuals. At the same time, we wanted to be sure that the findings are not simply a reflection of confounding with other aspects of society such as the sex ratio, age structure, racial composition, and income inequality. For instance, our conceptualization of the status of women is based on the idea that gender inequality has an effect on rape independent of the variables representing the sociodemographic structure of society. Consequently, the multiple regression analyses included age, income inequality, urbanization, and other variables as controls. The resulting regression coefficients indicate the degree of association between the status of women and rape, after subtracting out any confounding with these other aspects of social organization.

SPECIFICATION ERROR. Specification error refers to defects in the theoretical model being tested (Asher, 1980; J. Cohen and P. Cohen, 1983; Pedhazur, 1982). There are three general sources of specification error: (1) violation of the assumptions guiding regression, such as curvilinearity or abnormal distributions; (2) inclusion of superfluous variables in the regression equation; and (3) exclusion of essential variables from the regression equation. Although a model can never be perfectly specified, if a coherent theory is used to guide the analysis it reduces the likelihood of misspecifying the model. In order to guard against specification error, independent variables were chosen on the basis of theoretical and empirical work on the precursors of criminal violence. Additionally, all combinations of independent and dependent variables were checked for deviations from linearity, outliers, skewness, and unequal variances among the variables (see appendix C for details).

Terminology

Researchers who report findings based on multiple regression customarily refer to *testing* a model and use such terms as *effect* and *explain* to describe the results. It is important for readers to understood, though, that since we are using cross-sectional data, the regression coefficients or the coefficients of multiple determination (multiple R^2) do not provide evidence of a cause-effect relationship.

TESTING A MODEL. When we report the test of a theoretical model, the results need to be interpreted with considerable caution. The finding of a statistically significant relationship consistent with a theoretical model means only that the data fit the model. Such findings cannot prove or disprove the causal theory that underlies the model, because there are almost always plausible rival interpretations of the findings. Rather, findings from testing a causal model, such as those reported in this book, should be interpreted as either supporting the theory if the findings are consistent with the model or failing to support the theory if they are not. The point is that in many fields of science, and especially the social sciences, critical experiments which definitively prove or disprove a theory do not exist. Instead, theories tend to be confirmed or disconfirmed by a long series of studies, none of which is definitive but whose cumulative effect gradually leads to the validation or invalidation of the theory.

USE OF THE TERM *EXPLAIN*. Suppose that we report a multiple R square of .60 based on a regression analysis relating a set of independent variables to the rape rate. In making the statement that these variables *explain* 60% of the variance in rape, we are describing a statistical relationship. That statistic tells us how much of the state-to-state variation in rape is associated with state-to-state variation in a linear combination of the independent variables. As we noted in the section on causal inference, covariation is necessary, but not sufficient, to infer a causal relationship.

PREDICTORS AND DETERMINANTS. The term *predict* should be used only to describe findings from a prospective study (a panel or other time series study in which the values of variables at time 2 are shown to be a function of some set of variables at time 1). Similarly, *determinant* and *determinants* should be used only to describe relationships of a causal nature. However, it is customary to refer to the independent variables in a regression analysis as the "predictor variables" or to describe the results of a regression analysis as showing that variables $X1$ and $X2$ are determinants of Y, even when the data are cross sectional. Therefore, when the terms predictor or determinants are used, they should be understood as being synonymous with independent variable, and not as implying prediction in the chronological sense or as denoting causation.

Ratio Variables

Most of the variables used in this research are expressed as rates, typically per 1,000 or 100,000 population. The fact that relationships among such variables may be confounded with the common population component (the denominator used in computing the rate) has been a source of concern and disagreement since Pearson and Yule debated the issue at the turn of the century. A study by S. B. Long (1979) shows that ratio variables are particularly sensitive to measurement error, sometimes to the extent of reversing the sign of correlations. However, Long's study also indicates that this occurs if there is an important measurement error in the shared term. Since the shared terms for this research are population figures, and since population counts are among the most accurate data available to social scientists, the use of ratio variables may not be a serious problem for the current research. Nevertheless, in accordance with Bolen and Ward's (1980) suggestion, we substituted non-ratio variables for rates (for example, median income rather than income per capita). When this was not possible, we replicated some of the key analyses using the raw score versions of the dependent and independent variables and included the state population as one of the independent variables in the regression equation. Of course, the regression coefficients produced by these analyses differed from those in the original model, but the same set of variables was significant in the replications (Baron and Straus, 1984). We interpret these findings as providing cross validation for the analyses using ratio variables.

SUMMARY AND CONCLUSION

The most controversial aspects of the methods to be used in this research are the appropriateness of using the 50 states as societal units and the validity of the Uniform Crime Reports data on rape. In respect to states as social units, there are both advantages and disadvantages, as is the case when one uses other units such as cities, counties, or nations. The main reasons for using states are that (1) much of the data needed for empirical research on the theories tested in this study are available only for states; (2) there is no firm evidence that data at a lower level of aggregation would produce more valid findings; and (3) evidence that, despite their heterogeneity, there is sufficient variation among the states on a large number of theoretically important variables (Straus, 1985).

With respect to the appropriateness of the UCR data on rape, we are again faced with a situation in which the alternative, the NCS rape data, has its own set of limitations. These include the fact that the NCS interview depends on the respondent volunteering information about whether a specific assault involved rape, as contrasted with asking about this crime directly; and the fact that NCS rape data are available only for the ten largest states. Although we believe that the UCR rates of rape known to the police are the best data now available for investigating macrosociological theories of rape, the limitations and cautions described in this chapter must be considered when evaluating the findings of this study.

3

RAPE IN AMERICAN
STATES AND REGIONS

There are a number of simple but fundamental questions about rape and rape statistics that need to be answered as a first step toward the goal of understanding the structural sources of rape. Answers to these questions are also needed as a basis for examining the issues to be dealt with in later chapters.

- How much do the states differ in respect to the incidence of rape?
- How consistent over time are state-to-state patterns in the rape rate?
- Do the state differences reflect regional patterns?
- Does rape in rural areas show the same pattern of state-to-state differences as do rates for the urban parts of the states?
- To what extent is the rape rate correlated with certain social and economic characteristics of the states, such as urbanization, economic inequality, and the age structure of the states?

STATE-TO-STATE AND YEAR-TO-YEAR VARIATIONS IN RAPE

Our data on the incidence of rape come from two sources. The first is rapes that are known to and reported by the police, as given in the Uniform Crime Reports (UCR).[1] The second is reports by victims of rape, as given in the National Crime Survey (NCS).[2] Since NCS data are available for only ten states, the major focus of this chapter and the book as a whole is the UCR data.

1. Rape is defined in the UCR as: "(T)he carnal knowledge of a female forcibly and against her will. Assaults or attempts to commit rape by force or threat of force are also included; however, statutory rape (without force) and other sex offences are not included in this category" (Federal Bureau of Investigation, 1981:14).
2. Rape is defined in the NCS as: "Carnal Knowledge through the use of force or the threat of force, including attempts. Statutory rape (without force) is excluded. Includes both heterosexual and homosexual rape" (Bureau of Justice Statistics, 1983:98–99).

Ranking of the States

The first question that needs to be answered about the incidence of rape, as reported in the UCR, is whether the differences among states are large enough and consistent enough to make state-to-state differences in rape an issue worth exploring.

Table 3.1 shows that there are very large state-to-state differences in rapes known to the police and that these differences have remained relatively constant over the 21-year time span between 1960 and 1980.[3] In 1960, for example, the top ranking state (Alaska) had a rate of 20.8 rapes per 100,000 population. This was 9.5 times the rate for North Dakota, the lowest ranking state. Twenty-one years later in 1980, the rape rates had tripled, but Alaska remained near the top and North Dakota still had the lowest incidence of rape. Moreover, the multiple by which the rape rate in the top state exceeded the rate for the low state has remained remarkably consistent over this 21-year period.

As with any other generalization, there are important exceptions. One advantage of the format used in table 3.1 is that it encourages going beyond these generalizations to examine individual states. Take the case of Hawaii. In 1960 it was near the bottom as the 45th-ranking state. By 1970 it had moved up to 34th position and to 18th in 1980. Hawaii therefore did not follow the general pattern of year-to-year stability relative to other states. Instead, it experienced a steady climb from having one of the lowest rates in 1960 to a position well above the median in 1980.

Consistency over Time

Table 3.2 presents more precise measures of the extent to which there has been consistency over time in rape rates. It shows the correlation of rape rates for a given year with the rape rate for later years in 10-year intervals. All the correlations are substantial. Even data for 1960 have a correlation of .62 with the data for 1980, despite a 21-year interval. As might be expected, the correlations measuring agreement over 10 years are higher ($r = .81$ and .74). In addition to the correlations shown in table 3.2, we computed the correlations for each year since 1975 to obtain 1-year consistency measures. The mean of these five correlations is .97.

These statistics do not reveal anything that would lead us to doubt the

3. We began with 1960 data because this was the first census year that UCR rape rates became available by state. We ended with 1980 because it was the most current year for which data were available at the time this project began.

Table 3.1

UCR Rape Rate Per 100,000 Population, Arrayed in Rank Order by State,
1960, 1970, 1980

	1960 Rate			1970 Rate			1980 Rate	
Rank	State	v1085*		State	v1095*		State	ckf29*
1	Alaska	20.8		Colorado	36.0		Nevada	67.2
2	California	18.3		California	35.1		Alaska	62.5
3	Arizona	16.1		Missouri	27.4		California	58.2
4	Colorado	13.3		Arizona	27.0		Florida	56.9
5	Oklahoma	12.8		Alaska	26.1		Washington	52.7
6	Nevada	12.6		Maryland	23.9		Colorado	52.5
7	Illinois	12.4		Louisiana	23.1		Texas	47.3
8	Michigan	12.4		Michigan	22.9		Michigan	46.6
9	New Mexico	12.0		Florida	22.2		Arizona	45.2
10	Missouri	11.0		New Mexico	21.7		Louisiana	44.5
11	Louisiana	9.5		Texas	21.0		Georgia	44.3
12	Utah	9.5		Illinois	20.4		New Mexico	43.4
13	South Carolina	9.4		Nevada	19.6		Oregon	41.5
14	Oregon	9.3		Alabama	18.5		Maryland	40.1
15	Texas	9.3		Oregon	18.0		South Carolina	37.5
16	Pennsylvania	9.0		Washington	18.0		Tennessee	37.4
17	Arkansas	8.7		Indiana	17.9		Oklahoma	36.3
18	Florida	8.4		Arkansas	17.1		Hawaii	34.7
19	Alabama	8.3		South Carolina	17.1		Ohio	34.3
20	Delaware	8.3		Delaware	16.8		Indiana	33.1
21	New Jersey	7.9		Georgia	16.1		Missouri	32.6
22	Georgia	7.6		Ohio	16.0		Kansas	31.5
23	Maryland	7.3		Oklahoma	15.6		New York	30.9
24	Montana	7.3		New York	15.5		New Jersey	30.7
25	North Carolina	7.3		Tennessee	15.5		Alabama	30.0
26	Virginia	7.3		Virginia	15.4		Vermont	29.1
27	Idaho	7.0		Kansas	14.5		Wyoming	28.6
28	Wyoming	7.0		Kentucky	13.7		Utah	27.7
29	New York	6.3		New Jersey	12.9		Virginia	27.4
30	Ohio	6.0		North Carolina	12.6		Massachusetts	27.3
31	Washington	5.9		Idaho	12.3		Illinois	26.9
32	Kentucky	5.5		Wyoming	12.3		Arkansas	26.7
33	South Dakota	5.4		Massachusetts	12.0		Mississippi	24.6
34	Kansas	5.3		Hawaii	11.8		Delaware	24.2
35	Tennessee	5.2		Pennsylvania	11.3		Minnesota	23.2
36	Mississippi	5.1		South Dakota	11.1		Nebraska	23.2
37	Maine	5.0		Utah	10.9		Pennsylvania	23.0
38	Massachusetts	5.0		Montana	10.5		North Carolina	22.7
39	Indiana	4.7		Vermont	10.3		Idaho	22.4
40	West Virginia	4.4		Minnesota	9.7		Connecticut	21.6
41	Connecticut	4.2		Nebraska	9.3		Montana	21.0
42	Nebraska	4.2		Connecticut	9.1		Kentucky	19.2
43	New Hampshire	4.1		Mississippi	8.9		New Hampshire	17.3
44	Iowa	3.7		Maine	7.0		Rhode Island	17.1
45	Hawaii	3.3		West Virginia	6.7		West Virginia	15.8
46	Wisconsin	2.8		Wisconsin	6.7		Wisconsin	14.9
47	Minnesota	2.5		Iowa	6.2		Iowa	14.3
48	Rhode Island	2.3		North Dakota	6.2		Maine	12.9
49	Vermont	2.3		New Hampshire	6.0		South Dakota	12.5
50	North Dakota	2.2		Rhode Island	3.6		North Dakota	9.5

* These are the variable identification codes used in the State and Regional Indicators Archive.

Table 3.2

Temporal Consistency of UCR Rape Rates, 1960, 1970, and 1980

Year	Between Year Correlations*		
	1960	1970	1980
1960	—	.81	.62
1970		—	.74
1980			—

*All Correlations are statistically significant at the .001 level.

reliability of the UCR rape rates. The fact that for six consecutive years (1975–80), the correlations between adjacent years is almost perfect suggests that, whatever the processes underlying the production of these rates, they are consistent. At the same time, the gradual decrease in the correlations as the time interval between measurements increases suggests that the rates can and do reflect changes over time, either in the true incidence rate or the recording methods. It remains to be seen whether the former or the latter are the cause of the changes.

REGIONAL PATTERNS

The consistently high ranking of such states as California, Colorado, Alaska, Arizona, and Nevada suggests that rape is most frequent in the Mountain and Pacific regions. To more accurately determine the extent of such regional differences, we categorized the states into the four census regions and the nine census divisions. Analysis of variance was computed to measure the statistical significance of differences among the regions and divisions.[4]

The top half of figure 3.1 shows that in both 1970 and 1980 there were large and statistically significant differences in rape among census divisions.

4. These calculations were done using each state as an equal unit, regardless of the size of the state. Consequently, the figures for regions in this book differ from those given in other sources. See section "Statistics on Regions" in chapter 2 for elaboration.

Figure 3.1
Rape Rates by Division and Region, 1980 and 1970

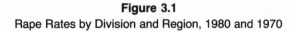

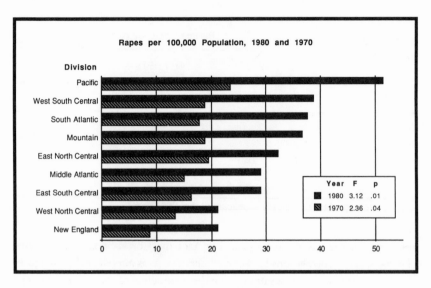

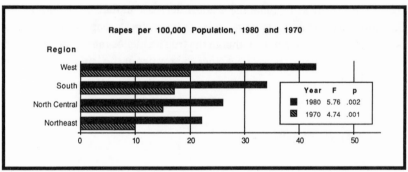

The Pacific division (Washington, Oregon, California, Alaska, Hawaii) has a much higher incidence of rape than any other area, although the West South Central division (Arkansas, Louisiana, Oklahoma, Texas), the South Atlantic division (Delaware, Maryland, Virginia, West Virginia, North Carolina, South Carolina, Georgia, and Florida), and the Mountain division (Montana, Idaho, Wyoming, Colorado, New Mexico, Arizona, Utah, and Nevada) also have high average rape rates. The West North Central States (Minnesota, Iowa, Missouri, North Dakota, South Dakota, Nebraska, Kansas) and New England (Maine, New Hampshire, Vermont, Massachusetts, Rhode Island, Connecticut) have the lowest average rape rate.

The lower half of figure 3.1 shows the Census Bureau's regional breakdown of rape rates for the years 1970 and 1980. It can be seen that the incidence of rape has increased considerably in each region between 1970 and 1980 but that the relative ranking of each region has remained the same. Moreover, there are statistically significant differences among the regions in the incidence of rape in both 1970 and 1980. In 1980 the West led all other regions in the incidence of rape with 42.9 rapes per 100,000 population. In fact, states in the western region had almost twice as many reported rapes as did the Northeast and 6.5 rapes per 100,000 population more than the national average of 36.4 per 100,000 population.

These large, statistically significant, and temporally consistent differences among states and regions in the incidence of rape show that states are still highly diverse, despite the continuing homogenization that has been going on since the nineteenth century (Gastil, 1975; Sharkansky, 1970). In fact, differences between the top and bottom states and between the top and bottom census divisions are as large or larger than the differences in rape among nations (Schiff, 1973). What factors might account for these differences? The analyses that follow were designed to investigate some of the more obvious possibilities, such as the degree to which a state is urbanized or has a disproportionate number of men and women in the high rape age group.

RURAL AND URBAN PATTERNS IN RAPE

The rape rate per 100,000 population is much higher in urban than in rural areas. In 1976, the SMSAs[5] of the United States had a rate of 29.4 per 100,000 population, the other cities had a rate of 17.1, and the rural areas of the United States had a rate of 15.4. The corresponding figures for 1980 were 40.5, 21.6, and 18.2. During both years, twice as many rapes were reported to the police in the metropolitan areas than in the rural areas.

Since states vary in respect to the degree of urbanization from almost completely rural (such as Vermont and Wyoming) to almost completely urban (for example, New Jersey), the large differences among states in the incidence of rape might reflect the largely urban nature of some states and the largely rural nature of other states. Consequently, it is essential to compare the rape

5. See note 2 in chapter 2 for the definition of SMSA.

Table 3.3

UCR Rape Rate per 100,000 Population for SMSAs, Other Cities, and Rural Areas, 1980

Rank	SMSAs State	ckf25r	Other Cities State	ckf26r	Rural Areas State	ckf27r
1	Nevada	75.9	Alaska	74.0	New Jersey	48.2
2	Washington	61.4	New Mexico	40.0	Michigan	38.8
3	Florida	60.4	Washington	39.7	Alaska	37.6
4	Georgia	60.1	California	39.6	Hawaii	36.2
5	California	60.0	Florida	38.8	Wyoming	35.9
6	Colorado	59.4	South Carolina	34.7	Massachusetts	35.0
7	Louisiana	57.5	Oregon	32.3	Florida	34.5
8	New Mexico	55.9	Arizona	32.0	California	33.0
9	Texas	55.4	Hawaii	29.6	New Mexico	31.0
10	Tennessee	52.2	Georgia	28.0	Vermont	30.7
11	Oregon	51.2	Vermont	27.3	Nevada	29.5
12	Oklahoma	50.6	Wyoming	24.4	Arizona	26.4
13	Kansas	50.5	Montana	24.2	Washington	24.8
14	Arizona	50.4	Idaho	24.1	South Carolina	23.3
15	Michigan	50.1	Mississippi	23.8	Oregon	22.0
16	South Carolina	48.6	New Jersey	23.7	Colorado	21.9
17	Arkansas	46.7	Colorado	23.5	Louisiana	21.6
18	Missouri	45.0	North Carolina	22.9	Georgia	19.3
19	Maryland	44.1	Massachusetts	22.3	Maryland	18.7
20	Nebraska	42.8	Louisiana	22.0	Delaware	16.8
21	Indiana	41.3	Kansas	21.9	Montana	16.6
22	Mississippi	41.3	Michigan	21.9	Mississippi	15.5
23	Ohio	39.9	Oklahoma	21.5	New Hampshire	14.5
24	Alabama	38.9	Nevada	20.5	Connecticut	14.0
25	Idaho	38.7	Tennessee	20.1	New York	13.6
26	Hawaii	34.6	Missouri	19.8	Idaho	13.4
27	Virginia	34.2	Virginia	19.4	Oklahoma	12.9
28	New York	33.5	Alabama	19.0	North Carolina	12.9
29	Minnesota	31.7	Texas	18.2	Texas	12.9
30	Utah	31.5	Maryland	18.1	Alabama	12.6
31	New Jersey	31.1	Arkansas	17.4	Kentucky	12.6
32	North Carolina	30.5	Indiana	17.3	Virginia	12.6
33	Illinois	30.4	Ohio	17.2	Indiana	12.2
34	South Dakota	30.3	Delaware	16.7	Pennsylvania	12.2
35	Delaware	27.8	Rhode Island	15.9	Utah	12.1
36	Massachusetts	27.4	Illinois	14.5	West Virginia	11.8
37	Kentucky	27.3	New Hampshire	14.4	Arkansas	11.1
38	Iowa	27.2	Utah	14.1	Maine	11.1
39	Pennsylvania	26.4	Connecticut	13.4	Ohio	10.5
40	Montana	24.9	Kentucky	12.6	Illinois	8.8
41	West Virginia	24.3	Nebraska	12.5	Missouri	8.6
42	New Hampshire	23.8	Maine	12.0	Tennessee	8.1
43	Connecticut	22.7	South Dakota	11.8	Kansas	7.2
44	Wisconsin	19.6	Minnesota	11.1	Wisconsin	6.0
45	Rhode Island	17.2	West Virginia	9.8	Minnesota	5.9
46	Maine	16.1	New York	8.9	North Dakota	5.2
47	North Dakota	15.3	Wisconsin	8.6	Iowa	3.9
48	Alaska	Missing	North Dakota	8.3	Nebraska	3.1
49	Vermont	Missing	Iowa	8.0	South Dakota	1.5
50	Wyoming	Missing	Pennsylvania	6.7	Rhode Island	Missing

Note: There are missing data because some states had no SMSAs and some had no areas classified as rural.

rates for equivalent areas of each state. This will show if the state-to-state differences apply to the rural as well as the urban parts of the states.

To answer this question we computed the residence-specific rape rate for 1980 using the figures on number of rapes occurring in the SMSAs, the other cities, and in the rural areas of each state.[6] Table 3.3 arrays the states in rank order according to these rates.

Visual inspection of the rank-order distributions suggests that states which have high rape rates in their metropolitan areas also have high rape rates in their nonmetropolitan areas. This impression was tested by correlating the rates for each type of community. The resulting correlations are shown in table 3.4.

The column headed Rural Areas in table 3.4 shows that there is a strong tendency for the rape rate in rural areas to be associated with the rape rate for SMSAs and for other cities. The column headed Other Cities also shows a strong association. Thus, the higher the rape rate in the SMSAs of the state, the higher the rape rate in the other cities, and the higher the rape rate in the rural areas.

It is especially noteworthy that the rural areas of each state tend to follow

Table 3.4
Correlation of Rape Rates for SMSAs, Other Cities,
Rural Areas, and States, 1980

Community Type	Correlations*		
	Other Cities	Rural Areas	States
SMSAs	.67	.40	.89
Other Cities	–	.66	.67
Rural Areas		–	.57

* All correlations are significant at p < .001.

6. The Uniform Crime Reports gives the *number* of crimes separately for the Standard Metropolitan Statistical Areas, for other cities, and for the rural areas of each state. It also gives the estimated population of the areas included in the UCR reporting system. However, for reasons which are not stated in the three editions of the UCR which we checked, the UCR does not report crime *rates* separately for each residential area. We therefore computed the rates reported in this chapter by dividing the number of crimes by the estimated populations, as given in the UCR.

the same pattern in respect to rape as do the largest urban centers of the state. It appears, then, that there may be something in the social organization or culture of such states as California, Washington, and Florida which makes for a high incidence of rape throughout the state and not just in the most urban parts of the state.

SOCIAL ORGANIZATION AND RAPE

In chapter 1 we suggested that rape, rather than being only a manifestation of individual differences in criminal tendencies, grows out of the structure of society itself. That idea has already received support from the data which show that the rape rate in some states is five or six times higher than the rate in other states, and from the data which show that the rape rate in urban areas is about double the rate in rural areas.

The higher crime rates of urban areas is well known. Indeed, it is so well known that it is easy to overlook the fact that this is an example of the general principle that crime is a function of the way society is organized. Because of these rural-urban differences, it seems likely that the degree of urbanization is one of the factors which accounts for a much higher incidence of rape in some states than others. The following analysis provides information on that question.

There are many aspects of the social organization and culture of the states that need to be investigated, far more than can be included in this book. As stated in chapter 1, we chose to focus on theories that view rape as a consequence of sexual inequality, pornography, social disorganization, and cultural support for violence. However, there are other aspects of society which are likely to have a pervasive effect either because they might obscure the relationship between rape and the variables of key theoretical interest, or because they might produce a spurious correlation. To deal with this possibility, we investigated eight variables that are known to be associated with rape and other crimes of violence:

Percent of the population residing in SMSAs, 1980
Percent of the population below poverty level income, 1980
Gini Index of income inequality, 1979
Percent of the population black, 1980
Percent of the population age 18–24, 1980
Ratio of males to females age 15–24, 1980
Percent single of the male population age 15 and older, 1979
Percent of the civilian labor force unemployed, 1980

Table 3.5(a and b) shows the rank order of the states for each of the eight variables, and table 3.6 shows the regional differences. These variables represent aspects of the social organization of the states that are important from both a theoretical and a practical perspective. The following sections explain the reasons for including each variable and present correlations between these variables and the average rape rate for the years 1980–82 per 100,000 popula-

Table 3.5a

Ranking of the States on Social Organizational Variables*

	Percent of the Population Residing in SMSAs		Percent of Population Below Poverty Level		Gini Index of Income Inequality		Percent of Population Black	
Rank	State	met80	State	pov80	State	gini79fx	State	blk80
1	California	94.9	Mississippi	24.5	Mississippi	39.5	Mississippi	35.2
2	Rhode Island	92.2	Louisiana	18.9	Louisiana	37.8	South Carolina	30.4
3	New Jersey	91.4	Arkansas	18.7	Georgia	37.4	Louisiana	29.4
4	New York	90.1	Kentucky	18.4	Kentucky	37.4	Georgia	26.8
5	Maryland	88.8	Alabama	17.9	Tennessee	37.2	Alabama	25.6
6	Connecticut	88.3	New Mexico	17.4	Alabama	37.1	Maryland	22.7
7	Florida	87.9	Tennessee	17.0	Arkansas	36.9	North Carolina	22.4
8	Massachusetts	85.3	Georgia	16.4	New Mexico	36.7	Virginia	18.9
9	Michigan	82.8	South Dakota	16.1	Florida	36.3	Arkansas	16.3
10	Nevada	82.0	South Carolina	15.9	Texas	36.1	Delaware	16.1
11	Pennsylvania	81.9	Texas	14.8	Oklahoma	35.9	Tennessee	15.8
12	Illinois	81.0	North Carolina	14.6	New York	35.8	Illinois	14.7
13	Colorado	80.9	West Virginia	14.5	South Carolina	35.6	Florida	13.8
14	Washington	80.4	New York	13.7	South Dakota	35.5	New York	13.7
15	Ohio	80.3	Oklahoma	13.3	West Virginia	35.2	Michigan	12.9
16	Texas	80.0	Florida	13.0	North Dakota	35.0	New Jersey	12.6
17	Utah	79.0	Maine	12.9	California	35.0	Texas	12.0
18	Hawaii	79.0	North Dakota	12.8	North Carolina	35.0	Missouri	10.5
19	Arizona	75.1	Idaho	12.7	Missouri	34.9	Ohio	10.0
20	Indiana	69.8	Arizona	12.4	Delaware	34.8	Pennsylvania	8.8
21	Virginia	69.6	Missouri	12.4	Virginia	34.7	California	7.7
22	Delaware	67.0	Montana	12.4	Arizona	34.6	Indiana	7.6
23	Wisconsin	66.8	Delaware	11.9	Idaho	34.6	Kentucky	7.1
24	Missouri	65.3	Illinois	11.5	Hawaii	34.2	Connecticut	7.0
25	Oregon	64.9	Virginia	11.5	Nebraska	33.9	Oklahoma	6.8
26	Minnesota	64.6	Vermont	11.4	Michigan	33.9	Nevada	6.4
27	Louisiana	63.4	California	11.3	Maine	33.9	Kansas	5.3
28	Tennessee	62.8	Oregon	11.3	Oregon	33.8	Massachusetts	3.9
29	Alabama	62.0	Michigan	11.1	Montana	33.7	Wisconsin	3.9
30	Georgia	60.0	Utah	10.7	Colorado	33.7	Colorado	3.5
31	South Carolina	59.8	Ohio	10.5	New Jersey	33.7	Alaska	3.4
32	Oklahoma	58.5	Pennsylvania	10.5	Vermont	33.6	West Virginia	3.3
33	North Carolina	52.7	Nebraska	10.4	Kansas	33.5	Nebraska	3.1
34	New Hampshire	50.7	Rhode Island	10.3	Alaska	33.4	Rhode Island	2.9
35	Kansas	46.8	Colorado	10.2	Illinois	33.2	Arizona	2.8
36	Kentucky	44.5	Kansas	10.2	Massachusetts	33.2	Washington	2.6
37	Nebraska	44.1	Washington	10.2	Rhode Island	33.2	New Mexico	1.8
38	Alaska	43.4	Alaska	10.1	Maryland	33.1	Hawaii	1.8
39	New Mexico	42.3	Hawaii	10.0	Ohio	33.0	Iowa	1.4
40	Iowa	40.1	Maryland	9.9	Washington	33.0	Oregon	1.4
41	Arkansas	39.2	Indiana	9.8	Minnesota	32.9	Minnesota	1.3
42	West Virginia	37.1	Massachusetts	9.8	Pennsylvania	32.8	Wyoming	0.7
43	North Dakota	35.9	New Jersey	9.7	Iowa	32.7	Utah	0.6
44	Maine	33.0	Iowa	9.4	Utah	32.7	North Dakota	0.4
45	Mississippi	27.1	Minnesota	9.3	Indiana	32.5	New Hampshire	0.4
46	Montana	24.0	Connecticut	8.7	Nevada	32.3	Maine	0.3
47	Vermont	22.3	New Hampshire	8.7	Connecticut	32.2	South Dakota	0.3
48	Idaho	18.3	Nevada	8.5	Wisconsin	32.1	Idaho	0.3
49	South Dakota	15.8	Wisconsin	8.5	New Hampshire	31.8	Montana	0.2
50	Wyoming	15.3	Wyoming	8.0	Wyoming	31.1	Vermont	0.2

* The data for all the social organization variables are for the year 1980 with the exception of the Gini Index and Percent of Single Males which are based on 1979 data.

Table 3.5b

Ranking of the States on Social Organizational Variables

Rank	Percent of Population Age 18-24 State	yng80	Ratio of Males to Females Age 15-24 State	c78s	Percent of Single Males Age 15+ State	cp62r	Percent of Civilian Labor Force Unemployed State	cb107r
1	North Dakota	14.9	Hawaii	54.5	Hawaii	36	Michigan	10.95
2	Alaska	14.9	Alaska	54.3	Massachusetts	35	Alaska	9.75
3	Hawaii	14.8	Wyoming	52.0	New York	34	Kentucky	8.54
4	Utah	14.8	North Dakota	51.5	California	33	West Virginia	8.45
5	Wyoming	14.7	North Carolina	51.4	Alaska	33	Oregon	8.27
6	Colorado	14.5	Virginia	51.4	Colorado	32	Montana	8.25
7	South Carolina	14.3	South Carolina	51.3	Vermont	32	Idaho	7.97
8	Louisiana	14.2	Kansas	51.3	Rhode Island	32	Ohio	7.97
9	Texas	14.0	Washington	51.2	Minnesota	32	Indiana	7.81
10	Delaware	14.0	California	51.2	North Dakota	32	Maine	7.62
11	North Carolina	14.0	Oklahoma	51.2	Connecticut	32	Alabama	7.51
12	Virginia	13.9	Kentucky	51.1	Maryland	32	Pennsylvania	7.41
13	Vermont	13.9	Colorado	51.0	Delaware	31	Tennessee	7.40
14	Kansas	13.8	Montana	50.8	New Jersey	31	Washington	7.39
15	South Dakota	13.8	Nevada	50.8	Wisconsin	31	Illinois	7.15
16	Rhode Island	13.7	Texas	50.8	Illinois	31	Mississippi	7.15
17	New Mexico	13.7	Arizona	50.6	Michigan	30	New York	7.14
18	Massachusetts	13.7	South Dakota	50.5	Pennsylvania	30	New Mexico	7.10
19	Minnesota	13.7	Georgia	50.4	Virginia	30	Rhode Island	7.04
20	Wisconsin	13.7	Rhode Isalnd	50.3	South Dakota	30	Arkansas	6.92
21	California	13.7	Maine	50.2	South Carolina	30	Missouri	6.90
22	Arizona	13.6	Florida	50.2	North Carolina	29	New Jersey	6.67
23	Michigan	13.6	Idaho	50.2	New Hampshire	29	Wisconsin	6.58
24	Nebraska	13.4	New Mexico	50.1	Louisiana	29	California	6.55
25	Washington	13.4	Nebraska	50.1	Washington	29	Vermont	6.29
26	Mississippi	13.4	Tennessee	50.1	Mississippi	29	Delaware	6.29
27	Indiana	13.4	Louisiana	50.0	New Mexico	28	Arizona	6.20
28	Georgia	13.4	Mississippi	50.0	Alabama	28	South Carolina	6.07
29	Kentucky	13.4	Illinois	50.0	Maine	28	Louisiana	6.00
30	Oklahoma	13.3	Missouri	49.9	Montana	28	Nevada	5.93
31	Iowa	13.3	Connecticut	49.9	Texas	28	Georgia	5.86
32	Alabama	13.2	Iowa	49.9	Georgia	28	Maryland	5.76
33	Montana	13.2	Wisconsin	49.9	Nevada	28	North Carolina	5.48
34	Illinois	13.2	New Jersey	49.8	Utah	28	Utah	5.46
35	Nevada	13.2	Oregon	49.8	Nebraska	28	Minnesota	5.41
36	Tennessee	13.1	Maryland	49.8	Ohio	28	North Dakota	5.34
37	New Hampshire	13.1	Arkansas	49.7	Arizona	28	Florida	5.11
38	Ohio	13.1	New Hampshire	49.7	Kansas	27	Massachusetts	5.05
39	Maryland	13.1	Indiana	49.7	Oregon	27	Iowa	5.04
40	Idaho	13.0	Alabama	49.7	Tennessee	27	Colorado	5.00
41	Missouri	12.9	West Virginia	49.7	Iowa	27	Virginia	4.97
42	Pennsylvania	12.7	Michigan	49.6	Missouri	27	South Dakota	4.92
43	Oregon	12.6	Minnesota	49.6	Indiana	27	New Hampshire	4.80
44	Maine	12.6	Pennsylvania	49.6	Wyoming	27	Hawaii	4.73
45	West Virginia	12.5	Ohio	49.5	Kentucky	27	Connecticut	4.66
46	Connecticut	12.4	Vermont	49.4	Idaho	26	Wyoming	4.14
47	New York	12.3	Massachusetts	49.3	West Virginia	26	Oklahoma	4.11
48	Arkansas	12.2	New York	49.1	Florida	26	Texas	4.00
49	New Jersey	11.8	Utah	49.1	Oklahoma	25	Kansas	3.98
50	Florida	11.7	Delaware	49.0	Arkansas	24	Nebraska	3.70

tion.[7] The three-year average rape rate will be used as the dependent variable for the remainder of the book, unless otherwise indicated.[8] The rank-order distribution for the 1980–82 average rape rate is presented in table 3.7.

7. We decided to use the mean rape rate for a three-year period rather than just one year in order to reduce the possibility of chance fluctuations in the rape rate for any given year.

8. Initially, we computed rape rates per 100,000 *females* and correlated them with rape rates per 100,000 *population*. The correlations for the years 1975 to 1980 were almost perfect ($r = .99$). Consequently, we decided to use the published rate per 100,000 population.

Table 3.6

Regional Differences in Social Organization

Variable	Regions			
	Northeast	North Central	South	West
Percent Residing in SMSAs, 1980	70.5	57.7	60.0	59.9
Gini Index, 1979***	33.3	33.6	36.2	33.7
Percent Below Poverty Level Income, 1980***	10.6	11.0	15.8	11.1
Percent Black, 1980***	5.5	5.9	18.9	2.5
Percent Age 18-24, 1980*	12.9	13.5	13.3	13.8
Percent Male of Population Age 15-24, 1980**	49.7	50.1	50.4	51.2
Percent Single Males Age 15+, 1979	31.4	29.1	28.0	29.4
Percent Unemployed, 1980	6.2	6.3	6.2	6.6

Note: *p<.05, **p<.01, ***p<.001.

Percentage of the Population Living in Standard Metropolitan Statistical Areas

As was shown in "Rural and Urban Patterns in Rape" in this chapter, there are large differences between rural and urban areas in per capita rape rates. This is consistent with studies that report a direct relationship between the conditions of urban life and violent crime. Although criminologists have been unable to agree on the reasons for a higher rate of violent crime in urban areas, some of the explanations include the stresses and strains of urban life, the erosion of community ties, the impersonal and alienating nature of cities, greater population density, and increased residential mobility (Crutchfield, Geerken, and Goven, 1982; Harries, 1980; J. D. McCarthy, Galle, and Zimmerman, 1975; Nettler, 1984; Roncek, 1975). Whatever the reasons, states that are more urbanized can be expected to have a higher rape rate. As expected, a significant correlation of .36 was found.

That moderate correlation is an important finding in itself. However, within the context of this study, the chief significance of the correlation between the urbanness of states and the rape rate is methodological. This is

Table 3.7
UCR Rape Rate Per 100,000
Population 1980–1982

Rank	State	rap3
1	Alaska	83.3
2	Nevada	64.5
3	Florida	55.5
4	California	55.0
5	Washington	49.6
6	Colorado	47.5
7	Michigan	46.9
8	New Mexico	46.3
9	Texas	46.0
10	Georgia	42.1
11	Louisiana	41.9
12	Oregon	41.0
13	Arizona	40.6
14	Maryland	38.7
15	South Carolina	37.5
16	Tennessee	36.8
17	Oklahoma	36.2
18	Hawaii	34.6
19	Vermont	32.3
20	Ohio	31.7
21	New Jersey	30.5
22	New York	30.4
23	Wyoming	30.3
24	Indiana	30.1
25	Missouri	29.4
26	Kansas	29.0
27	Delaware	27.8
28	Alabama	27.3
29	Massachusetts	26.6
30	Utah	26.6
31	Virginia	26.5
32	Arkansas	26.3
33	Mississippi	25.7
34	Illinois	24.0
35	Minnesota	23.9
36	North Carolina	22.4
37	Pennsylvania	22.0
38	Connecticut	21.8
39	Nebraska	21.4
40	Kentucky	20.0
41	Idaho	19.8
42	Montana	19.3
43	Rhode Island	18.1
44	New Hampshire	16.6
45	West Virginia	15.3
46	Wisconsin	14.9
47	Iowa	13.4
48	Maine	13.0
49	South Dakota	11.8
50	North Dakota	9.3

because the urban states might also be higher than the rural states in respect to the key theoretical variables of this study (for example, circulation of pornography). Consequently, if in the analyses to be presented later we find a relationship between the circulation rate of pornography and the rape rate, the finding could be spurious. That is, it might be the result of the confounding of these three variables rather than a relationship due to pornography per se.

Percentage of the Population with Incomes below the Poverty Level

We had intended to use the percent of the population with incomes below the poverty level as an independent variable because previous research indicates that violent crime is associated with poverty (Blau and Golden, 1986; Curtis, 1978; Loftin and Hill, 1974; M. D. Smith and Bennett, 1985; M. D. Smith and Parker, 1980; K. R. Williams, 1984; Wolfgang and Ferracuti, 1967). Studies also indicate that rapists are more likely to come from areas with the greatest poverty and urban decay (Amir, 1971; Katz and Mazur, 1979; Schwendinger and Schwendinger, 1983). However, a substantial correlation ($r = .93$) was found between the poverty measure and the Gini Index of income inequality. A correlation of such magnitude suggests that these variables are likely to be measuring the same underlying construct. Since we are using multiple regression in chapter 8, the inclusion of both variables would inflate the standard error and produce unstable regression coefficients. Consequently, we decided to exclude percentage below the poverty level from further analysis.

Gini Index of Income Inequality

Perhaps part of the reason that researchers have found a relationship between poverty and rape is that poverty is typically accompanied by economic inequality. Since the Gini Index measures the degree of income dispersion in states relative to the mean income in each state, we decided to use the Gini Index as an indicator of economic inequality. The Gini Index was computed using 1979 data on family income. The theoretical range of scores on the Gini Index is from 0 to 100; however, the actual state scores range from a low of 31.1 in Wyoming to a high of 39.5 in Mississippi. States with higher index scores have greater income inequality.

Research indicates that income inequality is positively associated with criminal violence (Baron and Straus, 1987, 1988; Blau and Blau, 1982; Braithwaite, 1979; Loftin and Hill, 1974; Messner, 1980; O'Brien, 1983; Rosenfeld, 1986; Simpson, 1985; Stack and Kanavy, 1983). These studies suggest that the structure of inequality within states may generate a climate of antagonism that is conducive to rape. The correlation between the Gini Index and the rape rate does not support this conjecture, however, since the coefficient is low ($r = .09$) and not statistically significant.

Percent Black

In absolute numbers, most rapes are committed by whites. However, blacks represent only a small portion of the nation's population (11.8% in 1980). Relative to the rest of the population, blacks commit several times more rapes than would be expected by their number (Amir, 1971; Curtis, 1975; Hindelang and Davis, 1977; Katz and Mazur, 1979; MacDonald, 1971; Rabkin, 1979). Moreover, an important fraction of all rapes are intraracial, which means that black women are at higher risk of being raped than white women (Amir, 1971; Katz and Mazur, 1979; LaFree, 1982; O'Brien, 1987; Russell, 1984).[9] Therefore, the percentage of blacks residing in a state might be expected to affect the rape rate. Contrary to this expectation, the correlation between percent black and the incidence of rape is low and not statistically significant ($r = .15$).

Percent Age 18–24

It is well established that a disproportionate number of violent crimes are committed by young men (Curtis, 1978; Hirschi and Gottfredson, 1983; Wolfgang, 1978). Similarly, rapists, and also their victims, are predominantly young, usually in their late teens or early twenties (Amir, 1971; Hindelang and Davis, 1977; Katz and Mazur, 1979; MacDonald, 1971; Rabkin, 1979). Thus, states with a youthful population would be expected to have higher rates of rape. To our surprise, this turned out to be only minimally true ($r = .14$).

This low correlation is probably a function of the relatively small differences among states in the percent of the population in this age group. For most of the variables in this study, the figures for the high scoring states are two, three, or more times the figures for the low scoring states. However, in respect to the percent of the population who are age 18–24, there is not much variation among the states. Florida, for example, has the lowest proportion of its population in this age group (11.7%), while North Dakota and Alaska, the

9. There is evidence, though, that interracial rapes are increasing. LeFree's (1982) exhaustive review of the literature on interracial rape and his original research on this issue suggest that rapes consisting of black perpetrators and white victims have become more prevalent since the late 1950s due to desegregation.

two states with the highest proportion of 18- to 24-year-olds in the nation, have only 14.9%.

Ratio of Males to Females Age 15–24

Some investigators have suggested that rape may be a function of the sexual composition of the population (Brownmiller, 1975; Harries, 1972; Messner and Blau, 1987; Shorter, 1977; Svalastoga, 1962; Von Hetig, 1951). They argue that when there are considerably more men than women, a larger proportion of men might use force as a means of obtaining sexual access. This principle seems to be illustrated by Alaska, since that state has the second highest ratio of men to women and the highest average rape rate. Consistent with this reasoning, we found a statistically significant correlation between the sex ratio and the rape rate ($r = .38$).

Percent Single of the Male Population Age 15 and Older

As might be expected from the large proportion of young men involved in rape, a high percentage of these men are single (Amir, 1971; Svalastoga, 1962). It has been suggested that the lifestyle of many single men includes a number of activities such as drinking and "chasing women" that may increase the likelihood of rape (MacNamara and Sagarin, 1977; Rabkin, 1979). Therefore, states that have a large proportion of single men might also have a high rape rate. Contrary to this prediction, we found a correlation between the percent single and the rape rate of .09.

Percent of the Civilian Labor Force Unemployed

Studies investigating the influence of unemployment on criminal violence have yielded mixed results. Some research suggests that high rates of unemployment are associated with high rates of homicide (Brenner, 1978; Ehrlich, 1975; Henry and Short, 1954; Krohn, 1976) and high rates of rape (De-Fronzo, 1983; Sommers, 1982; Stack and Kanavy, 1983). Other research suggests that the influence of unemployment is too slight to significantly effect rates of criminal violence (Cook and Zarkin, 1985; Freeman, 1983; S. K. Long and Witte, 1981; Orsagh, 1980; Wilson and Hernstein, 1985). Perhaps the strongest evidence in support of the link between unemployment and criminal violence is Chirocos' (1987) extensive literature review of 63 studies published since 1960. Of the 38 studies that investigated the relationship between unemployment and homicide, 66% yielded a positive association and

34% yielded a negative association. The findings for rape provide even stronger support for the criminogenic character of unemployment. Of the 17 studies that examined the relationship between unemployment and rape, 71% showed a positive association compared to 29% that showed a negative association.

On the basis of these studies it seems plausible that a heavy concentration of unemployed individuals could generate a climate of powerlessness and hostility that might be conducive to rape. Therefore, we decided to include in the analysis the percentage of the civilian labor force unemployed. The correlation between the percentage unemployed and the rape rate is .17. Although the correlation is in the predicted direction, it is low and not statistically significant.

SUMMARY AND CONCLUSIONS

The first half of this chapter compared the incidence of rapes known to the police in the states and regions of the United States. We found very large differences in the frequency of rape among individual states. Depending on the year examined, the states with the highest incidence of rape tended to have from five to ten times as many rapes per 100,000 population as did the states with a low incidence of rape. These differences tended to follow a regional pattern. Rapes occur much more frequently in the West, followed by the South, the North Central, and then the Northeast. Moreover, this regional ranking has been relatively constant since 1960. We also found substantial consistency between the rape rate for the state as a whole and the rates found in different parts of the states. States that have a high rape rate in their urban areas tend to have a high rate in their rural areas. Similarly, states that have a low rape rate in their urban areas also tend to have a low rate in their rural areas, relative to the rate in the rural parts of other states.

The second half of this chapter described several variables that represent the social and demographic structure of states and reported zero-order correlations between these variables and the average rape rate for the years 1980–82. The correlation analysis showed that more urbanized states and states with a high ratio of males to females are associated with higher rates of rape. The variables that did not have significant associations with the rape rate were the Gini Index of economic inequality, the percent of black persons residing in the states, the percentage of the state's population between the ages of 18 and 24, the percentage of single males age 15 and older, and the percent of the civilian labor force unemployed.

The findings just summarized are important for two reasons. First, they have methodological implications. In later analyses, we will examine the extent to which state-to-state variation in rape can be explained by sexual inequality, cultural supports for violence, the level of social disorganization, and the circulation of soft-core pornographic magazines. In those analyses, the variables discussed in this chapter will be introduced as statistical controls. Second, the findings reported in this chapter support the central theoretical assumption of the book: rape is a socially patterned phenomenon, not just a manifestation of individual psychopathology or other defects of personality, character, or physiology.

Part II

FOUR THEORIES OF RAPE

4

GENDER INEQUALITY

In chapter 1 we pointed out that a major theme in feminist theories of rape is the idea that rape functions as a mechanism of social control in patriarchal societies (Brownmiller, 1975; Riger and Gordon, 1981). Feminist scholars who take this position believe that rape and the fear of rape enable men to assert their power over women and maintain the existing system of gender stratification (Adamec and Adamec, 1981; Barry, 1979; Brownmiller, 1975; Riger and Gordon, 1981; Russell, 1984; Sanday, 1981). Clark and Lewis (1977) argue that rape is more likely to occur in societies where women are regarded as the sexual and reproductive possessions of men. In such societies, men sustain their power and privilege and enforce their sexual rights through threat and the use of force. On the other hand, the opposite argument is also plausible. Russell (1975), for example, maintains that some men rape because they feel threatened by the women's movement and the prospect of women obtaining equality. Thus, as the status of women increases relative to men, some men may retaliate by trying to put women "back in their place."

A related theme in feminist scholarship is the idea that traditional gender-role attitudes encourage rape (Burt, 1980; Check and Malamuth, 1983; Cherry, 1983; Curtis, 1975; Russell, 1975; K. Weis and Borges, 1977). According to this view, norms associated with masculinity such as dominance and aggression encourage men to sexually exploit women. Because the acquisition of sexual scripts is closely allied to the development of gender-role identities (Gagnon and Simon, 1973), it seems likely that male sexual behavior is infused with the traditional masculine traits of dominance and aggression.

A continuing obstacle to empirical research on the gender inequality theory of rape has been the lack of a suitable societal-level measure of the degree to which the society is stratified along gender lines. Within the United States we know of no broadly based measure available for each state. Consequently, early in the project we began to develop such a measure. Before that could be done, however, a theoretical analysis was necessary to specify the meaning of terms such as the *status of women* and *gender equality*. The results of that effort are presented in the first section of this chapter. Specifically, we decompose the concept of *status of women* and identify and describe two key aspects: gender attainment and gender equality.

In addition to this theoretical analysis, the chapter is also intended as a methodological contribution to macrosociological research. On the basis of the theoretical analysis we created a multi-indicator measure of gender equality. The methodological contribution consists of making this measure available to the research community. This chapter describes the methods used to create these indicators and provides preliminary evidence of reliability and convergent and discriminant validity.

THE CONCEPT OF THE STATUS OF WOMEN

The status of women has been conceptually and operationally defined in a number of different ways. Mason (1986) describes it as a "much used but ill-defined term." Rather than weighing the merits of one approach over others, we find it is more useful to conceptualize the status of women as a multidimensional phenomenon. One aspect of this is the difference between theories and empirical studies which focus on the *absolute* degree to which women have attained valued social characteristics versus research which focuses on the status of women *relative* to men.

Gender Attainment and Gender Equality

A key dimension in understanding the differences and similarities among various studies of the status of women concerns whether the conceptualization and measurement focus on gender status *attainment* (from now on referred to as gender attainment) or on gender *equality*.

GENDER ATTAINMENT. Gender attainment, as used in this chapter, refers to the extent to which members of a particular gender have achieved such socially valued statuses as education, economic resources, and physical and mental health (Bianchi and Spain, 1983; Curtin, 1982; Powers, 1983). Empirical studies of the gender attainment aspect of the status of women are illustrated in the Population Reference Bureau's publication "Status of Women: A Comparative Analysis of Twenty Developing Countries" (Curtin, 1982). The status of women in that study refers to the extent to which women in these countries have achieved literacy or some other level of education, the percentage of women employed in the paid labor force, and life expectancy.

GENDER EQUALITY. Some feminist scholars, and some of the literature on social stratification, tend to use the idea of women's status in a different sense.

They are concerned with whether women have as much education *as men*, earn as much, and live as long. Hommes (1978:27), for example, defined the status of women as "the position women have as a group, compared with men as a group, in different fields of society." The term *partriarchy* as used by several feminist writers (for example, Dobash and Dobash, 1979) refers to gender *in*equality as an institutionalized aspect of the social structure typical of all social institutions, including the family, church, political, educational, and legal institutions. This facet of the status of women refers to the degree to which there is equality between the sexes (gender equality).

RELATION BETWEEN GENDER ATTAINMENT AND GENDER EQUALITY. The gender attainment and gender equality conceptualizations are related, but by no means unidimensional. The stereotypical upper-middle-class suburban women of the 1950s has a high absolute level of education attainment, lived in affluence relative to most of the world, and had a very low risk of dying in childbirth. Thus, the level of gender attainment was high. At the same time, but under the influence of the "feminine mystique" (Friedan, 1963), middle class housewives occupied subordinate roles relative to their husbands and relative to middle class men in almost all spheres of life.

The opposite combination is also possible. Education, material standard of living, and life expectancy can be low, but gender equality can be high. When viewed as an aspect of social stratification, women can have high status relative to men but low levels of gender attainment if both men and women are equally uneducated, equally poor, and have an equally short life expectancy. Thus, women are said to have high status in foraging societies such as the Kung!, even though neither men nor women are literate (Blumberg, 1978). Women are closer to being equal in areas valued by Kung! society than in areas valued by most other societies such as family and household matters, subsistence activities, and political power to influence the larger group.

We do not mean to suggest that gender equality and gender attainment are in conflict, or even that they are completely separate. In fact, an issue of major theoretical and practical importance is the extent to which equality between men and women is associated with the absolute level of gender attainment and other indicators of social and psychological well-being.[1]

CORRELATES OF EQUALITY. There is a growing body of empirical evidence supporting the idea that equality is not only desirable as an end in itself, but

1. Johnston (1985:233) points to the same distinction by differentiating between the *situation* of women versus the *status* of women. The latter can be determined "by comparing their situation, however measured, with some reference group or standard, such as the corresponding situation among men in the same society, or among women in another society or sub-culture."

that it also brings other benefits to society. Jacobs and Britt (1979), for example, compared the states of the United States and found that the greater the degree of economic equality, the lower the crime rate. Within the family, it has been found that egalitarian marriages, as opposed to male-dominant marriages, have the lowest incidence of violence (Coleman and Straus, 1986; Straus, 1973; Straus, Gelles, and Steinmetz, 1980). Another example is research which suggests that women's subordinate position and restricted social roles partly explain their high rate of depression (Aneshensel, Fredrichs, and Clark, 1981; Barnett and Baruch, 1985; Gove, 1979; Gove and Tudor, 1973). Each of these is an empirical question which might be addressed using a measure of gender equality such as the one described in this chapter.

METHOD OF CONSTRUCTING THE GENDER EQUALITY INDEX

As the name Gender Equality Index indicates, this instrument is intended to measure the attainments of women *relative to men.* There are several reasons for choosing this aspect of the status of women. First, equality between the sexes is presumed to be an issue of broad concern in almost all societies. Second, it is a universally applicable comparative frame. Third, it focuses on the status of women as an aspect of social stratification and therefore makes available the theoretical and methodological tools developed for research on social class and other aspects of social stratification.

Computation of Equality Indicators

Guided by the conceptualization outlined up to this point, we selected measures that could be used to assess the extent to which women have the same access to economic resources, legal rights, or positions of political power as men in each of the 50 states. In the case of the economic and political dimensions, this was achieved by expressing the gender attainment score of women in the state as a percentage of the gender attainment score of men in the state.[2] For example, one of the economic equality indictors is the median income of employed women in a particular state divided by the median income of employed men in the same state, multiplied by 100. For the United States

2. It should be noted that the method of computing indicators of equality used in this research results in a figure which can be substantially higher than the percentage of women among those having a given characteristic. Suppose there are 150 members of a legislature, of which 25 are women. This is a 16% female membership. However, using our method of computing indicators

as a whole, this was 59% in 1980. However, as will be seen, there are large differences among states.[3] The indicators of legal equality consist of statutes which grant legal rights to women, or legislation which protects existing but previously ignored rights, such as a fair employment practices act or legislation which prohibits sex discrimination in housing.

Composite Indexes

In addition to considering each of the separate indicators, we investigated the degree to which they formed a consistent pattern and calculated composite indexes to represent the cumulative effect of the economic indicators, the political indicators, the legal indicators, and all three subindexes combined to form an overall Gender Equality Index (GEX) for each state.

---

of equality (the female percentage divided by the male percentage) results in an equality index of 20 rather than 16:

$$((25/150) / (125/150)) * 100 = 20.$$

Essentially this is because gender equality in the legislature is achieved with 50% women members, not with 100%.

Another method of measuring gender equality was proposed by Johnston (1985). Johnston's method was to sum the squared differences between the proportion of the members of a particular gender who hold a specific social status and the proportion of the individuals of a particular gender in the overall population. For example, this indicator would first square the difference between the proportion of women who hold professional or technical jobs and the proportion of women in the civilian labor force. A similar squared difference is computed for men and the two resultant values are summed. Consequently, as the proportion of individuals of a specific gender who are in a particular valued social status approaches the proportion of gender members in the more general population, this indicator approaches the value of zero.

One problem with Johnston's proposal is that it does not offer the researcher direction regarding any potential between-gender differences. For example, a value of 50 may represent either that women are overrepresented in that social status or that men are overrepresented. In the present conceptualization, the former situation is shown by values below 100 while the latter situation results in values above 100. Consequently, one should theoretically expect a U-shaped curvilinear relationship between the indicator that Johnson (1985) proposes and the indicators employed in the present analysis.

3. Similarly, since being employed is a more highly valued status than being unemployed, one of the indicators in the economic subindex assesses the percent of the female civilian labor force who were employed relative to the percent of male civilian labor force who were employed. This ratio was then multiplied by 100. This permits an interpretation of gender equality if the indicator resulted in a value of 100. If the resultant indicator value is less than 100, it suggests that women in a specific state have a lower status than men in that state.

Table 4.1

Initial Pool of Economic Gender Equality Indicators

Indicators	Description	Year
Civilian Labor Force	Percent of females age 16 and older who are in the civilian labor force relative to the percent of males age 16 and older who are in the civilian labor force	1982
Professional and Technical Occupations	Percent of women in professional and technical occupations relative to the percent of men in professional and technical occupations	1982
Managers and Administrators	Percent of women who are managers and administrators in non-farm occupations relative to the percent of men who are managers and administrators in non-farm occupations	1982
Employment	Percent of female labor force members age 16 and older who are employed relative to the percent of male labor force members age 16 and older who are employed	1982
Median Income	The median income of full-time female workers age 15 and older relative to the median income of full-time male workers age 15 and older	1979
Loans by Small Business Administration	Percent of Small Business Loans given to women relative to the percent of Small Business loans given to men	1977
Amount Lent by Small Business Administration	Percent of Small Business Loan money lent to women relative to the percent of Small Business Loan money lent to men	1977
Households Above Poverty Level	Percent of female headed households with incomes above the poverty level relative to the percent of male headed households with incomes above the poverty level	1979

ECONOMIC EQUALITY

Given the considerable attention that researchers have focused on gender differences in the economic sphere (for example, Friedl, 1975; Roos, 1983; Treiman and Roos, 1983), a gender economic equality index was created. Eight indicators of gender equality with respect to economic status were compiled and are listed in table 4.1. Table 4.2(a and b) array the states in rank order according to each of these indicators. There are large state-to-state differences in respect to most of the eight economic equality indicators.

State-to-State Differences

LABOR FORCE PARTICIPATION AND PROFESSIONAL EMPLOYMENT. The first column of table 4.2a shows that women's labor force participation ranged from 56% of the rate for men in West Virginia to 78% of the male rate in Hawaii.

Table 4.2a

Rank Order of the States on Economic Gender Equality Indicators

Rank	Percent of Women Relative to Men in Civilian Labor Force		Percent of Women Relative to Men in Professional and Technical Occupations		Percent of Women Relative to Men who are Administrators in Non-Farm Occupations		Percent of Women who are Employed relative to Men who are Employed	
	State	swre1	State	swre2	State	swre3	State	swre4
1	Hawaii	78.0	West Virginia	178	Nevada	70.6	West Virginia	104
2	Minnesota	75.3	North Dakota	163	Oregon	64.7	Iowa	103
3	Alaska	75.0	South Dakota	162	Alaska	64.4	Pennsylvania	103
4	Nevada	74.6	Kentucky	147	New Mexico	61.3	Wisconsin	102
5	Wisconsin	73.2	Iowa	139	Washington	60.0	Alaska	102
6	North Carolina	73.1	Georgia	135	Montana	60.0	Ohio	102
7	Virginia	72.3	North Carolina	133	Hawaii	59.4	Montana	102
8	Wyoming	72.2	Mississippi	132	Arizona	58.2	Wyoming	102
9	Delaware	72.0	Arkansas	124	Kentucky	58.2	Delaware	101
10	Vermont	71.8	Wyoming	121	Idaho	57.6	Kansas	101
11	South Carolina	71.7	Nebraska	121	California	57.3	Oklahoma	101
12	Maryland	71.6	Indiana	120	Missouri	57.1	Washington	101
13	Massachusetts	71.5	Montana	120	Oklahoma	56.9	Indiana	101
14	Rhode Island	71.3	Louisiana	117	Iowa	56.9	Illinois	101
15	Nebraska	71.0	Maine	115	Florida	55.7	Idaho	101
16	Colorado	70.8	Texas	114	Texas	54.7	Hawaii	101
17	Arizona	70.8	Florida	114	Colorado	53.1	Minnesota	101
18	California	70.7	Wisconsin	113	Maine	52.3	Massachusetts	101
19	Florida	70.7	Oklahoma	111	Virginia	52.2	Kentucky	101
20	Connecticut	70.5	Alabama	110	Tennessee	52.1	Colorado	101
21	Georgia	70.4	Ohio	109	South Carolina	52.1	Nebraska	100
22	New Hampshire	70.3	Vermont	109	Wyoming	51.5	Nevada	100
23	South Dakota	69.7	Tennessee	108	Alabama	51.1	California	100
24	Washington	69.5	New Jersey	108	West Virginia	50.3	Michigan	100
25	Arkansas	69.5	Alaska	108	Maryland	50.6	Arizona	100
26	Kansas	69.5	Michigan	108	Vermont	50.6	Connecticut	100
27	Idaho	69.2	Oregon	108	Minnesota	50.0	Maine	100
28	Maine	68.9	South Carolina	107	Mississippi	49.7	Maryland	100
29	Iowa	68.9	Utah	107	Louisiana	49.6	Utah	100
30	Indiana	68.8	Illinois	106	Wisconsin	49.1	Missouri	100
31	Oregon	68.7	Missouri	106	Georgia	49.0	Oregon	100
32	North Dakota	68.4	Pennsylvania	104	Ohio	48.5	New York	99
33	Missouri	68.3	New York	104	Michigan	47.6	Vermont	99
34	Michigan	68.1	Virginia	102	South Dakota	47.1	Florida	99
35	Montana	67.9	Kansas	102	New Jersey	47.0	North Dakota	99
36	Illinois	67.5	Idaho	102	Utah	47.0	South Carolina	99
37	New Jersey	67.4	Rhode Island	101	Illinois	46.6	New Hampshire	99
38	Tennessee	67.3	Massachusetts	100	Arkansas	45.8	South Dakota	99
39	Texas	67.2	Nevada	100	Indiana	45.2	Texas	99
40	Ohio	66.9	Arizona	98	Massachusetts	44.8	Mississippi	99
41	Mississippi	66.7	New Mexico	98	Pennsylvania	44.6	New Jersey	99
42	Oklahoma	66.2	Hawaii	97	New York	44.2	Rhode Island	98
43	Kentucky	66.1	Washington	97	Kansas	43.8	Alabama	98
44	New Mexico	65.8	Maryland	97	North Dakota	43.8	Georgia	98
45	Utah	65.5	New Hampshire	96	Nebraska	43.1	Virginia	98
46	Pennsylvania	65.5	Connecticut	95	New Hampshire	42.5	New Mexico	98
47	New York	65.3	Minnesota	91	Delaware	41.6	Tennessee	98
48	Alabama	64.2	California	90	Connecticut	37.7	North Carolina	97
49	Louisiana	60.2	Colorado	87	Rhode Island	37.7	Arkansas	97
50	West Virginia	55.8	Delaware	85	North Carolina	37.7		

The second column of table 4.2a, which gives female employment in professional and technical occupations as a percentage of the male employment in
these occupations, also shows large differences among states. However, column 2 also shows some surprising statistics; most of the figures are greater
than 100, which indicates a larger percentage of women than men are employed in professional and technical occupations. This is because so many
women are employed as teachers and nurses, occupations which, although

Table 4.2b

Rank Order of the States on Economic Gender Equality Indicators

Rank	Median Income of Female Workers Relative to Median Income of Male Workers		Percent of SBA Loans given to Women Relative to Percent Given to Men		Percent of SBA Loan Money Lent to Women Relative to Percent Lent to Men		Percent of Female Headed Families Above Poverty Level Relative to Male Headed Families Above Poverty Level	
	State	swre5	State	swre6	State	swre7	State	swre8
1	Hawaii	69.2	Idaho	58.7	Idaho	53.8	Nevada	83.5
2	North Carolina	66.0	Kansas	56.2	Kansas	40.8	North Dakota	82.3
3	South Carolina	64.6	Alaska	49.2	Delaware	36.9	Minnesota	82.2
4	Vermont	64.4	Oregon	44.9	Maryland	31.5	Nebraska	81.6
5	New York	64.3	Delaware	38.8	Oregon	31.5	Arizona	81.4
6	Alaska	63.9	Maryland	35.1	Alaska	28.2	Iowa	80.6
7	Maine	63.5	Arizona	33.3	Arizona	26.5	Wyoming	80.5
8	Massachusetts	62.5	Oklahoma	31.5	Oklahoma	23.4	Missouri	80.0
9	Virginia	62.2	Kentucky	28.2	Missouri	21.9	California	79.6
10	Georgia	62.0	Pennsylvania	25.0	Montana	19.0	Utah	78.9
11	Maryland	61.9	Missouri	25.0	Hawaii	19.0	Hawaii	78.5
12	South Dakota	61.7	New Hampshire	25.0	Wisconsin	19.0	Alaska	78.4
13	Arkansas	61.6	Rhode Island	23.4	Pennsylvania	17.6	Vermont	78.2
14	Nevada	61.6	Montana	23.4	Rhode Island	17.6	Maryland	78.1
15	California	61.2	Wisconsin	23.4	Ohio	17.6	Oregon	77.4
16	Florida	60.5	Ohio	23.4	New Hampshire	17.6	Kansas	77.4
17	Colorado	60.1	Virginia	21.9	Connecticut	16.2	Colorado	77.1
18	Mississippi	60.1	New York	21.9	Kentucky	14.9	New Hampshire	76.9
19	Rhode Island	59.5	New Jersey	21.9	Virginia	13.6	West Virginia	76.8
20	New Hampshire	59.3	West Virginia	20.4	New York	13.6	Florida	76.5
21	Tennessee	59.3	Connecticut	20.4	West Virginia	12.3	Pennsylvania	76.3
22	Connecticut	59.0	South Carolina	20.4	North Carolina	12.3	Wisconsin	76.2
23	Kansas	58.9	Alabama	19.2	New Jersey	12.3	Massachusetts	75.8
24	Idaho	58.9	Georgia	19.0	Mississippi	12.3	Indiana	75.8
25	Arizona	58.8	Hawaii	17.6	Wyoming	12.3	Maine	75.6
26	Wisconsin	58.6	North Carolina	17.6	Illinois	12.1	Oklahoma	75.3
27	Nebraska	58.6	North Dakota	17.6	Louisiana	11.1	Texas	75.3
28	Oregon	58.5	Wyoming	17.6	South Carolina	11.1	Kentucky	75.0
29	Iowa	58.5	Washington	16.2	Georgia	11.1	Ohio	75.0
30	Minnesota	58.4	Mississippi	16.2	Washington	9.8	North Carolina	74.8
31	Oklahoma	58.4	Arkansas	14.9	Utah	9.8	Delaware	74.7
32	New Mexico	58.3	Louisiana	14.9	California	9.8	South Carolina	74.5
33	Delaware	58.3	Illinois	14.9	Florida	9.8	South Dakota	74.4
34	Pennsylvania	58.3	South Dakota	13.6	South Dakota	9.8	Washington	73.9
35	Texas	57.7	Nevada	12.3	North Dakota	8.7	Connecticut	73.9
36	Missouri	57.6	Massachusetts	12.3	Arkansas	8.7	New Jersey	73.4
37	New Jersey	57.5	California	12.3	Nevada	8.7	Arkansas	73.2
38	Washington	57.3	Indiana	12.3	Indiana	7.5	Rhode Island	72.8
39	Kentucky	57.1	Texas	12.3	Alabama	7.5	Montana	72.3
40	North Dakota	57.0	Florida	12.3	Texas	6.3	Michigan	72.1
41	Alabama	56.8	Utah	9.8	Massachusetts	6.3	Alabama	72.0
42	Michigan	56.7	Michigan	9.8	Michigan	6.3	Georgia	71.6
43	Illinois	56.6	Iowa	9.8	Iowa	6.3	Virginia	71.2
44	Ohio	56.5	Tennessee	9.8	Maine	5.2	Illinois	71.1
45	Montana	55.7	Colorado	9.8	Colorado	4.1	Tennessee	71.0
46	Indiana	55.6	Nebraska	7.5	Tennessee	4.1	Idaho	70.3
47	Utah	54.2	Vermont	6.3	New Mexico	4.1	New York	68.4
48	Louisiana	53.2	New Mexico	5.2	Vermont	3.0	New Mexico	67.4
49	West Virginia	51.4	Minnesota	5.2	Minnesota	3.0	Louisiana	64.3
50	Wyoming	50.2	Maine	5.2	Nebraska	3.0	Mississippi	60.4

professions, are not highly rewarded, either in money or prestige. On the other hand, when employment as managers or administrators is considered, column 3 of table 4.2a shows that the female rate is only half that of the male rate in the median state, and only 38% of the male rate in three states (Connecticut, Rhode Island, and North Carolina).

EMPLOYMENT. The last column of table 4.2a presents data on the female employment rate (the percentage of women in the labor force who actually have jobs) as a percentage of the male employment rate. The median score is 100, indicating that women have slightly more freedom from unemployment than men. Two factors can contribute to this finding. First, this low comparative unemployment rate probably reflects the sale of skilled and dependable female labor at bargain rates and specifically at an average of 59% of male wages. Second, it is possible that unemployed women may withdraw from the labor force more rapidly, which might not be mirrored in the unemployment rate.

INCOME. The first column of table 4.2b arrays the states according to the most widely used measure of the economic equality of women—the percentage that the earnings of women employed full-time are of the earnings of men who are employed full-time. The median is the well-known figure of 59%. What is not well known is that there are large state-to-state differences. The range is from 50% in Wyoming to 69% in Hawaii. Nowhere do women come close to equality with men.

ACCESS TO CAPITAL. The second and third columns of table 4.2b show extremely large differences in the extent to which women have secured business capital through the Small Business Administration. In most states women obtain fewer than one-fifth of the loans and less than 12% of the funds. Even in Idaho, the top ranking state, the figure is only 59% of the loans and 54% of the amount lent to men.

ABOVE-POVERTY HOUSEHOLDS. Although women are moving toward economic equality with men in certain ways, they are losing ground in other ways. One example of this feminization of poverty (D. Pearce and McAdoo, 1981) is the proportion of female-headed households with incomes below the federal poverty line. In every state, a smaller proportion of female-headed households have incomes above the poverty line than is true of households containing an adult male. The range is from 60% in Mississippi to 84% in Nevada. In the median state, the rate of nonpoor female-headed households is only 76% of the male rate.

SUMMARY. With respect to six of the eight indicators of economic status, women are far from reaching equality with men. This is not only the typical situation but also applies to the states in which women fare best. The maximum female attainment of these six economic statuses among the states falls short of gender equality with men. Moreover, a closer examination of the two indicators which manifestly indicate equality suggests that even this situation may be illusory.

Table 4.3

Regional Differences in Economic Gender Equality Indicators

Indicators	Northeast	North Central	South	West
Percent of Women Relative to Men in Civilian Labor Force, 1982	69.2	69.6	67.8	70.7
Percent of Women Relative to Men in Professional and Technical Occupations, 1982*	104.0	120.4	120.1	102.9
Percent of Women Relative to Men who are Administrators in Non-Farm Occupations, 1982**	44.6	48.2	50.5	58.8
Percent of Women who are Employed Relative to Men who are Employed, 1982*	100.3	101.2	99.7	100.9
Median Income of Female Workers Relative to Median Income of Male Workers, 1979	60.9	57.9	59.4	59.1
Percent of SBA Loans Given to Women Relative to Percent Given to Men, 1977	17.9	18.2	20.8	23.9
Percent of SBA Loan Money Lent to Women Relative to the Percent Lent to Men, 1977	12.2	13.0	14.2	18.2
Percent of Female Headed Families Above Poverty Level Relative to Male Headed Families Above Poverty Level, 1979*	74.6	77.4	72.8	76.9
Economic Subindex (P-Index), 1977-1982	54.2	55.1	55.0	58.3

Note: * p < .05, ** p < .001.

Regional Patterns

Table 4.3 shows the extent to which the four major regions of the United States differ with respect to economic equality. One point of special interest concerns the South. The low per capita income in the South (U.S. Department of Commerce, 1984) might lead one to expect a tendency for southern states to have low economic status scores. That would be a reasonable expectation if the indicators measured economic *attainment*. Because all eight of the indicators measure economic *equality*, not economic attainment, there is no necessary correlation. In fact, examination of tables 4.2 and 4.3 provides only the most minimal support for regional differences in economic gender equality, particularly with regard to comparing the South to other regions. Other researchers have reached similar conclusions (Martin, Wilson, and Dillman, 1986).

The paucity of regional differences on the economic equality indicators illustrates the difference between gender attainment and gender equality. The first column in table 4.2b shows that women come closest to equality with men in Hawaii and North Carolina. The median income of women in Hawaii ($10,910 in 1979) was over $2,000 more than in North Carolina ($8,781). However, the proportion that women's income is of men's income is not very different in the two states (69 and 66% of male income). In Hawaii, wage rates are relatively high for women as well as men, and in North Carolina wage rates are low for both men and women. At the other end of the continuum, women in West Virginia earn only 51% of male income and women in Wyoming only 50% of male income, despite the fact that one is a low income state and the other a high income state.

Economic Equality Index

Each of the eight indicators measures a different aspect of gender equality in economic status. Consequently, it seemed desirable to determine if a composite measure could be constructed which would gauge the cumulative effect of all eight indicators. An internal consistency reliability analysis was therefore computed using the Statistical Package for the Social Sciences (SPSS) (Nie et al., 1975) reliability program, as shown in table 4.4.

Two criteria were required for the exclusion of an indicator in the creation of the final index. First, the correlated item-total correlation (the correlation between the indicator and the subindex after adjusting for the fact that the indicator is part of the index) had to fall below .30. Second, the exclusion of the indicator would result in an increase in the alpha coefficient of reliability

Table 4.4

Reliability Analysis of Economic Gender Equality Index

Indicators	Inter-Item Correlations							All Indicators		Final Set of Indicators	
	1	2	3	4	5	6	7	r*	Alpha if Item Deleted	r*	Alpha if Item Deleted
Percent of women relative to men in the civilian labor force, 1982	—							.25	.37	.38	.52
Percent of women relative to men in professional and technical occupations, 1982	-.43	—						-.28	.59	—	—
Percent of women relative to men who are administrators in non-farm occupations, 1982	.09	-.10	—					.18	.40	.21	.58
Percent of women who are employed relative to percent of men who are employed, 1982	-.05	.07	.19	—				.27	.36	.23	.58
Median income of female workers relative to median income of male workers, 1979	.61	-.24	.05	-.31	—			.03	.46	.10	.59
Percent of SBA Loans given to women relative to percent given to men, 1977	.05	-.14	.12	.25	.01	—		.42	.28	.45	.50
Percent of SBA Loan money lent to women relative to percent lent to men, 1977	.11	-.23	.08	.27	.01	.95	—	.41	.29	.47	.48
Percent of female headed families above poverty level relative to male headed families above poverty level, 1979	.43	-.03	.17	.40	.03	.01	.02	.32	.33	.31	.55
Standardized Alpha Coefficient								.43		.59	

Note: Prior to computing the reliability coefficients, all of the indicators were transformed to Z-scores and outliers were adjusted.

* r = Corrected Item-Total Correlation. See text for explanation.

for the index. Both these requirements had to be satisfied before an indicator was eliminated from a subindex.

The correlation of the eight economic equality indicators with each other is presented in the left panel of table 4.4. The two right panels give the corrected item-total correlation in the columns headed r, and the alpha coefficients of reliability if the item were to be deleted.

The second row in the panel headed All Indicators shows that Professional and Technical Occupations has a negative correlation of $-.28$ with the other indicators. This is consistent with the fact that a large proportion of the professional positions held by women are as teachers and nurses. In addition, the "Alpha if item is deleted" coefficient of .59 shows that elimination of this indicator would result in an index with a substantially higher reliability than if it were retained as part of the Economic Equality Index. We therefore computed the index by summing the Z-scored version of the seven remaining indicators. The right-hand panel of table 4.4 shows the item analysis statistics for the final version of the Economic Equality Index and the alpha coefficient (Cronbach, 1970) of reliability of .59. This index has a mean of 56 and a standard deviation of 4.

POLITICAL EQUALITY

Another sphere in which it is important to assess gender equality is the political. The low female representation in legislatures and other elected offices is probably one of the factors maintaining inequality in other spheres. In addition, a number of researchers (including Huber, 1986; Sacks, 1974; and Sapiro, 1983) have suggested that the more women are involved in nondomestic work, the greater their ability to participate in societal decision-making and the greater their political power. Although it is beyond the scope of the present chapter, the indicators presented in this section might be used to test this hypothesis.

Table 4.5 identifies the six indicators of political equality, and tables 4.6(a and b) array the states in rank order on these six variables. Examination of tables 4.6a and b suggests that, in general, women have achieved even less political equality than economic equality. For these six variables, women in the median states have achieved only between 0 and 16% of equality with men. In addition, the state-to-state differences are greater for the political equality indicators than they are for the economic equality indicators, mainly because there are a large number of states where the political power of women is at or near zero.

Table 4.5

Initial Pool of Political Gender Equality Indicators

Indicators	Description	Year
Congress	Percent of U.S. Congress members who are women relative to the percent of U.S. Congress members who are men	1983
State Senate	Percent of State Senate members who are women relative to the percent of State Senate Members who are men	1983
State House	Percent of State House members who are women relative to the percent of State House members who are men	1983
Judges	Percent of major trial and appellate court judges who are women relative to the percent of major trial and appellate court judges who are men	1979
Mayors	Percent of mayors who are women relative to the percent of mayors who are men	1983
Governing Boards	Percent of Governing Board members who are women relative to the percent of Governing Board members who are men	1983

The zero, or near zero, level of political officeholding by women is well illustrated by the first of the variables in table 4.6a. This shows that in two-thirds of the 50 states, there are no women members of either the U.S. House of Representatives or U.S. Senate.

Women do somewhat better in terms of membership in *state* legislatures. The second and third columns of table 4.6a show that there are five states where women have about 25% of the state senate positions needed for equality with men. With respect to the lower houses, there are about a dozen states where women have 24% or more of the positions held by men. Nevertheless, in the median state, women occupy only about 9% as many state senate seats as men and only 16% of the number of state house seats which would be necessary for equal representation.

The situation is not greatly different with respect to mayoralties, where women have only about 8% of the mayoral positions held by men (see table 4.6b). Even in Delaware, the state with the largest ratio of women to men mayors, women have only 28% of the mayoralties needed for equality in this aspect of political status. In respect to judgeships on major appeal and trial courts, the figures in the first column of table 4.6b show that the appointment of Sandra Day O'Connor to the U.S. Supreme Court is far from indicative of the situation in the state courts. In the median state, women have only 2% of the seats needed for equality with men; and even in the top ranking state, Hawaii, women are only 10% of the way toward equal status with men.

The indicator of political status on which women come closest to men is

Table 4.6a

Rank Order of the States on Political Gender Equality Indicators

Rank	Percent of U.S. Congress Members who are Women Relative to Percent who are Men		Percent of State Senate Members who are Women Relative to Percent who are Men		Percent of State House Members who are Women Relative to Percent who are Men	
	State	swrp1	State	swrp2	State	swrp3
1	Nevada	50.0	New Hampshire	33.3	Colorado	44.4
2	Maryland	42.8	Florida	29.0	Wyoming	42.2
3	Maine	33.3	Connecticut	28.5	New Hampshire	40.3
4	Connecticut	33.3	Oregon	25.0	Connecticut	31.3
5	Rhode Island	33.3	Hawaii	25.0	Hawaii	30.7
6	Nebraska	25.0	Maine	22.2	Maryland	30.5
7	Kansas	16.6	Arizona	20.0	Oregon	30.4
8	Colorado	16.6	Washington	19.5	Arizona	30.4
9	Louisiana	11.1	Alaska	17.6	Wisconsin	30.2
10	Tennessee	11.1	Massachusetts	17.6	Maine	30.1
11	Ohio	8.7	Colorado	16.6	Washington	25.6
12	Indiana	8.3	Delaware	16.6	Vermont	23.9
13	Illinois	8.3	Illinois	15.6	Idaho	20.6
14	Florida	6.2	Minnesota	15.5	Delaware	20.5
15	New Jersey	6.2	Vermont	15.3	Kansas	20.1
16	California	4.6	Nebraska	13.9	Illinois	19.1
17	New York	2.5	Idaho	12.9	Iowa	19.0
18	Hawaii	0.0	North Carolina	11.1	Montana	19.0
19	New Hampshire	0.0	Rhode Island	11.1	North Carolina	18.8
20	Montana	0.0	Wyoming	11.1	Florida	18.8
21	Alaska	0.0	Nevada	10.5	South Dakota	18.6
22	Vermont	0.0	West Virginia	9.6	California	17.6
23	Wisconsin	0.0	South Dakota	9.3	Minnesota	16.5
24	Massachusetts	0.0	New York	8.9	North Dakota	16.4
25	Iowa	0.0	Indiana	8.7	Missouri	16.4
26	Utah	0.0	North Dakota	8.1	Rhode Island	16.2
27	Oklahoma	0.0	Kansas	8.1	Indiana	16.2
28	Texas	0.0	New Mexico	7.6	West Virginia	16.2
29	Kentucky	0.0	South Carolina	6.9	Michigan	14.5
30	Minnesota	0.0	Maryland	6.8	Alaska	14.2
31	North Carolina	0.0	Wisconsin	6.4	Massachusetts	14.2
32	Delaware	0.0	Montana	6.3	New York	12.7
33	South Carolina	0.0	Missouri	6.2	New Jersey	12.6
34	South Dakota	0.0	Kentucky	5.5	Ohio	12.5
35	Washington	0.0	Michigan	5.5	Virginia	12.3
36	Pennsylvania	0.0	Virginia	5.2	Oklahoma	12.2
37	West Virginia	0.0	California	5.2	Utah	11.9
38	Arkansas	0.0	Georgia	3.7	Nevada	10.5
39	Oregon	0.0	Utah	3.5	Georgia	10.4
40	Georgia	0.0	Ohio	3.1	Texas	9.4
41	Michigan	0.0	Tennessee	3.1	New Mexico	9.3
42	Alabama	0.0	Alabama	2.9	Tennessee	8.7
43	Mississippi	0.0	Arkansas	2.9	Kentucky	8.7
44	Virginia	0.0	New Jersey	2.5	South Carolina	7.8
45	Missouri	0.0	Oklahoma	2.1	Arkansas	6.3
46	Wyoming	0.0	Iowa	2.0	Alabama	5.0
47	Idaho	0.0	Pennsylvania	2.0	Pennsylvania	4.6
48	Arizona	0.0	Louisiana	0.0	Louisiana	2.9
49	New Mexico	0.0	Texas	0.0	Mississippi	2.5
50	North Dakota	0.0	Mississippi	0.0	Nebraska	Missing

positions on municipal governing boards. However, although women are 67% of the way toward equality with men in Michigan, this relatively high figure is an outlier. In the next highest ranking state, Connecticut, women have only 27% of the seats needed for equality with men. Moreover, the median is only 14%. Finally, seats on municipal governing boards, although important, are not usually positions of great political prestige or power.

Table 4.6b

Rank Order of the States on Political Gender Equality Indicators

	Percent of Major Trial and Appellate Court Judges who are Women Relative to Percent who are Men		Percent of Mayors who are Women Relative to Percent who are Men		Percent of Governing Board Members Who are Women Relative to Percent who are Men	
Rank	State	swrp4	State	swrp5	State	swrp6
1	Hawaii	9.8	Delaware	28.2	Michigan	66.6
2	Rhode Island	9.8	California	19.0	Connecticut	26.5
3	Wisconsin	8.7	Washington	17.6	Arizona	26.5
4	Connecticut	8.7	New Mexico	14.9	Oregon	25.0
5	Kansas	7.5	Oregon	14.9	Wyoming	23.4
6	Arkansas	6.3	Indiana	14.9	Alaska	23.4
7	New Mexico	6.3	Massachusetts	13.6	New Mexico	21.9
8	Maryland	5.2	New Jersey	13.6	Colorado	20.4
9	Arizona	5.2	Maine	13.6	Rhode Island	20.4
10	Minnesota	5.2	Kentucky	12.3	Washington	19.0
11	Michigan	5.2	New Hampshire	12.3	Kentucky	19.0
12	Massachusetts	5.2	Wyoming	12.3	West Virginia	17.6
13	Oregon	4.1	Arizona	12.3	Maryland	17.6
14	California	4.1	Idaho	11.1	Montana	17.6
15	New York	4.1	Michigan	11.1	California	17.6
16	Pennsylvania	4.1	Colorado	11.1	Florida	16.2
17	Florida	4.1	Montana	9.8	Delaware	16.2
18	Mississippi	3.0	Connecticut	9.8	Alabama	16.2
19	New Jersey	3.0	North Carolina	8.7	Virginia	14.9
20	Washington	3.0	Minnesota	8.7	Idaho	14.9
21	Oklahoma	3.0	Florida	8.7	Mississippi	13.6
22	Texas	2.0	Maryland	8.7	Utah	13.6
23	South Dakota	2.0	Alaska	8.7	New Jersey	13.6
24	Ohio	2.0	West Virginia	8.7	Kansas	13.6
25	Colorado	2.0	South Dakota	7.5	Texas	13.6
26	Kentucky	2.0	Oklahoma	7.5	Iowa	13.6
27	Indiana	2.0	Arkansas	7.5	Hawaii	12.3
28	North Carolina	2.0	New York	7.5	North Carolina	12.3
29	Illinois	2.0	Texas	7.5	South Carolina	12.3
30	Iowa	1.0	Nevada	6.3	Arkansas	11.1
31	Tennessee	1.0	Virginia	6.3	Oklahoma	11.1
32	Alabama	1.0	Vermont	6.3	Louisiana	11.1
33	Georgia	1.0	Kansas	6.3	North Dakota	9.8
34	Wyoming	0.0	Alabama	6.3	Maine	9.8
35	Maine	0.0	Mississippi	6.3	Nevada	9.8
36	Montana	0.0	South Carolina	5.2	Massachusetts	9.8
37	Utah	0.0	Utah	5.2	South Dakota	9.8
38	Nevada	0.0	Nebraska	5.2	Tennessee	8.7
39	Virginia	0.0	Louisiana	5.2	Ohio	7.5
40	Alaska	0.0	Illinois	5.2	Nebraska	7.5
41	West Virginia	0.0	North Dakota	5.2	Illinois	6.3
42	Missouri	0.0	Wisconsin	4.1	Missouri	6.3
43	North Dakota	0.0	Missouri	4.1	New Hampshire	6.3
44	South Carolina	0.0	Iowa	4.1	Georgia	6.3
45	Delaware	0.0	Georgia	3.0	Pennsylvania	6.3
46	Idaho	0.0	Pennsylvania	2.0	Minnesota	5.2
47	Vermont	0.0	Tennessee	2.0	Vermont	5.2
48	Louisiana	0.0	Ohio	2.0	Indiana	4.1
49	New Hampshire	0.0	Rhode Island	0.0	Wisconsin	Missing
50	Nebraska	0.0	Hawaii	Missing	New York	Missing

Regional Differences

In contrast to the lack of a clear regional pattern in economic equality, the means for each region in table 4.7 do reveal some consistent tendencies for political equality. Specifically, the South has the lowest score of any region on five of the six indicators, and the Northeast and West tend to be regions in

Table 4.7

Regional Differences on Political Gender Equality Indicators

Indicators	Northeast	North Central	South	West
Percent of U.S. Congress members who are women relative to percent who are men, 1983	12.08	5.59	4.46	5.49
Percent of State Senate members who are women relative to percent who are men, 1983*	15.76	8.58	6.62	13.94
Percent of State House members who are women relative to percent who are men, 1983**	20.72	18.19	11.98	23.65
Percent of major trial and appellate court judges who are women relative to percent who are men, 1979	3.92	2.99	1.95	2.69
Percent of mayors who are women relative to percent who are men, 1983	8.79	6.58	8.30	11.98
Percent of State House members who are women relative to percent who are men, 1983	12.31	13.72	13.66	18.93
Political Subindex (P-Index Version B), 1979-1983**	14.43	11.64	10.14	17.45

Note: * p < .05, ** p < .01.

Table 4.8

Reliability Analysis of Political Gender Equality Index

Indicators	Inter-Item Correlations					All Indicators		Final Set of Indicators	
	1	2	3	4	5	r*	Alpha if Item Deleted	r*	Alpha if Item Deleted
Percent of U.S. Congress members who are women relative to percent who are men, 1983	—					.18	.68	—	—
Percent of State Senate members who are women relative to percent who are men, 1983	.16	—				.55	.53	.59	.62
Percent of State House members who are women relative to percent who are men, 1983	.21	.69	—			.56	.53	.63	.59
Percent of major trial and appellate court judges who are women relative to percent who are men, 1979	.28	.13	.03	—		.25	.65	—	—
Percent of mayors who are women relative to percent who are men, 1983	-.13	.40	.38	.01	—	.33	.62	.49	.68
Percent of State House members who are women relative to percent who are men, 1983	.06	.22	.31	.35	.36	.41	.59	.36	.75
Standardized Alpha Coefficient						.64		.72	

Note: Prior to computing the reliability coefficients, all of the indicators were transformed to Z-scores and substitutions were made for missing values.
* r = Corrected Item-Total Correlation. See text for explanation.

which women have achieved far more political equality than in either the South or the North Central regions. Taking all six indicators together in the form of a composite index gives the edge to the western states.

Political Equality Index

As with the Economic Equality Index, we investigated the feasibility of combining the six indicators to form a composite index which might measure the political equality of women in a more comprehensive and reliable way than is possible with any one of the indicators by itself.[4]

The initial reliability analysis of the six indicators is presented in table 4.8 in the panel headed All Indicators. Examination of this analysis suggests that two indicators be dropped from the subindex: percent of U.S. Congress members and percent of judges. After this was done, the panel headed Final Set of Indicators shows that the resulting four-item index has an alpha coefficient of .72, which is high for an index containing only four indicators.[5] This index has a mean of 13.1 and a standard deviation of 5.8.

4. Missing values and outliers were a particular problem in computing the Economic Equality Index and the other composite indexes because, with a population of only 50, loss of even a single state results in 2% reduction in the number of cases. Consequently, rather than deleting states with a missing value or an outlier, we tried to substitute meaningful estimated values.

Substitution for missing values was needed primarily for the political subindex because four states (Nebraska, Hawaii, New York, and Wisconsin) had a missing datum point. For example, Wisconsin lacks data on the percent of women on municipal governing boards. The estimate for this indicator was based on the ranking of the state on the indicator which we believed to be most similar—the percent of mayors who are female. The rank position of Wisconsin in respect to women mayors was used to estimate the percentage of women on municipal governing boards by assigning Wisconsin a percentage that corresponds to that rank in the distribution of members of municipal governing boards. Similarly, since Nebraska has a unicameral state legislature, we used the percentage of women in that body as the best estimate for both houses of the state legislature.

In respect to outliers, we did not want to permit any one of the indicators in an index to exert an overwhelming influence on the score of a state. Consequently, we inspected the data to locate values which were more than 2.5 standard deviations from the mean and more than 1.0 standard deviations from either the next highest or lowest value for that indicator. Values which met these two criteria were replaced by values that were just higher or lower than the next most extreme score. Six such outlier adjustments were made.

5. This evaluation of the .71 coefficient is based on the fact that alpha is a function of both the interitem correlation and the number of items. Psychological tests, which typically consist of a great many test items, have higher alpha coefficients despite having *lower* average item-to-item correlations because they usually contain a large number of items. Of course, from an absolute perspective, a reliability coefficient of .71 leaves much to be desired.

Table 4.9

Initial Pool of Legal Gender Equality Indicators, 1980

Indicators	Description
SWL1	State passed fair employment practices act
SWL2	Women may file lawsuit personally under fair employment practices act
SWL3	State passed equal pay laws
SWL4	Women may file lawsuit personally under equal pay laws
SWL5	Sex discrimination law in the area of public accommodations
SWL6	Sex discrimination law in the area of housing
SWL7	Sex discrimination law in the area of financing
SWL8	Sex discrimination law in the area of education
SWL9[R]	State requires that wife must change name when married
SWL10	Statutes provide for civil injunction relief for victims of abuse
SWL11	Statutes provide temporary injunction relief during a divorce, separation, or custody proceedings
SWL12	Statutes that define the physical abuse of a family or household member as a criminal offense
SWL13	Statutes that permit warrantless arrest based on probable cause in domestic violence cases
SWL14	Statute that requires data collection and reporting of family violence by agencies that serve these families
SWL15	Statutes that provide funds for family violence shelters or established standards for shelter operations

Note: All indicators were scored 1 = yes and 0 = no, except for the indicator superscripted (R) which was reverse scored.

LEGAL EQUALITY

The laws which a community enacts regarding the rights of women as compared to the rights of men offer another perspective on gender equality. Lerman and Livingston (1983) and Stanko (1981) noted wide variation in state statutes designed to protect women from domestic violence. L. M. Williams (1982) reviewed the rape laws of 15 countries and found that those countries whose rape laws derogated rape victims and treated women as sexual objects had significantly lower female participation in the labor force (especially fewer women in the professional labor force) than those countries whose rape laws were less biased. The primary focus of this section is sex discrimination statutes in and out of the workplace and domestic violence statutes.

The indicators used to measure the legal equality of women differ from those used for the economic and political equality in two important respects. First, each indicates the presence or absence of a statute which grants legal rights to women or which protects existing but presumably ignored rights. Second, it follows from this that these are measures *intended* to provide for equality rather than measures of actual equality.

State and Regional Differences

The distinction between the indicators used for the economic or political dimensions and the legal indicators can be grasped from considering the first of the indictors listed in table 4.9—whether the state has passed a fair employment practices act. It is all too obvious that, important as such statutes are, their passage does not immediately produce a situation of gender equality in employment.

The pool of items used to index the legal equality of women consists of all the statutes for which state-by-state data are given in Ross and Barcher (1983). Table 4.10 shows which states have passed each of these 15 laws, and table 4.11 displays the regional differences in the legal gender equality indicators.

Legal Equality Index

Each of the legal indicators was scored so that the presence of a statute that protected the rights of women in a state resulted in that state gaining a point on the Legal Equality Index. For example, if a state had enacted a fair employment practice law, the state was coded with a 1; if not, it was coded with a 0. Consequently, the presence of all the statutes in the state law would result in a score of 15. These scores were then transformed to a percentage. A state which had passed five of these laws would have a score of 33, indicating 33% of the maximum points.

Table 4.12 gives the results of the reliability analysis of this index. Since all these items were scored either zero or one, no Z-score transformations were done. The initial analysis (shown in the panel headed All Indicators) suggested that 2 of the 15 indicators should be eliminated. These two indicators were (1) whether the state required that the wife change her name when married, and (2) whether the state had a statute that provided temporary injunction relief during a divorce, separation, or custody proceedings. The deletion of these two indicators resulted in an index with an alpha coefficient of .76. This 13-item scale had a mean score of 55.8 and a standard deviation of 23.5.

Table 4.10

States Enacting 15 Legal Equality Measures, 1980

Statute	States Which Enacted
1. Fair employment practices law	Alaska, Arizona, California, Colorado, Connecticut, Delaware, Georgia, Hawaii, Idaho, Illinois, Indiana, Iowa, Kansas, Kentucky, Maine, Maryland, Massachusetts, Michigan, Minnesota, Missouri, Montana, Nebraska, Nevada, New Hampshire, New Jersey, New Mexico, New York, North Carolina, Ohio, Oklahoma, Oregon, Pennsylvania, Rhode Island, South Dakota, Utah, Vermont, Washington, West Virginia, Wisconsin, Wyoming
2. Fair employment personal suits	Alaska, Arizona, California, Colorado, Connecticut, Georgia, Idaho, Maine, Michigan, Montana, Nevada, Oregon, Washington
3. Equal pay law	Alaska, Arizona, Arkansas, California, Colorado, Connecticut, Florida, Georgia, Hawaii, Idaho, Illinois, Indiana, Iowa, Kansas, Kentucky, Maine, Maryland, Massachusetts, Michigan, Minnesota, Missouri, Montana, Nebraska, Nevada, New Hampshire, New Jersey, New York, North Dakota, Ohio, Oklahoma, Oregon, Pennsylvania, Rhode Island, South Dakota, Tennessee, Texas, Utah, Vermont, Virginia, Washington, West Virginia, Wisconsin, Wyoming
4. Equal pay personal suits	Alaska, Arizona, Arkansas, California, Colorado, Connecticut, Florida, Georgia, Hawaii, Idaho, Indiana, Kentucky, Maryland, Massachusetts, Michigan, Minnesota, Missouri, Nebraska, New Hampshire, New Jersey, North Dakota, Ohio, Oregon, Rhode Island, South Dakota, Tennessee, Virginia, Washington, West Virginia, Wyoming
5. Public accommodations law	Alaska, California, Colorado, Connecticut, Delaware, Idaho, Indiana, Iowa, Kansas, Kentucky, Louisiana, Maine, Maryland, Massachusetts, Michigan, Minnesota, Missouri, Montana, Nebraska, New Hampshire, New Jersey, New Mexico, New York, North Dakota, Ohio, Oregon, Pennsylvania, South Dakota, West Virginia
6. Housing law	Alaska, California, Colorado, Connecticut, Delaware, Georgia, Hawaii, Idaho, Indiana, Iowa, Kansas, Kentucky, Maine, Maryland, Massachusetts, Michigan, Minnesota, Missouri, Montana, Nevada, New Hampshire, New Jersey, New Mexico, New York, Ohio, Oregon, Pennsylvania, Rhode Island, South Dakota
7. Loan law	Alaska, California, Colorado, Connecticut, Delaware, Florida, Georgia, Hawaii, Idaho, Illinois, Iowa, Kansas, Kentucky, Louisiana, Maine, Maryland, Massachusetts, Michigan, Minnesota, Missouri, Montana, Nevada, New Jersey, New Mexico, New York, North Carolina, Ohio, Oklahoma, Pennsylvania, Rhode Island, South Dakota, Virginia, Washington

8. Education law

Alaska, California, Hawaii, Idaho, Illinois, Indiana, Iowa, Louisiana, Maine, Massachusetts, Michigan, Minnesota, Montana, New Jersey, New York, Oregon, Pennsylvania, Rhode Island, South Carolina, Tennessee, West Virginia

9. Name change not required at marriage

Alaska, Arizona, Arkansas, California, Colorado, Delaware, Florida, Georgia, Hawaii, Idaho, Indiana, Kansas, Louisiana, Maryland, Massachusetts, Michigan, Minnesota, Mississippi, Missouri, Montana, Nebraska, Nevada, New Hampshire, New Jersey, New Mexico, New York, North Carolina, North Dakota, Ohio, Oklahoma, Pennsylvania, Rhode Island, South Carolina, South Dakota, Tennessee, Texas, Utah, Virginia, Washington, West Virginia, Wisconsin, Wyoming

10. Civil injunction for abuse cases

Alaska, Arizona, California, Colorado, Connecticut, Delaware, Florida, Hawaii, Illinois, Iowa, Kansas, Kentucky, Maine, Maryland, Massachusetts, Minnesota, Missouri, Montana, Nebraska, Nevada, New Hampshire, New York, North Carolina, North Dakota, Ohio, Oregon, Pennsylvania, Tennessee, Texas, Utah, Vermont, West Virginia, Wisconsin

11. Injunction relief during divorce or separation

Alaska, Arizona, California, Colorado, Delaware, Hawaii, Illinois, Indiana, Kansas, Massachusetts, Michigan, Missouri, Montana, Nebraska, New Hampshire, New York, Oregon, Rhode Island, South Carolina, Vermont, Virginia, Washington, West Virginia, Wisconsin, Wyoming

12. Physical abuse defined as a crime

Arizona, Arkansas, California, Hawaii, Maine, Maryland, Massachusetts, Michigan, Minnesota, Nebraska, New Hampshire, New York, North Carolina, Ohio, Oregon, Rhode Island, Tennessee, Utah, Washington, Wisconsin

13. Warrantless arrest for domestic violence

Alaska, Arizona, Florida, Hawaii, Illinois, Iowa, Kentucky, Maine, Maryland, Massachusetts, Michigan, Minnesota, Missouri, Nebraska, Nevada, New Hampshire, New Mexico, New York, North Carolina, North Dakota, Ohio, Oregon, Pennsylvania, Rhode Island, Tennessee, Utah, Virginia, Washington, Wisconsin

14. Requires report for family violence

Connecticut, Florida, Georgia, Illinois, Iowa, Kentucky, Louisiana, Maine, Maryland, Michigan, Minnesota, Montana, Nebraska, New Hampshire, New York, Ohio, Oregon, Texas, Washington

15. Statutes that provide funds for shelters

Alaska, California, Connecticut, Florida, Indiana, Kansas, Louisiana, Maine, Maryland, Massachusetts, Michigan, Minnesota, Montana, Nebraska, New Jersey, New York, Ohio, Oklahoma, Oregon, Texas, Utah, Virginia, Washington, Wisconsin

Note: See the corresponding numbered row of Table 4.9 for a more complete identification of variables.

Table 4.11

Regional Differences in Legal Gender Indicators

Indicators	Percent of States in Each Region			
	Northeast	North Central	South	West
State passed fair employment practices act**	100	92	44	100
Women may file lawsuit personally under fair employment practices act**	22	8	6	69
State passed equal pay laws**	100	100	63	92
Women may file lawsuit personally under equal pay laws	56	67	50	69
Sex discrimination law in the area of public accommodations*	78	83	31	54
Sex discrimination law in the area of housing**	89	67	25	69
Sex discrimination law in the area of financing	78	67	56	69
Sex discrimination law in the area of education	67	42	25	46
State requires that wife must change name when married [R]	67	83	88	92
Statutes provide for civil injunction relief for victims of abuse	78	75	50 .	69
Statutes that provide temporary injunction relief during a divorce, separation, or custody proceedings	56	58	25	69
Statutes that define the physical abuse of a family or household member as a criminal offense	56	42	25	46
Statutes that permit warrantless arrest based on probable cause in domestic violence cases	67	75	38	62
Statutes that require data collection and reporting of family violence by agencies that serve these families	44	50	38	23
Statutes that provide funds for family violence shelters or established standards for shelter operations	56	58	37	46
Legal Subindex (P-Index)**	68	63	38	63

Note: * $p < .05$, ** $p < .01$. All indicators were scored 1 = yes and 0 = no, except for the indicator marked with a superscript ([R]), which was reverse scored.

GENDER EQUALITY INDEXES AND THEIR INTERRELATIONSHIP

State Rankings on the Four Indexes

The first three columns of table 4.13 array the states according to the economic, political, and legal equality indexes. The far-right-hand column of the table also shows how the states rank on the overall Gender Equality Index, which consists of the mean of the three subindexes. In the case of the economic, political, and overall indexes, a score of 100 means complete equality with men. In the case of the legal index, 100 means that the state enacted all 13 of the laws included in the index.

Table 4.12

Reliability Analysis of Legal Gender Equality Index

Indicators	All Indicators		Final Set of Indicators	
	Corrected Item - Total Correlation	Alpha if Item Deleted	Corrected Item - Total Correlation	Alpha if Item Deleted
Fair Employment Practices Law	.52	.70	.50	.73
Fair Employment Personal Suits	.31	.72	.31	.74
Equal Pay Law	.48	.71	.48	.73
Equal Pay Personal Suits	.30	.72	.26	.75
Public Accommodations Law	.46	.70	.48	.73
Housing Law	.55	.69	.59	.71
Loan Law	.34	.72	.37	.74
Education Law	.29	.72	.27	.75
Name Change Not Required at Marriage	-.05	.75	—	—
Civil Injunction for Abuse Cases	.29	.72	.31	.75
Injunction Relief During Divorce or Separation	.19	.74	—	—
Physical Abuse Defined as a Crime	.36	.71	.32	.74
Warrantless Arrest for Domestic Violence	.33	.72	.34	.74
Requires Report for Family Violence	.30	.72	.38	.74
Statutes that Provide Funds for Shelters	.35	.71	.34	.74
Standardized Alpha Coefficients	.73		.76	

Note: See Table 4.9 for complete identification of the variables.

The median state had a score of 55 in respect to the Economic Equality Index, 12 in respect to the Political Equality Index, and 54 in respect to the Legal Equality Index. This can be interpreted as showing that in a typical state, women have achieved only 55% of what is necessary for economic equality with men, only 12% of what is needed for political equality, and only 54% of the statutory protections which will enable further progress toward gender equality. The median score of 42 on the overall Gender Equality Index can be interpreted as showing that, in the typical American state, women have achieved less than half of what is needed for equal status with men. Moreover, figure 4.1 shows that no region stands out as having a sharply higher score on the overall Gender Equality Index than any other. The main divergence from the national average is the significantly lower score of states in the South. This is due primarily to the South's lower scores on the political and legal subindexes.

Table 4.13

Rank Order of the States on Gender Equality Indexes

	Economic Subindex		Political Subindex		Legal Subindex		Composite Gender Equality Index	
Rank	State	swxe2	State	swxp2b	State	swxl2	State	swx2b
1	Idaho	67.1	Michigan	24.4	Oregon	92.3	Oregon	59.9
2	Alaska	66.0	Hawaii	24.2	Michigan	92.3	Michigan	56.1
3	Kansas	64.0	Connecticut	24.0	Minnesota	92.3	Alaska	55.5
4	Oregon	63.7	Oregon	23.8	Maine	92.3	Maine	54.7
5	Arizona	61.4	Colorado	23.1	Maryland	84.6	Maryland	53.9
6	Maryland	61.3	New Hampshire	23.1	Alaska	84.6	Minnesota	52.5
7	Delaware	60.6	Arizona	22.3	California	84.6	California	51.8
8	Hawaii	60.4	Wyoming	22.2	New York	84.6	Connecticut	51.6
9	Oklahoma	59.0	Washington	20.4	Ohio	84.6	Hawaii	51.3
10	Nevada	58.8	Delaware	20.4	Massachusetts	84.6	Massachusetts	50.6
11	Missouri	58.6	Maine	18.9	Connecticut	76.9	New York	49.7
12	Wisconsin	57.5	Florida	18.2	Montana	76.9	New Hampshire	49.4
13	Kentucky	57.2	Alaska	16.0	New Hampshire	69.2	Montana	49.1
14	Montana	57.2	Maryland	15.9	Hawaii	69.2	Ohio	48.9
15	South Carolina	56.3	Idaho	14.9	Washington	69.2	Washington	48.4
16	Virginia	56.0	California	14.9	Nebraska	69.2	Idaho	47.8
17	California	55.9	Massachusetts	13.8	Iowa	69.2	Colorado	46.1
18	New Hampshire	55.9	New Mexico	13.4	Kentucky	69.2	Kentucky	45.9
19	Pennsylvania	55.8	Montana	13.2	Rhode Island	61.5	Arizona	45.8
20	Ohio	55.8	West Virginia	13.0	Colorado	61.5	Iowa	44.6
21	Washington	55.5	Vermont	12.7	Idaho	61.5	Nebraska	44.3
22	Wyoming	55.2	North Carolina	12.7	Missouri	61.5	Kansas	43.3
23	Florida	55.0	Kansas	12.0	Pennsylvania	61.5	Missouri	42.8
24	Iowa	55.0	Rhode Island	11.9	New Jersey	61.5	Rhode Island	42.6
25	Georgia	54.6	Wisconsin	11.8	Florida	53.8	Florida	42.3
26	Rhode Island	54.5	Illinois	11.6	Arizona	53.8	New Jersey	42.1
27	North Carolina	54.2	Minnesota	11.5	Nevada	53.8	Nevada	40.6
28	New Jersey	54.1	Nebraska	11.4	Kansas	53.8	Pennsylvania	40.4
29	Connecticut	54.0	Kentucky	11.4	Illinois	53.8	Delaware	39.8
30	North Dakota	53.9	South Dakota	11.3	Georgia	53.8	Illinois	39.4
31	New York	53.9	Indiana	11.0	Indiana	53.8	Indiana	39.0
32	Colorado	53.7	New York	10.7	Wisconsin	46.1	Wisconsin	38.4
33	South Dakota	53.7	New Jersey	10.6	Utah	46.1	Georgia	38.1
34	Minnesota	53.7	North Dakota	9.9	West Virginia	46.1	West Virginia	37.4
35	Massachusetts	53.5	Virginia	9.7	South Dakota	46.1	South Dakota	37.0
36	Vermont	53.4	Iowa	9.7	Tennessee	46.1	Utah	35.6
37	Texas	53.3	Nevada	9.3	Delaware	38.4	North Carolina	35.1
38	West Virginia	53.1	Utah	8.6	Virginia	38.4	Virginia	34.7
39	Maine	53.0	Missouri	8.3	North Carolina	38.4	Tennessee	34.5
40	Arkansas	52.9	Oklahoma	8.2	New Mexico	38.4	New Mexico	34.4
41	Illinois	52.9	South Carolina	8.1	North Dakota	38.4	North Dakota	34.1
42	Alabama	52.8	Texas	7.6	Louisiana	38.4	Wyoming	33.5
43	Indiana	52.4	Alabama	7.6	Oklahoma	30.7	Oklahoma	32.7
44	Nebraska	52.2	Arkansas	6.9	Texas	30.7	Louisiana	31.2
45	Utah	52.2	Ohio	6.3	Wyoming	23.0	Texas	30.5
46	Mississippi	52.1	Georgia	5.9	Vermont	23.0	Vermont	29.7
47	Tennessee	51.7	Tennessee	5.6	Arkansas	23.0	Arkansas	27.6
48	Michigan	51.6	Mississippi	5.6	South Carolina	7.6	South Carolina	24.0
49	New Mexico	51.5	Louisiana	4.8	Alabama	0.0	Alabama	20.1
50	Louisiana	50.3	Pennsylvania	3.7	Mississippi	0.0	Mississippi	19.2

Z-Scored Version of the Overall Gender Equality Index

Although the overall Gender Equality Index in table 4.13 has the advantage of presenting the data in a metric which has intrinsic meaning (percent of equality), it also has a potential disadvantage. The disadvantage is in not being able to control for the contribution of each component to the total index. An index composed of the average of the component indicators will be disproportion-

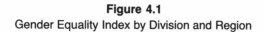

Figure 4.1
Gender Equality Index by Division and Region

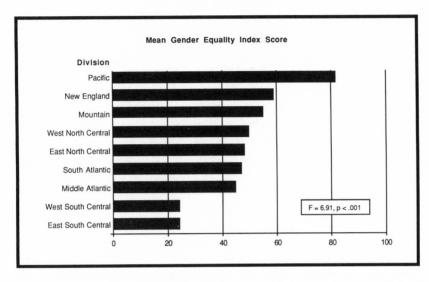

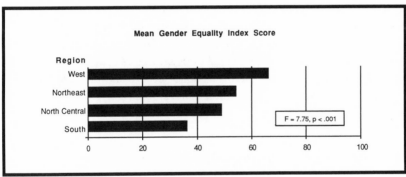

ately influenced by the component with the highest variance. To deal with this problem we computed a second version of the overall Gender Equality Index (SWX2BZ). In this version, the variances of the subindexes were equalized by transformation to Z scores before combining them to form the overall index, with the result that each of the components contributes approximately equally to the total index score. In the absence of a theoretical basis for weighting one component more than another, this version of the Gender Equality Index is probably best for purposes of investigating the relationship of gender equality to other variables.

Table 4.14 gives the results of a reliability analysis performed using the Z-scored indicators. The correlations of the subindexes with one another is shown in the panel labeled Inter-Index Correlations. The item-total correlations and alpha coefficients in the right panel do not call for deleting any of the components. The Z-scored overall Gender Equality Index (GEX), which is the version which will be used in the balance of this chapter, has an alpha coefficient of .59. The reliability of the index is high, considering that it consists of only three indicators. However, this should not lead one to overlook the fact that the correlations among each of the three dimensions are low to moderate. The three dimensions may be correlated but they are also distinct. Thus, our cross-state comparative analysis leads to the same conclusion as Whyte's (1978) study of 93 preindustrial cultures—that women can be relatively powerless in one sphere of life and relatively powerful in another.

VALIDITY OF THE INDEX

Thus far we have demonstrated that it is possible to construct indexes to measure gender equality in American states, and that there are large state-to-state differences in gender equality as measured by these indexes. However, aside from showing that the southern states are furthest from equality between women and men, we have not related these indicators to other characteristics of the states. It is essential that this be done because knowledge of the correlates of these indexes provides information regarding convergent and discriminant validity of the indexes.

Sociodemographic Characteristics and Gender Equality

The top section of table 4.15 gives the correlation of four sociodemographic variables with the Gender Equality Indexes. The right-hand column headed Composite Gender Equality gives the correlations with the overall Gender Equality Index. The first two correlations in this column suggest that there is a nonsignificant tendency for more urban states and states with an older population to have greater gender equality. A look at the other three columns in these two rows shows, however, that this correlation is due almost entirely to the legal component in the overall GEX. This is an example of the point emphasized by Mason (1986)—that it is important to distinguish specific types of gender equality or inequality.

The next two rows of table 4.15 show that the higher the socioeconomic status of a state (as measured by median years of education and median

Table 4.14

Reliability Analysis of the Composite Gender Equality Index

Subindex	Inter-Index Correlations		Corrected Item - Total Correlation	Alpha if Item Deleted
	1	2		
1. Legal	–		.43	.43
2. Economic	.25	–	.29	.32
3. Political	.41	.30	.44	.14

Standardized Alpha Coefficient = .59

Note: Each subindex was Z-scored prior to this analysis.

Table 4.15

Correlation of Selected Characteristics of the States with Gender Equality Indexes

Socio-Demographic Variables	Subindexes			Composite Gender Equality Index
	Economic	Political	Legal	
Percent of Population Residing in SMSAs (z251)	-.05	.04	.35*	.17
Median Age (ea8)	-.05	.06	.27*	.15
Median Years of Education (ec14)	.36**	.61***	.49***	.68***
Median Income (cp274)	.39**	.38**	.49***	.60***

Social-Psychological Variables	Subindexes			Composite Gender Equality Index
	Economic	Political	Legal	
NOW Members per 100,000 Population (z94r3)	10*	.17	.48***	36**
Sexual Liberalism Index (xgs1a)	.33*	.48**	.64***	.68***
Non-traditional Sex Roles Attitude Index (xgs4a)	.20	.42**	.45**	.52***
Violence Approval Index (xgs2a)	.23	.15	-.19	.08
Violent Behavior Index (xgs3a)	.01	.12	-.40**	-.13

Note: $^*p < .05$, $^{**}p < .01$, $^{***}p < .001$.

income), the higher the degree of gender equality. The tendency for states with higher socioeconomic status to be high in gender equality applies to each of the subindexes as well as to he overall index. The average correlation is sufficiently high ($r = .48$) to support the plausible notion that high education and high income populations tend to be liberal in a number of dimensions, including gender roles. Yet, at the same time, the coefficient is not so high as to indicate that the GEX is only a measure of socioeconomic level in disguise, since correlations of about .50 mean that 75% of the state-to-state variance in gender equality is *not* explained by these socioeconomic level variables.

Social-Psychological Characteristics and Gender Equality

The social-psychological variables in the bottom section of table 4.15 reveals some extremely interesting patterns.

MEMBERSHIP IN THE NATIONAL ORGANIZATION FOR WOMEN. This correlation shows that states with an active feminist movement tend to be states with a higher level of actual gender equality. With cross-sectional data one cannot tell which variable is the cause and which is the effect, or whether there is a feedback loop. However, that was not the purpose of computing the correlation. Rather, the correlation was computed to provide information on convergent validity, and the significant positive correlations do provide some evidence in support of the convergent validity of the GEX.

SEXUALLY LIBERAL ATTITUDES. The second row of the bottom section of table 4.15 shows that states with a high score on the Gender Equality Index also tend to have greater tolerance of alternative sexual lifestyles.[6]

NONTRADITIONAL SEX ROLE ATTITUDES. This variable is essentially a measure of attitudes about gender equality.[7] Consequently, the correlations in this row

6. The Sexual Liberalism Index and the Nontraditional Sex Roles Attitude Index are described in detail in Jaffee and Straus (1987). Both use items from the General Social Survey (Davis and Smith, 1985).

The Sexual Liberalism Index uses 20 indicators, each of which is the percentage of respondents in a state who agree with 20 items judged to reflect tolerance for alternative sexual behavior, such as the percentage who would not object to a homosexual teacher in college, the percentage who would object to having books favoring homosexuality removed from a public library, the percentage who oppose restrictions on abortion, and the same for pornography. This index has an alpha coefficient of reliability of .96.

7. The Nontraditional Sex Roles Attitude Index uses 5 indicators, specifically the percentage who, when asked to rate the most important qualities for a child, ranked "that he acts like a boy (she acts like a girl)" as least important of the 7 traits; disagreed that women should care for the home while men run the country; approved of women working outside the home; would vote for a

of table 4.15 provide the most direct evidence of convergent validity for the GEX.

VIOLENT ATTITUDES AND VIOLENT BEHAVIOR. [8] In contrast to the measures of sexual liberalism and nontraditional gender role attitudes, proviolence attitudes were not found to be significantly related to the GEX, or any of the subindexes. This can be considered as evidence of discriminant validity for the GEX. On the other hand, the GEX is negatively correlated with the violent *behavior* index, which is a measure of a state population's experience with violence. This relationship is due primarily to the Legal Equality Index. That finding is consistent with the fact that several of the indicators in the Legal Equality Index (such as laws criminalizing domestic violence) are concerned with the prevention of violence. It seems that states with a population that has experienced a relatively high level of violence are less likely to pass legislation aimed at limiting intrafamily violence.

Correlation with Measures Used to Test Theories of Rape

Some of the most interesting and potentially important correlates of the GEX are with the variables used to measure concepts needed to test the other theories of rape in this study. These are the Social Disorganization Index, the Sex Magazine Circulation Index, the Legitimate Violence Index, and the Gini Index of income inequality. These measures and detailed statistical analyses are presented in other chapters. At this point, only the bivariate correlations will be presented and briefly discussed.

SOCIAL DISORGANIZATION. The Social Disorganization Index, described in chapter 6, was found to have a correlation of .51 ($p < .001$) with the GEX.

---

woman president; and disagreed with the statement that men are better suited emotionally for politics than women. This index has an alpha coefficient of reliability of .95.

8. The Violence Approval Index and the Violent Behavior Index were computed from General Social Survey data (Davis and Smith, 1985). The Violence Approval Index is composed of the percent of respondents in each state who endorsed 14 questions judged to reflect approval of the use of violence. The conceptualization and indexing procedure used to construct the Violence Approval Index are presented in chapter 7.

The Violent Behavior Index consists of the percentage of respondents in each state who reported having been punched or beaten by another adult, punched or beaten as a child, punched, pushed, or beaten as an adult more than once, threatened with a knife or gun or shot at as an adult, threatened with a knife or gun or shot at as a child, and threatened with a knife or gun or shot at as an adult more than once; having any gun in the home, having a handgun in the home, and whether the respondent or other members of the household hunt. This index has an alpha coefficient of reliability of .85.

Therefore, as the level of social disorganization increases, gender equality increases. At first glance this might seem to be an implausible result, but it illustrates the reconstructive potential of social disorganization, as discussed in chapter 6. Thus, by disturbing the status quo, social disorganization tends to erode traditional norms and social relationships, including norms of male superiority and privilege.

SEX MAGAZINE CIRCULATION. The Sex Magazine Circulation Index, described in chapter 5, was found to have a correlation of .56 ($p < .001$) with the GEX. Thus, as the availability of sexually explicit materials increases, gender equality increases. Although this correlation is at odds with feminist conjectures about pornography and women's oppression, it is consistent with the experience of the most gender-equal countries (for example, Sweden and Denmark), where pornography is easily accessible and women enjoy the highest level of gender equality in the Western world (Reiss, 1986). Nonetheless, we suspect that there is probably some underlying factor that accounts for this association, such as political tolerance. Therefore, in more politically tolerant societies, we expect to find a greater abundance of sexually explicit materials and greater equality between men and women.

INCOME INEQUALITY. The measure of income inequality among families, described in chapter 3, was found to have a correlation of $-.55$ ($p < .001$) with the GEX. Thus, as the level of economic inequality in society increases, gender equality decreases. This suggests that economic inequality tends to diminish the status of women.

LEGITIMATE VIOLENCE. The Legitimate Violence Index, described in chapter 7, was found to have a correlation of $-.26$ ($p < .05$) with the GEX. Thus, as the level of legitimate violence increases, gender equality decreases. This suggests that cultural support for violence tends to reduce the status of women in society.

SUMMARY. These correlations provide preliminary evidence that the social disruption of sexist norms and practices, greater availability of sexually explicit materials, higher levels of economic equality, and lower levels of cultural support for violence constitute a set of societal characteristics that contribute to gender equality. The determinants of gender equality will be further explored in chapter 8 in the context of an integrated theory of rape.

Gender Equality and Rape

The correlations just presented offer considerable evidence in support of the convergent and construct validity of the GEX, and therefore the appropriateness of using it to test the gender inequality theory of rape. As a first step in that process we computed the simple correlation between the GEX and the average rape rate for the years 1980–82. We found a correlation of .23, which is not statistically significant. It should be kept in mind, though, that this is only a bivariate correlation, and quite different results can occur when a more adequately specified model is tested, as will be done in chapter 8.

SUMMARY AND CONCLUSIONS

The first part of this chapter was devoted to an attempt to systematize some of the divergent meanings attached to the concept of the status of women. We suggested that some of the confusion can be avoided by distinguishing between *status attainment* and *gender equality*. Status attainment, or in this case *gender attainment*, refers to the level of physical, educational, economic, political, legal, and psychological well-being achieved by women in a society. *Gender equality* refers to women having the same level of status attainment as men. A society can be low in gender attainment and high in gender equality, and vice versa.

The next part of the chapter described the methods used to construct a Gender Equality Index (GEX) for each of the states of the United States, and presented findings on state-to-state and regional differences in gender equality. Indexes were constructed to measure gender equality in respect to three spheres of life—economic, political, and legal—as well as an overall Gender Equality Index. Each of the four indexes is scaled from 0 to 100, with zero meaning that women have attained none of the status attributes included in the index (for example, no women members of the state legislature) and 100 meaning that women have attained complete parity with men (for example, as many women members of the legislature as men).

The use of these indexes revealed large differences among states for all four of the gender equality measures. The scores ranged from a low of 50 to a high of only 67 in economic equality, from 4 to 24 in political equality, from 0 to 92 in legal equality, and from 19 to 60 on the overall GEX. Thus, even in the state with the highest score on the GEX, women have achieved only 60% equality with men. The medians are also important because they show that in a typical state, women have achieved only 55% of what is necessary for economic equality with men, only 12% of what is needed for political equality, and only 54% of the statutory protections which will enable further progress toward gender equality. When all three subindexes are combined, the median score of 42 on the overall GEX shows that, in the typical American state, women have achieved less than half of what is needed for equal status with men.

The final section of the chapter examined the relationship of the gender equality indexes to selected demographic and social psychological characteristics of the states, as a means of providing preliminary data on the validity of the indexes. These analyses revealed a number of relationships which suggest that the indexes described in this chapter have both convergent and discriminant validity. In addition, some of the findings are substantively interesting. They suggest that the movement toward gender equality is most likely to take place in (1) a highly educated affluent society in which women have organized to promote their own welfare; (2) in a society where many aspects of the traditional social order are disintegrating, as reflected in a high level of social disorganization; and (3) in a society that rejects traditional norms which restrict sexuality and encourage violence. Despite these promising findings, the GEX was found to have only a low and nonsignificant correlation with rape. However, that is not a sufficient basis for rejecting the gender inequality theory of rape. That can be done only based on the results of a multivariate analysis which includes appropriate controls and other theoretically important variables. Such a test will be presented in chapter 8.

5

PORNOGRAPHY

Pornography has relatively few advocates in the world of scholarship or public affairs. Notable exceptions are therapists and sex educators who believe that pornography can help sexually inhibited people overcome their anxiety about sex and perhaps produce a new generation with less sexual guilt (Dallas, 1982; Gillan, 1978; Yaffé, 1982). On the other hand, opposition to pornography has many roots and many adherents. Those whose opposition is rooted in Christian theology make the argument that pornography corrupts man's spiritual nature and leads to a nihilistic rejection of a biblical moral order (Court, 1980; Falwell, 1980; Gallagher, 1981; Kirk, 1985; Wildmon, 1986). Among political conservatives there is opposition to pornography on secular moral grounds. Conservatives charge that pornography disinhibits men and loosens their commitment to absolute values, thus promoting autoeroticism, sexual promiscuity, and decadence (Berns, 1971; Kristol, 1971; van den Haag, 1970). Finally, there is feminist opposition to pornography on the grounds that pornography leads to violence against women (Barry, 1979; Dworkin, 1979, 1985; Lederer, 1980; MacKinnon, 1984; Russell, 1988).

This chapter focuses on the argument of antipornography feminists and provides a preliminary analysis of the relationship between the availability of pornography and rates of rape. We also review several definitions of pornography, evaluate their usefulness as guides for empirical research, and present our own definition. Pornography is measured in this study with a Sex Magazine Circulation Index (SMCX2), which is based on the combined circulation rates of eight sexually explicit magazines. The indexing method, the internal consistency reliability of the SMCX2, and evidence of its discriminate validity are also presented.

FEMINISM AND THE POLITICS OF PORNOGRAPHY

Pornography and Rape

Antipornography feminists theorize that pornography causes rape (Dworkin, 1979, 1985; MacKinnon, 1984; Morgan, 1980; Ratterman, 1982; Russell, 1988). This theory is based on three interrelated points.

1. *Pornography Both Reflects and Promotes Male Dominance in Society.*
Feminist criticism of pornography begins from the premise that male domination is the basis of violence against women (Brownmiller, 1975; Barry, 1979;
Dworkin, 1979). Antipornography feminists argue that sexism and male supremacy are represented and celebrated in pornography. Furthermore, pornography is said to express the power of men over women, and in turn,
communicate to those who use pornography that women are inferior to men.
Consequently, images of women as objects of sexual exploitation are believed
to promote and legitimate male sexual violence.

2. *Pornography Sexually Objectifies Women.* Antipornography feminists claim
that pornography encourages men to treat women as sex objects. Sexual
objectification entails the fragmentation of a woman's body and eroticization
of her body parts. They argue that pornography dehumanizes and degrades
women, glamorizes violence, and makes sexism sexy (Barry, 1979; Dworkin,
1979, 1985; Lederer, 1980; Russell, 1977). MacKinnon (1982) claims that
sexual objectification is the root of women's oppression. Presumably, then, it
is through the process of sexual objectification that women become identified
as the appropriate victims of sexual violence.

3. *Pornography Depicts Physical Assaults against Women That Serve as Behavioral Models.* According to antipornography feminists, pornography is mis-
ogynistic propaganda that presents violence against women in a positive light
(Barry, 1979; Dworkin, 1979; Longino, 1980; MacKinnon, 1984; Morgan,
1980). Feminist opponents of pornography claim that violent pornography has
become more prevalent and that images of women who enjoy being coerced,
brutalized, and raped are now omnipresent (Barry, 1979; Dworkin, 1979;
Longino, 1980). On the basis of these observations, these feminists surmise
that pornography provides behavioral and ideational support for actual violence against women.

Feminist Controversy over Pornography

The issue of pornography has bitterly divided the feminist movement. Many
will recall the Scholar and Feminist IX Conference, known as the sexuality
conference, held at Bernard College in 1982. The conference was disrupted
by members of Women Against Pornography who alleged that the conference
organizers were advocating sadomasochism and trivializing the danger posed
by pornography (Vance, 1984). During the same year, Robin Morgan (1982)
accused Diedre English, Amber Hollibaugh, Gayle Rubin, and Ellen Willis of
being pseudofeminists and Nazi sympathizers for expressing heterodox opinions about pornography. Andrea Dworkin now employs a polemical strategy
that includes labeling feminist critics of her sectarian view of pornography

antifeminist and refusing to debate her feminist critics in a public forum (Math, 1985–86).

While feminists continue to battle over pornography, New Right moralists have aligned with feminist opponents of pornography to restrict the accessibility of sexually explicit materials. Phyllis Schlafly's (1984) discussion of pornography aptly illustrates this strange bedfellow alliance. Employing the rhetoric of feminist antipornography crusaders, Schlafly argues that pornography degrades and demeans women and encourages acts of physical violence. Schlafly also supports the feminist antipornography legislation, drafted by Catharine MacKinnon and Andrea Dworkin, which would permit women to sue producers and distributors of pornography on the basis of sexual discrimination. Despite the fact that advocates of this legislation claim that it is not a censorship measure, if it were to be enacted, a court of law would have the authority to prohibit sexual depictions that meet the legislation's definition of pornography.

To the uninitiated this must seem a bit bewildering. Why are feminists unable to put their differences aside and provide a united front against the pornography industry? Why does Schlafly adopt the idiom of antipornography feminists and support the MacKinnon/Dworkin antipornography legislation, while a significant number of feminists have organized to defeat it?[1] Although there is no definitive answer to these questions, one possible answer is that support for the legal restriction of pornography among some feminists has engendered both the internecine warfare between feminists[2] and the alliance between antipornography feminists and right-wing moralists. In fact, there is

1. Considering Schlafly's consistent efforts to undermine the feminist movement, one might have expected her to rehearse the conservative line that pornography corrupts public morals, promotes homosexuality, encourages premarital and extramarital sex, and undermines the nuclear family. Does Schlafly's support for the MacKinnon/Dworkin antipornography legislation signal a change in her ideological commitments? Certainly not. Schlafly is willing to support this legislation only because the censorship of pornography is consistent with her conservative agenda. If the MacKinnon/Dworkin proposal were to become law, one could only speculate on whether Schlafly and Dworkin would find the same sexual depictions actionable.

2. The feminist split over pornography does not lend itself to any simple categorization of supporters and critics. Nevertheless, it is possible to distinguish between those feminists who have united in support of the MacKinnon/Dworkin antipornography legislation (e.g., Women Against Pornography) and those feminists who have organized to oppose it (e.g., the Feminist Anti-Censorship Taskforce). Feminists who support the legislation are motivated by the conviction that pornography stimulates violence against women and constitutes a flagrant violation of women's civil rights. Feminists who oppose the legislation fear that its passage would lead to the prohibition of unconventional feminist erotica, expand social controls over women's sexuality, and undermine women's First Amendment rights. Given their disparate concerns, we refer to feminist supporters of the legislation as *antipornography feminists* and feminist opponents of the legislation as *anticensorship feminists*.

empirical evidence that both antipornography feminists and right-wing opponents of pornography mutually support the governmental regulation of pornography (Jelen, 1986).

Pornography and the State

Canadian feminist Varda Burstyn (1985) maintains that there are good historical reasons to be suspicious of coalitions between feminists and right-wing groups. Drawing from Judith Walkowitz's (1980) analysis of prostitution in nineteenth-century Britain, Burstyn uses the example of the Contagious Diseases Acts (CDAs), which feminists and social purists joined forces to repeal in the 1870s and 1880s, to illustrate her argument. According to Burstyn, the ostensible purpose of the CDAs was to control the spread of venereal disease. This was to be accomplished by requiring prostitutes to file their names with local police officials and forcing them to endure a medical examination every two weeks. Although the CDAs did not accomplish the goal of stopping the spread of venereal disease, they did function to stigmatize and control prostitutes.

Burstyn notes that, contrary to the feminists who protested the CDAs because they violated the civil rights of prostitutes, social purists opposed the CDAs because they lent tacit legitimation to prostitution. Convinced that prostitution threatened the institution of the family, social purists sought to have prostitution outlawed rather than merely regulated. At the same time, feminists felt ambivalent toward prostitution and believed that monogamy was their best protection against contracting venereal disease. Despite their differences, feminists believed that they could channel the righteous indignation of social purists in the direction of achieving feminist goals. Consequently, feminists joined forces with social purists and were able to successfully overturn the CDAs. Burstyn convincingly argues that repeal of the CDAs represented a pyrrhic victory for feminists because feminist interests had been eclipsed by the political agenda of the purity movement. Thus the CDAs were repealed, only to be replaced by more repressive criminal sanctions against prostitution.

The lesson to be learned from this historical example is that feminists unite with right-wing groups at their own peril. Burstyn makes the cogent observation that the patriarchal state cannot be counted on to guarantee the rights of feminist women.[3] Applying these insights to recent proposals to censor por-

3. For an extended discussion of the patriarchal state see Eisenstein (1984).

nography, Burstyn notes that once such proposals are passed, feminists will have very little control over the interpretation and enforcement of such laws. Consequently, feminists must be careful when invoking the power of the state. Burstyn makes clear that laws designed to ban "degrading" sexual images of women can just as easily be used to suppress sexual images that women find arousing and empowering.

These concerns are especially salient for sexual minorities. As Valverde and Weir (1985) point out, whatever gains lesbians have made toward constructing a lesbian culture could be subverted by censorship laws. In view of the intolerance that currently prevails toward same-gender sexual relationships, new legal remedies to censor pornography could be used to harass the sellers of lesbian pornography.[4] Since there is no reason to believe that police officers and judges are any less homophobic than the surrounding culture, Valverde and Weir advise against investing law enforcement authorities with the legal clout to further oppress sexual minorities.

The Victim Ideology of Antipornography Feminists

Anticensorship feminists have criticized antipornography feminists for promoting a victim ideology (Echols, 1983, 1984; Elshtain, 1982; Snitow, 1985; Vance, 1984). This ideology is based on the idea that female subordination is rooted in male sexual aggression. Feminist critics of the antipornography movement argue that the exclusive concern of antipornography feminists with sexual politics marks a dramatic break from the concerns of radical feminists prior to 1970. Previously, radical feminists had addressed such issues as sex-role stereotyping, the patriarchal nuclear family, and economic inequality, whereas antipornography feminists focus their attention on compulsory heterosexuality, sexual slavery, and images of eroticized violence. This change in political priorities is also reflected in much radical feminist theory, which characterizes men as sexual predators, women as helpless victims, and heterosexuality as rape (for example, Barry, 1979; Brownmiller, 1975; Daly, 1973, 1978; Dworkin, 1979, 1987; Morgan, 1980). It was in this intellectual climate that Catharine MacKinnon and Andrea Dworkin developed the ideas underlying their civil rights antipornography legislation.

4. Valverde and Weir (1985) correctly point out that lesbian pornography has typically been produced by men for men and does not accurately portray lesbian sexuality. In light of this, it is encouraging to report that three lesbian sex magazines, created by lesbian collectives, have recently been published. These magazines are named *Bad Attitude*, *On Our Backs*, and *Outrageous Women*.

The MacKinnon/Dworkin Civil Rights Antipornography Legislation

In an effort to use the powers of the state to eliminate pornography, antipornography legislation was drafted by attorney Catharine MacKinnon and social activist Andrea Dworkin and introduced in such cities as Los Angeles, Cambridge, Minneapolis, and Indianapolis.[5] The legislation is based on the idea that pornography discriminates against women and violates their civil rights. MacKinnon and Dworkin define pornography as "the graphic sexually explicit subordination of women" (MacKinnon, 1984:321). This definition is consistent with their belief that pornography constitutes a *discriminatory practice*. In their view, pornography is not fantasy or simulated activity; it is documentary evidence of *actual* crimes against real women.[6] The remedy that they propose is civil rights legislation which would allow women to bring a cause of action, on behalf of all women, against those involved in the production and sale of pornography.

This approach is quite different from existing obscenity law, which emphasizes the salaciousness of a depiction and its effect on the moral fiber of the community. In several publications, MacKinnon and Dworkin disassociate themselves from tradition obscenity doctrine by arguing that pornography is "not a moral issue." Rather, they argue that pornography is about male power, male sexual coercion, and female victimization.

As stated in the proposed legislation, a depiction must meet three criteria for it to be considered pornographic. First, the depiction must be sexually explicit. Second, the depiction must show women in a subordinate position. And third, it must entail one or more of nine general conditions (see table 5.1 for the exact wording). These conditions include "women presented as dehumanized sexual objects"; or "women presented as sex objects who enjoy pain or humiliation"; or "women presented in postures of sexual submission or sexual servility, including inviting penetration"; or "women presented as whores by nature"; or "women presented as being penetrated by objects or

---

5. In 1985, feminist opponents of pornography introduced antipornography legislation in Los Angeles, but it was defeated by the City Board of Supervisors. During the same year, Cambridge put a modified version of the model antipornography ordinance up for referendum, but it was defeated by more than 3,000 votes (Moore, 1985). The Minneapolis City Counsel twice passed antipornography ordinances, but both times the ordinance was vetoed by Mayor Donald Fraser. The Indianapolis city council passed antipornography legislation in 1984, but it was held unconstitutional in federal district court (*American Booksellers, Inc. V. Hudnut*, 771 F.2d 323 (7th Cir. 1985), aff'd 106 S.Ct. 1172 (1986).

6. We have drawn from the following sources in our discussion of the MacKinnon/Dworkin antipornography legislation: Dworkin, 1985; Dworkin and MacKinnon, 1988; MacKinnon, 1984, 1985.

animals." The legislation also has provisions for trafficking, forcing pornography on a person, and violence that is caused by pornography. One of the most controversial aspects of the legislation is a section that deals with "coercion into pornographic performances." This would permit a woman who works in the sex industry to sue her employer for coercion even if she was well aware that she was making pornography, consented to participate, and signed a contract.

Feminist Criticism of the MacKinnon/Dworkin Proposal

The most devastating critique of the MacKinnon/Dworkin legislation was written by three founding members of the Feminist Anti-Censorship Taskforce, Lisa Dugan, Nan Hunter, and Carole Vance (1985). Their objections to the legislation may be summarized as follows. First, they argue that the language used in the ordinance is vague and open to interpretation. For instance, it is not at all clear what an image would have to look like to depict women as "whores by nature," in "postures of sexual submission," or "in scenarios of degradation." A related issue concerns who will ultimately decide the meaning of these ambiguous phrases. Since this is civil rights legislation, cases would presumably be brought before a magistrate who would determine if a particular image met the definition of pornography set out in the legislation. Thus, instead of empowering women, this legislation shifts power to legal authorities, who would decide which images are pornographic. Because many conservatives view masturbation, premarital sex, and same-gender sexual relations as degrading, this legislation could just as easily be used by right-wing forces to undermine feminist interests.

Second, the provision of the legislation dealing with coercion into pornographic performances suggests that women are not free to give their consent to work in the sex industry. Since the proposed law would make it illegal for a woman to enter into a contract to make pornography, the implicit assumption is that women are not competent to give their consent. Moreover, rather than preventing the production of pornography, which appears to be the intent of this provision, the effect would be to generate a thriving underground market and nullify whatever legal protections currently exist for women in the sex industry.

Finally, Dugan, Hunter, and Vance question whether this legislation really addresses the issue that MacKinnon and Dworkin purport to address, that is, violence against women. In fact, a close reading of the legislation shows that its central focus is not violence at all but sexual explicitness. This point can be illuminated with an example. Imagine, if you will, a movie that presents a *naked* woman in a "subordinate" pose. This depiction fits the legislation's definition of pornography and would be actionable. Now imagine a movie that showed a woman, *fully dressed*, being brutally stabbed to death. This depiction would not be actionable under the proposed legislation. What distinguishes these two portrayals is that the first would be considered sexually explicit and the second would not. The fact that only sexually explicit images are actionable, irrespective of the presence of violence, goes a long way toward explaining why right-wing groups support this legislation (for additional criticism of the MacKinnon/Dworkin antipornography legislation see Benson, 1986; Carr, 1987; Emerson, 1984; Lynn, 1986b; Stone, 1986; and Tigue, 1985).

At the present time, the MacKinnon/Dworkin antipornography legislation is no longer legally viable. The chain of events that led to this began in 1984, when the Indianapolis city council passed a slightly modified version of the model antipornography legislation. Almost immediately, its constitutionality was challenged in federal district court. Judge Sara Evans ruled that the legislation was unconstitutional because it violated the First Amendment right of free speech. This ruling was appealed to the Supreme Court, which summarily affirmed the decision of the lower court. In so doing, the Supreme Court made this legislation illegal across the country (*American Booksellers, Inc. v. Hudnut*, 771 F.2d 323 [7th Cir. 1985], aff'd 106 S.Ct. 1172 [1986]).

CONCEPTUALIZATION AND DEFINITION OF PORNOGRAPHY

The concept of pornography has been a source of considerable confusion and controversy. One reason for this is the subjective nature of what is pornographic. The same magazine or film may be defined as pornography by one group or person and a work of art by another. An additional problem is whether sexual content by itself makes a book or film pornographic, or whether the essence of pornography lies in the combination of sex with other elements such as violence or the depiction of women in demeaning poses. Pornography is also sometimes used as a pejorative to describe materials which are "degrading" to women, even though there is little or no sexual content to the materials.

These problems have led some social scientists to follow the example of the 1970 Commission on Obscenity and Pornography, which, despite the name of the commission and its report, decided not to use the term "pornography" at all. Instead, both the commission and those who follow its example in this respect use such terms as "sexually explicit materials," "sexually oriented materials," and "erotica" (Commission on Obscenity and Pornography, 1970:5). However, "pornography," "porn," and "porno" are so firmly established in everyday language that this approach is not likely to be successful. More important, simply using another term does not solve the difficult conceptual problems that are inherent in the analysis of such materials. Substituting another word can sometimes be a way of avoiding the difficult task of constructing a precise and carefully crafted definition.

Although the use of an alternative term for pornography is tempting, we decided to use the term "pornography" in the present study. Having made that decision, we were led to a review of the conceptual definitions used by feminists, social scientists, philosophers, clinicians, journalists, and others. This section presents an overview of these definitions and discusses the advantages and limitations of our own definition of pornography.

The Concept of Pornography

In the majority of empirical studies, researchers have failed to provide a nominal definition of pornography. The paucity of such definitions presents a problem for anyone trying to interpret the research findings, as well as for those trying to piece together a comprehensive understanding of the effect of pornography on behavior. It is regrettable to report that out of the 29 *empirical* studies that we examined on the effects of pornography on sexual and/or aggressive behavior (Baron and Straus, 1983), only two supplied nominal definitions of pornography. Thus, for one reason or another, social scientists have been reluctant to follow the standard scientific procedure of using a nominal definition in their research on pornography.

Table 5.1 displays several nominal definitions of pornography. The definitions included in table 5.1 are not intended to be exhaustive but illustrative of the different ways pornography has been conceptualized. We tried to include definitions from a wide variety of sources because how pornography is defined by important social groups is a necessary point of reference. Consequently, we include feminist definitions, three national commission definitions, dictionary definitions, and definitions offered by social scientists, philosophers, and a representative of the religious right.

Limitations of Past Definitions

Examination of the definitions in table 5.1 suggests that there are several problems with the way pornography has been conceptualized.

1. *The Use of Several Important Dimensions as Constants.* Since we consider

TABLE 5.1

Nominal Definitions of Pornography

Author/year	Definitions of Pornography
Feminists Gould 1977	Pornography—for either sex—has been defined as whatever turns the Supreme Court on. More seriously, the word is generally applied to the explicit depiction, in books, films or photographs, of sexual organs and sexual acts, in a manner designed to elicit a strong erotic response in the reader or viewer. The word itself derives from Greek terms that mean writing about harlots—thus, any graphic representation of illicit sexual material. (p. 285)
Dworkin 1979	The word *pornography* does not mean "writing about sex" or "depictions of sexual acts" or "depictions of nude bodies" or "sexual representations" or any other such euphemism. It means the graphic depiction of women as vile whores. (p. 200)
Steinem 1980	"Pornography" begins with a root "porno," meaning "prostitution" or "female captives," thus letting us know that the subject is not mutual love, or love at all, but domination and violence against women. (Though, of course, homosexual pornography may imitate this violence by putting a man in the "feminine" role of victim.) It ends with a root "graphos," meaning "writing about" or "description of," which puts still more distance between subject and object, and replaces a spontaneous yearning for closeness with objectification and voyeurism. . . . Perhaps one could simply say that erotica is about sexuality, but pornography is about power and sex-as-weapon—in the same way we

Note: The subcategories used to group the definitions are not mutually exclusive.

TABLE 5.1 *(Continued)*

Author/year	Definitions of Pornography
	have come to understand that rape is about violence, and not really about sexuality at all. (pp. 37–38)
Diamond 1980	(P)ornography is primarily a medium for expressing norms about male power and domination, thereby functioning as a social control mechanism for keeping women in a subordinate status. (p. 188)
Longino 1980	I define pornography as *verbal or pictorial explicit representations of sexual behavior that*, in the words of the Commission on Obscenity and Pornography, *have as a distinguishing characteristic "the degrading and demeaning portrayal of the role and status of the human female . . . as a mere sexual object to be exploited and manipulated sexually."* (p. 42)
Yeamans 1980	I define pornography, all of which I believe should be suppressed, *as any use of the media which equates sex and violence.* (p. 248)
Russell 1980	By *pornography*, I mean *explicit representations* of sexual behavior, verbal or pictorial, that have as a distinguishing characteristic the degrading or demeaning portrayal of human beings, especially women. Erotica differs from pornography by virtue of its not degrading or demeaning women, men, or children. (pp. 216–217)
Women Against Pornography 1982	We define pornography as "images which represent victimization and violence as sexually stimulating, or images which depict the objectification or humiliation of a

(continued)

TABLE 5.1 *(Continued)*

Author/year	Definitions of Pornography
	human being (usually it's a woman or a girl) in the name of sexual entertainment." (p. 1)
MacKinnon and Dworkin 1983	Pornography is the sexually explicit subordination of women, graphically depicted, whether in pictures or in words, that also includes one or more of the following: (i) women are presented dehumanized as sexual objects, things, or commodities; or (ii) women are presented as sexual objects who enjoy pain or humiliation; or (iii) women are presented as sexual objects who experience sexual pleasure in being raped; or (iv) women are presented as sexual objects tied up or cut up or mutilated or bruised or physically hurt; or (v) women are presented in postures of sexual submission, servility or display; or (vi) women's body parts— including but not limited to vaginas, breasts and buttocks—are exhibited, such that women are reduced to those parts; or (vii) women are presented as whores by nature; or (viii) women are presented being penetrated by objects or animals; or (ix) women are presented in scenarios of degradation, injury, torture, shown as filthy or inferior, bleeding, bruised, or hurt in a context that makes these conditions sexual. All versions of the ordinance also define "the use of men, children or transsexuals in the place of women" as pornography. (pp. 3–4)

Social Scientists, Philosophers, and Attorneys

Peckham 1971	"Pornography" is the presentation in verbal or visual signs of human sexual organs in a condition of stimulation. (p. 47)
Wilson 1973	Pornography in its original Greek derivation had to do with writing of, or about prostitutes, and by extension refers today to depictions that are sexually arousing. (p. 8)

TABLE 5.1 *(Continued)*

Author/year	Definitions of Pornography
Stoller 1976	By "pornography," I mean material made available (openly or secretively) for those who derive sexual stimulation by representations of sexual objects and erotic situations rather than the objects and situations themselves. These materials may consist of writings, drawings, paintings, sculpture, ceramics, and the like; private performances, recorded or spoken; performances for an audience, such as recitations, plays, dance, religious rites; and performances in which one is a participant. (p. 901)
Gagnon 1977	[Pornography] literally means stories about prostitutes, but has come to include all forms of erotic or sexually arousing materials in such media as literature, art, film. Has been used interchangeably with such expressions as obscenity. (p. 424)
MacNamara and Sagarin 1977	Written or pictorial material with overt sexual portrayal in a manner generally unacceptable in a society. (p. 263)
Eysenck and Nias 1978	The term "pornography" has been used in connection with practices which are believed to be harmful either to the victims or to the people engaged in them. (p. 13)
Gray 1982	Most contemporary research on pornography studies both soft-core and hard-core materials. Although the distinction between soft-core and hard-core is sometimes fuzzy, "soft-core" generally refers to depictions of nudity or semi-nudity, or depictions of sexual activity without explicit photographs or descriptions of genitals. "Hard-core" generally refers to depictions of nudes engaged in implied sexual activity with a focus upon the genitals. For the purpose

(continued)

TABLE 5.1 (*Continued*)

Author/year	Definitions of Pornography
	of this paper, I define pornography as both soft-core and hard-care depictions of sexual behavior, be they found in magazines, books, films, or audiotapes. (p. 338)
Kutchinsky 1983	(P)ornography means a product verbally or visually portraying sexual anatomy and behavior with the main purpose of eliciting sexual arousal. (p. 1078)
Feinberg 1985	(Pornography) is a purely descriptive word referring to sexually explicit writing and pictures designed entirely and plausibly to induce sexual excitement in the reader or observer. (p. 127)
Lynn 1986b	(P)ornography refers to written or visual material produced commercially to arouse sexual feelings or fantasies. (p. 30)
Soble 1986	*(P)ornography* refers to any literature or film (or other art-technological form) that describes or depicts sexual organs, preludes to sexual activity, or sexual activity (or related organs and activities) in such a way as to produce sexual arousal in the user or the viewer; and this effect in the viewer is either the effect intended by both producer and consumer or a very likely effect in the absence of direct intentions. (pp. 8–9)
Clergy Falwell 1980	The word came from *porne* (prostitute) and *graphein* (to write). Twenty-five years ago the word meant "writings, pictures, or any symbolic stimulus intended to arouse sexual desire." Now the word pornography goes on to include more than arousal of sexual drives. Pornography now includes in its meaning, "arousing sexual drives of deviations, perversions, and abnormal behavior." (pp. 198–199)

TABLE 5.1 *(Continued)*

Author/year	Definitions of Pornography

Government Commissions

Report of the Commission on Obscenity and Pornography 1970	The term "pornography" is not used at all in a descriptive context because it appears to have no legal significance and because it most often denotes subjective disapproval of certain materials, rather than their content or effect. The Report uses the phrase "explicit sexual material," or some variant thereof to refer to the subject matter of the Commission's investigations; the word "materials" in this context is meant to refer to the entire range of depictions or descriptions in both textual and pictorial form—primarily books, magazines, photographs, films, sound recordings, statuary, and sex "devices." (p. 5)
Report of the Special Committee on Pornography and Prostitution in Canada 1985	(W)e would say that a work is pornographic if it combines the two features of explicit sexual representations (content) and an apparent or *purported* intention to arouse its audience sexually. (p. 53)
Attorney General's Commission on Pornography 1986	(I)n this Report a reference to material as "pornographic" means only that the material is predominantly sexually explicit and intended primarily for the purpose of sexual arousal. (p. 229)

Dictionaries

Oxford English Dictionary 1970	1. (A) description of Prostitutes or of prostitution, as a matter of public hygiene. 2. Description of the life, manners, etc., of prostitutes and their patrons; hence, the expression or suggestions of obscene or unchaste subjects in literature or art; pornographic literature or art. (p. 1131)
American Heritage Dictionary 1976	Written, graphic, or other forms of communication intended to excite lascivious feelings (from Greek

(continued)

TABLE 5.1   *(Continued)*

Author/year	Definitions of Pornography
	pornographos, writing about prostitutes: *porne*, harlot, prostitute + GRAPH). (p. 1021)
Webster's Third New International Diction- ary 1976	Gk *pornographos* writing of harlots (fr. *porne* harlot + *graphos* writing) 1: a description of prostitutes or prostitution 2: a depiction (as in writing of licentiousness or lewdness: a portrayal of erotic behavior designed to cause sexual excitement. (p. 1767)

pornography to be a multidimensional phenomenon, a major limitation of the nominal definitions presented in table 5.1 is that many of the essential dimensions of pornography are either ignored or treated as constants instead of variables (Eysenck and Nias, 1978; Diamond, 1980; Longino, 1980; Steinem, 1980; Women Against Pornography, 1982; Yeamans, 1980). When dimensions such as coercion, violence, male domination, and physical injury are part of the definition itself, they must be present in the depiction for the materials to be considered pornography. Consequently, depictions which exclude these dimensions but include frontal nudity, fellatio, sodomy, group sex, or bestiality would not be deemed pornographic, even if they were intended to sexually arouse the viewer.

A related problem is that by including a specific dimension in the definition itself, such as physical violence, attention is shifted away from two important types of analysis. The first is a consideration of various combinations of these dimensions. Most definitions do not specify more than one of the dimensions mentioned. Yet, it may be that to understand pornography and to investigate what effects it has on consumers, the crucial point is whether the materials include certain combinations of dimensions, or perhaps all of them, one of them, or none. Second, by focusing on the presence or absence of one of these dimensions, one tends to ignore the *degree* of violence, explicitness, or injury.

2. Equation of Pornography with Degradation. A number of antipornography feminists conceptualize pornography in a way that defines most sexually explicit depictions of women as degrading, demeaning, and humiliating (for example, Barry, 1979; Dworkin, 1979, 1985; Longino, 1980; MacKinnon, 1984; MacKinnon and Dworkin, 1983; Ratterman, 1982; Russell, 1980; Women Against Pornography, 1982). A central problem with defining pornography according to what is "degrading," "demeaning," or "humiliating" is that these terms are so subjective and broad in scope that any activity found unacceptable or objectionable to the viewer might be labeled pornographic. For instance, members of the religious right consider depictions of homosexuality, masturbation, and extramarital sex to be degrading, whereas many feminists would not consider portrayals of these acts to be degrading. Anticensorship feminists object to the political implications of the term "degrading" because it has been used to delimit the lives of women:

> "Degrading to women" is a phrase that has been used consistently to justify limits on women's lives. Within the past century, paid employment, recognition of women's sexuality, and information about birth control have all been called degrading. (Feminist Anti-Censorship Taskforce, 1985:12)

3. *The Etymological Root of Pornography.* In many instances, the Greek derivation of the term "pornography" is used as part or all of the definition of pornography (American Heritage Dictionary, 1976; Dworkin, 1979; Falwell, 1980; Gagnon, 1977; Gould, 1977; Oxford English Dictionary, 1970; Webster's Dictionary, 1976; W. C. Wilson, 1973). In the Greek derivation, *graphos* means the writing of or about, and *porne* means harlot or prostitute. Thus, the original meaning of pornography is the writing of or about prostitutes. Although this definition has historical significance, it is too narrow to serve as an adequate framework for the analysis of pornography.

4. *Community Norms.* MacNamara and Sagarin (1977) hinge their definition of pornography on whether a sexual depiction is "generally unacceptable in society." Applied to the community level, this conception of *pornography* is similar to the current legal definition of *obscenity* (*Miller v. California*, 413 U.S. 15 1973).[7] Former Chief Justice Warren Burger, who wrote the majority opinion in *Miller*, argued that it is unrealistic to believe that a national standard could be established for obscene materials; however, the justices did feel that obscenity could be defined on a community-by-community basis. The standard established in the *Miller* case permits communities to censor materials that meet a three-part test:

7. Many people make the mistake of equating pornography with obscenity. However, there is no necessary correspondence between materials that an individual or group might consider pornographic and materials that a court of law might deem obscene. Although there is clearly an overlap between the two, they are certainly not synonymous (for elaboration see Feinberg, 1985).

1. whether the average person, applying contemporary community standards, would find that the work, taken as a whole, appeals to the prurient
   interest;
2. whether the work depicts or describes, in a patently offensive way,
   sexual conduct specifically defined by the applicable state law;
3. whether the work, taken as a whole, lacks serious literary, artistic,
   political, or scientific value.

There are many problems with the *Miller* test, among them the difficulty of
defining such terms as "average person," "prurient interest," and "patently
offensive." It is similarly unclear how a court of law could objectively determine whether a book or film has "serious value," or why the freedom of
expression should be based on a standard of seriousness.

The vague and subjective nature of the Supreme Court's definition of
obscenity is further illustrated by the community standard criterion. Apart
from the quandary of trying to apply the meaning of "community standards,"
the problem with leaving it up to individual communities to define obscenity is
that a book, magazine, or film that is acceptable in a major city such as New
York or Los Angeles may not be acceptable in a small town in New Hampshire, Utah, or Arkansas. If the same book were to be ruled obscene in one
place and not another, this would tell us much more about the community's
intolerance toward a particular book than it would about the nature of obscene
materials. Since the Supreme Court chose not to define pornography at all,
and left us with an imprecise definition of obscenity, it seems that the *Miller*
decision has done very little to settle the difficult conceptual issues plaguing
the meaning of pornography and obscenity.

5. *Neglection of the Intent to Sexually Arouse.* Several of the definitions presented in table 5.1 fail to acknowledge the intent of the producer of these
materials to sexually stimulate the viewer (for example, Diamond, 1980; Gagnon, 1977; Gray, 1982; Peckham, 1971; Russell, 1980; Stoller, 1976; W. C.
Wilson, 1973). In each of these definitions, the emphasis is on either the
ability of the depictions to elicit sexual arousal, the illicitness of the depiction,
or the depiction of genitals in a condition of sexual excitement. Because the
intention of the producer is omitted, *any* materials that have the above-
mentioned effects or characteristics could be considered pornography. Thus,
materials created for purposes *other* than sexual stimulation which nonetheless aroused the viewer, depicted men and women in sexual poses, or were
considered illicit would also be covered by these broad definitions. These
definitions would extend the meaning of pornography to include such materials as books and films that are used in sexuality courses and medical schools;

films, photographs, and audiotapes that are used to alter the behavior of sex offenders; sexually explicit materials that are used by sex therapists to assist them in treating sexual dysfunctions; much that is considered literature and art; a variety of feature films and documentaries; and a host of advertisements.

6. *Social Context of the Presentation.* Individuals do not automatically respond with sexual excitement to materials that are designed to sexually stimulate (Gagnon and Simon, 1973). How an individual labels and responds to sexual stimuli is dependent upon the social context. For example, men who look at sexually explicit photographs in the magazine section of a bookstore or supermarket, in clear view of other customers, are likely to have a different set of cognitive and physiological responses to these stimuli than they would if viewing the same photographs in private. Similarly, consciousness-raising efforts such as the Women Against Pornography Slide Show, which shows slides of sexually explicit photographs from pornographic magazines (while a prepared script is read), are likely to take on a different meaning when seen in a classroom than they would if the photographs were seen privately in their original context. Since the social context sets limits on acceptable response options, individuals will find themselves thinking about and responding to sexually explicit materials in ways that allow them to successfully coordinate the social context with their definition of the sexually stimulating material.

SUMMARY. In our estimation, the most useful definitions in table 5.1 are those that focus on the *intent* of the *producer* to sexually stimulate the viewer. As will be explained in the next section, we share this conceptual focus, although we acknowledge that it too has some limitations.

Definition of Pornography

The problems and limitations of many previous definitions led us to formulate the following alternative definition of pornography:

> *Pornography refers to written, pictorial, or audiovisual materials that are produced for the purpose of sexual arousal.*

There are two important aspects of this definition that we want to emphasize.

1. *Intent of the Producer.* The definition focuses on the intent of the producer of the material rather than the behavior of the consumer. Thus, a sexually explicit film like the feminist documentary *Not a Love Story*, which is intended to educate the public about the way some pornography demeans women, may have had the unintended effect of sexually stimulating some of the viewers.

We saw this film in two different cities and in both cases noticed that the majority of the viewers looked and acted like the typical audience of X-rated films, with the exception that the audiences were about 90% male rather than almost 100% male. Given that the movie was advertised in the newspaper as an X-rated film, it should not be surprising that some men viewed it as just another "skin flick."

The advantage of basing the definition of pornography on the intent of the producer, rather than its effect on the viewer, is that it permits us to avoid having to classify movies like *Not a Love Story* as pornography just because some of the audience may have become sexually aroused. Similarly, the fact that the pages of the *National Geographic Magazine* have been turned by millions of young boys looking for pictures of nude native women does not make it pornography except to the extent that sexual stimulation of adolescent boys was the intent of the publisher.

We do not mean to suggest by this definition that the producer's intention of sexually stimulating consumers is the only or even the most important consideration behind the production and distribution of pornography. It would be ignoring the obvious not to admit that selling pornography is an enormously lucrative business. According to one estimate, the pornography industry nets $7 billion a year (Attorney General's Commission on Pornography, 1986). At the same time, many producers of pornography believe that they are fulfilling an important social function to society by supplying the public with materials that provide educational information about sex. Other producers of pornography have the conviction that their materials have artistic significance, literary merit, or cinematic import. Thus, not unlike other commodities, there are multiple intentions behind the production of pornography. But the intent on the part of producers to sexually stimulate the consumers of these materials is what distinguishes pornography from other commodities.

2. *Context Dimensions.* A central feature of this definition is that it allows for empirical investigation of a number of dimensions of pornography by deliberately omitting a specification of the nature of the material that is produced for purposes of sexual arousal. Some questions that researchers might ask are: To what extent is simple nudity an important part of what makes up pornography? How important is the display of genitals? How critical is portrayal of sexual acts? To what extent is the depiction of aggression, either verbal or physical, an important aspect? How does the age or gender of the sexual actors influence whether or not a depiction is perceived as pornographic? These questions suggest that researchers need to isolate the various dimensions of sexually explicit materials and measure them separately. However, if the individual dimensions are included in the definition itself, then they become constants whose separate and joint effects cannot be studied because the dimension

must be present for the material to be defined as pornography. Therefore, the most heuristic definition is one which restricts the core conceptualization of pornography to the producer's intention to sexually arouse the viewer and treats all other aspects, such as type of sex acts depicted, as variables to be analyzed in empirical research.

Limitations of the Proposed Definition

1. *No Definition of Arousal.* One limitation of this definition is that it does not address the issue of what constitutes sexual arousal and how to measure it. Although we regard the conceptualization and measurement of sexual arousal to be an important issue, the proposed definition is not designed to address it. In fact, the inherent ambiguity in conceptualizing and measuring arousal was one of the problems which led us to formulate a definition based on *intent of the producer*.[8] If the producer believes that the material will be found stimulating and makes it available for that purpose, it fits our definition of pornography, regardless of whether those exposed to the material experience physiological arousal.

2. *Intent.* Although basing the definition on the intent of the producer avoids the problem of what may be stimulating to one sector of the population but not be stimulating to another, it does not free the definition from dependence on another subjective variable—the producer's intent. As was previously noted, producers of pornography are often quite explicit about their intention to arouse consumers and regard themselves as filling a vital individual and social need. However, even when the makers of sexually oriented materials are not explicit about their intent, it can be inferred from a multitude of clues such as a XXX-rating on the marquees of a movie theater, the type of store selling the materials (for example, an adults-only bookstore), the stylized poses of the models, explicit portrayals of sexual activity, and the illicitness of the depiction. Given the convergence of a number of these clues, few would fail to perceive that these materials are offered for the purposes of sexual arousal.

Summary

The definition of pornography set forth in this section has important limitations as well as advantages and is not offered as a universally appropriate

---

8. Laboratory research on the effects of pornography have utilized different measures of sexual arousal including self-reports, a penile transducer which measures blood flow in the genitals, heart rate, and blood pressure (Byrne and Kelley, 1984). Zuckerman (1971) reviewed the literature on physiological measures of arousal and concluded that the penile transducer provides the most accurate assessment. However, there is evidence that men can control their erections by shifting their attention away from the source of arousal (Rosen and Keefe, 1978).

definition. Definitions can and do vary according to the purposes at hand. Although a number of different definitions to describe the same concept can cause problems when trying to integrate a literature, that is much less of a problem than if authors fail to give any definition at all. Concepts and their definitions are tools used to achieve a given purpose. In order for definitions to be effective tools, they must be sharply delineated and stated in a way that facilitates empirical research.

MEASUREMENT OF PORNOGRAPHY

Sex Magazine Circulation Index

A Sex Magazine Circulation Index (SMCX2) was constructed to measure the prevalence of pornography. The raw data for this measure are the number of copies sold in 1979, both subscription and newsstand sales, for each of eight sexually explicit magazines (*Playboy, Hustler, Penthouse, Chic, Club, Gallery, Genesis,* and *Oui*). The data were obtained from the Audit Bureau of Circulation, which is an independent nonprofit organization that audits and certifies magazine sales figures. These are soft-core rather than hard-core sex magazines, in the sense that they do not show the penis erect or show acts of copulation. However, just a few years ago they would have been considered hard core because all show details of female genitalia. These magazines represent the most widely read sexually explicit materials in the United States; several sell millions of copies each month. They reach a much wider audience than other sex literature and are therefore important for both theoretical and policy reasons.

We began by converting the number of copies sold to a rate per 100 males

Table 5.2

Correlation Matrix of Sex Magazines

Sex Magazines	1	2	3	4	5	6	7	8
1. Playboy	1.00							
2. Hustler	.36	1.00						
3. Penthouse	.93	.41	1.00					
4. Chic	.43	.69	.43	1.00				
5. Club	.51	.67	.53	.63	1.00			
6. Gallery	.76	.48	.75	.56	.64	1.00		
7. Genesis	.66	.65	.65	.70	.73	.86	1.00	
8. Oui	.95	.30	.88	.45	.48	.80	.70	1.00
Mean	11.29	3.15	4.49	.48	1.11	1.23	.77	1.52
Standard Deviation	3.76	.90	1.15	.19	.39	.39	.29	.63

Table 5.3

Reliability Analysis of the Sex Magazine Circulation Index

Indicators	Corrected Item - Total Correlations	Alpha if Item Deleted
Playboy	.86	.83
Hustler	.45	.69
Penthouse	.92	.59
Chic	.56	.71
Club	.62	.70
Gallery	.83	.69
Genesis	.77	.70
Oui	.92	.65

Standardized Alpha Coefficient = .93

age 15 and older for each state. Next we examined frequency distributions for extreme scores and adjusted the outliers.[9] In a previous version of the index, the sex magazines were factor analyzed and all the magazines loaded on a single factor. As a result, we decided not to repeat the factor analysis and constructed an index based on the combined circulation rates of the eight magazines.[10] Table 5.2 displays a correlation matrix of the sex magazines.

The SPSS (Nie et al., 1975) reliability program was used to compute the internal consistency reliability of the index (Cronbach, 1970). Table 5.3 reports the item-to-total correlations and the alpha level if an item were to be deleted from the index. The standardized alpha coefficient of reliability is .93.

9. See appendix A for a more detailed discussion of the indexing method.

10. In an earlier paper (Baron and Straus, 1984), a different version of the Sex Magazine Circulation Index was constructed. We believe that the new version is an improvement over the old version for a number of reasons. First, in the previous version we computed the circulation rate of each magazine per 100,000 population, whereas in the new version we use a rate per 100 males age 15 and older. The new denominator better reflects the actual consumers of pornography because women purchase a very small proportion of these magazines and state law prohibits the sale of pornography to minors. Second, in the previous version *Forum* was used as one of the indicators, whereas in the new version *Forum* was dropped and *Penthouse* was added. We decided to drop *Forum* because, unlike the other magazines in the index, it is composed primarily of stories and drawings, not color photos of nude women. The data on *Penthouse* enabled us to include one of the most highly circulated pornographic magazines and has the advantage of content consistency with the other magazines in the index. *Penthouse* was not included in the previous version of the index because the data did not become available to us until 1985. Finally, the indicators in the previous version of the index were Z-scored in order to equalize the contribution of each maga-

Table 5.4a

Ranking of the States in Sex Magazine Circulation

	Playboy		Hustler		Penthouse		Chic	
Rank	State	ma239r2	State	ma151r2	State	ma411r2	State	ma59r2
1	Alaska	26.0	Alaska	8.29	Alaska	9.57	Alaska	1.46
2	Nevada	24.4	Nevada	6.57	Wyoming	8.16	Hawaii	1.05
3	Wyoming	21.2	Hawaii	4.90	Nevada	8.15	Nevada	0.88
4	Colorado	17.3	New Hampshire	4.53	Colorado	6.36	Michigan	0.75
5	Idaho	15.8	Delaware	4.48	Hawaii	6.00	Kansas	0.74
6	Oregon	15.3	Arizona	4.37	Montana	5.84	Oklahoma	0.73
7	Arizona	14.9	Kansas	4.04	Oregon	5.78	Ohio	0.72
8	Washington	14.5	Illinois	4.02	Idaho	5.70	Nebraska	0.63
9	Montana	14.3	Nebraska	4.00	Arizona	5.52	Texas	0.60
10	Hawaii	14.0	Texas	3.85	California	5.39	Oregon	0.56
11	California	13.7	Vermont	3.82	Washington	5.38	California	0.54
12	Oklahoma	13.2	Oregon	3.76	New Hampshire	5.35	Delaware	0.53
13	Minnesota	13.2	Michigan	3.72	Kansas	5.16	New Jersey	0.52
14	New Mexico	13.1	California	3.64	Minnesota	5.05	Wyoming	0.51
15	Kansas	12.9	West Virginia	3.51	Florida	5.05	Illinois	0.50
16	Iowa	12.2	South Dakota	3.49	Massachusetts	4.83	Georgia	0.50
17	Texas	11.8	Florida	3.38	New Mexico	4.74	North Dakota	0.50
18	Nebraska	11.5	New Jersey	3.38	Utah	4.66	Vermont	0.50
19	Vermont	11.4	New Mexico	3.28	Virginia	4.65	New Hampshire	0.49
20	New Hampshire	11.3	Wyoming	3.20	North Dakota	4.60	North Carolina	0.49
21	South Dakota	11.2	North Carolina	3.20	Georgia	4.56	Alabama	0.48
22	Utah	11.2	North Dakota	3.18	Texas	4.55	Maryland	0.47
23	Illinois	10.7	Ohio	3.18	Delaware	4.46	Florida	0.45
24	Georgia	10.6	Maryland	3.15	Michigan	4.40	New York	0.45
25	Florida	10.6	Washington	3.13	Nebraska	4.40	South Dakota	0.44
26	Michigan	10.5	Maine	3.09	Vermont	4.26	Virginia	0.44
27	Virginia	10.3	Kentucky	3.07	New York	4.23	Massachusetts	0.43
28	Delaware	10.3	Pennsylvania	3.06	Illinois	4.22	Indiana	0.43
29	Maryland	10.3	Massachusetts	3.01	Rhode Island	4.22	South Carolina	0.43
30	Wisconsin	10.2	Indiana	2.97	Maryland	4.21	Pennsylvania	0.43
31	Indiana	10.0	Virginia	2.91	South Dakota	4.20	Montana	0.42
32	North Dakota	9.7	Tennessee	2.89	New Jersey	4.14	West Virginia	0.42
33	Louisiana	9.4	New York	2.89	Oklahoma	4.06	Rhode Island	0.42
34	New Jersey	9.4	Alabama	2.87	Iowa	4.00	Kentucky	0.41
35	Connecticut	9.4	Louisiana	2.87	Wisconsin	3.98	Arizona	0.41
36	Ohio	9.2	Montana	2.79	Ohio	3.91	Tennessee	0.41
37	Massachusetts	9.1	Wisconsin	2.72	Connecticut	3.88	Wisconsin	0.40
38	Maine	9.0	Connecticut	2.63	Maine	3.88	Louisiana	0.39
39	Rhode Island	8.3	Colorado	2.56	Louisiana	3.83	Washington	0.38
40	Pennsylvania	8.2	South Carolina	2.48	Pennsylvania	3.53	Minnesota	0.37
41	Missouri	8.0	Mississippi	2.45	Indiana	3.48	Iowa	0.35
42	New York	7.7	Iowa	2.41	Missouri	3.44	Mississippi	0.35
43	Alabama	7.3	Georgia	2.39	South Carolina	3.36	Connecticut	0.33
44	North Carolina	7.2	Minnesota	2.37	North Carolina	3.10	Idaho	0.33
45	Kentucky	7.1	Arkansas	2.10	Tennessee	3.10	Missouri	0.31
46	Tennessee	7.0	Rhode Island	1.80	Kentucky	2.99	New Mexico	0.30
47	South Carolina	6.9	Missouri	1.72	West Virginia	2.84	Maine	0.29
48	Mississippi	6.2	Oklahoma	1.64	Alabama	2.72	Colorado	0.29
49	Arkansas	6.2	Idaho	1.35	Arkansas	2.52	Arkansas	0.28
50	West Virginia	6.0	Utah	0.90	Mississippi	2.38	Utah	0.03

Note: Rates per 100 males age 15 and older.

STATE AND REGIONAL DIFFERENCES IN THE CIRCULATION OF PORNOGRAPHY

There is substantial variation among states and regions in the circulation of sex magazines. Table 5.4(a and b) presents the rank-order distribution of the eight magazines. The first two columns of table 5.4a show the circulation rates

zine to the overall index. In the new version, the indicators were not standardized because we wanted the index to reflect the actual number of copies sold in each state.

Table 5.4b

Ranking of the States in Sex Magazine Circulation

	Club		Gallery		Genesis		Oui	
Rank	State	ma66r2	State	ma123r2	State	ma125r2	State	ma225r2
1	Hawaii	2.36	Alaska	3.56	Alaska	2.37	Alaska	5.94
2	Nevada	2.35	Nevada	2.59	Hawaii	1.75	Wyoming	3.45
3	Oregon	1.95	Oregon	2.08	Nevada	1.50	Nevada	3.29
4	Arizona	1.75	Georgia	2.05	Oregon	1.27	Idaho	2.33
5	Alaska	1.75	Arizona	2.02	Kansas	1.27	Arizona	2.22
6	New Jersey	1.68	Hawaii	1.85	Wyoming	1.13	Oregon	2.19
7	Kansas	1.61	Kansas	1.80	Arizona	1.12	Oklahoma	1.99
8	New Hampshire	1.57	Wyoming	1.70	New Hampshire	1.11	Hawaii	1.96
9	Idaho	1.44	Idaho	1.51	Georgia	0.95	Montana	1.96
10	Ohio	1.42	Oklahoma	1.50	New Mexico	0.94	Colorado	1.94
11	California	1.40	Colorado	1.46	Maryland	0.88	New Mexico	1.94
12	New York	1.37	New Hampshire	1.43	Maine	0.87	Kansas	1.87
13	Michigan	1.30	Maryland	1.37	Vermont	0.85	Utah	1.84
14	Illinois	1.28	North Dakota	1.36	Oklahoma	0.84	Washington	1.83
15	Texas	1.23	Washington	1.35	Florida	0.81	Georgia	1.77
16	Vermont	1.23	Vermont	1.34	Virginia	0.78	California	1.74
17	Maryland	1.22	Virginia	1.33	Illinois	0.78	Illinois	1.64
18	New Mexico	1.14	New Mexico	1.32	Tennessee	0.77	Vermont	1.63
19	Virginia	1.12	Florida	1.30	Delaware	0.76	Minnesota	1.62
20	Indiana	1.08	Illinois	1.20	Idaho	0.75	Texas	1.60
21	Georgia	1.08	Louisiana	1.20	North Dakota	0.73	Louisiana	1.42
22	Massachusetts	1.08	Delaware	1.19	Ohio	0.73	Iowa	1.41
23	Washington	1.06	California	1.18	South Carolina	0.72	North Dakota	1.40
24	Nebraska	1.03	Minnesota	1.17	Indiana	0.71	New Hampshire	1.38
25	Colorado	1.03	Indiana	1.10	Iowa	0.71	Michigan	1.37
26	Delaware	1.02	Ohio	1.09	Alabama	0.69	Wisconsin	1.37
27	Maine	1.00	Montana	1.09	Nebraska	0.67	Florida	1.36
28	South Dakota	0.99	Texas	1.08	Arkansas	0.67	Indiana	1.31
29	Connecticut	0.99	Michigan	1.06	Texas	0.67	Maryland	1.29
30	Iowa	0.98	Iowa	1.05	California	0.66	Virginia	1.25
31	Kentucky	0.98	Nebraska	1.04	Kentucky	0.65	Rhode Island	1.25
32	Wyoming	0.97	Alabama	1.04	North Carolina	0.65	New York	1.20
33	Pennsylvania	0.97	Maine	1.01	Michigan	0.64	Delaware	1.19
34	South Carolina	0.96	South Carolina	0.99	Massachusetts	0.63	Nebraska	1.18
35	Florida	0.96	North Carolina	0.99	Montana	0.63	Ohio	1.17
36	Louisiana	0.90	Massachusetts	0.97	New Jersey	0.62	Massachusetts	1.17
37	Alabama	0.90	Wisconsin	0.96	Washington	0.59	Alabama	1.14
38	North Carolina	0.88	Rhode Island	0.95	New York	0.58	New Jersey	1.13
39	Wisconsin	0.87	Utah	0.94	Wisconsin	0.57	Connecticut	1.07
40	Minnesota	0.86	Tennessee	0.94	Minnesota	0.56	Missouri	1.05
41	Oklahoma	0.85	New Jersey	0.94	Louisiana	0.55	South Dakota	1.04
42	Tennessee	0.84	Arkansas	0.94	Connecticut	0.54	Arkansas	1.01
43	West Virginia	0.83	South Dakota	0.93	Utah	0.54	Pennsylvania	0.99
44	Mississippi	0.76	West Virginia	0.93	Colorado	0.54	Tennessee	0.93
45	Montana	0.75	Kentucky	0.91	South Dakota	0.54	South Carolina	0.89
46	Arkansas	0.70	Pennsylvania	0.84	Pennsylvania	0.52	Kentucky	0.86
47	Rhode Island	0.55	New York	0.83	Mississippi	0.43	Maine	0.81
48	Missouri	0.53	Connecticut	0.77	Rhode Island	0.42	West Virginia	0.78
49	Utah	0.53	Mississippi	0.65	West Virginia	0.41	North Carolina	0.77
50	North Dakota	0.18	Missouri	0.57	Missouri	0.37	Mississippi	0.74

Note: Rates per 100 males age 15 and older.

of *Playboy* and *Hustler* for each state. A comparison of the top and bottom ranking states indicates that four times more copies of *Playboy* and eight times more copies of *Hustler* were sold in Alaska than in West Virginia and Utah, respectively. These two magazines were chosen for purposes of illustration because they are two of the largest circulation sexually explicit magazines and because of the contrast in the image that each presents. *Playboy* seeks to portray itself as a highbrow magazine and *Hustler* as a macho magazine. This difference between the two magazines led us to expect the moderate positive

Table 5.5

Regional Differences in Sex Magazine Circulation

Indicators	Regions			
	Northeast	North Central	South	West
Playboy***	9.36	10.81	8.81	16.63
Hustler	3.13	3.15	2.95	3.75
Penthouse***	4.26	4.24	3.65	6.25
Chic	0.43	0.51	0.46	0.55
Club*	1.16	1.01	0.95	1.42
Gallery***	1.01	1.11	1.15	1.74
Genesis**	0.68	0.69	0.70	1.06
Oui***	1.18	1.37	1.19	2.51

Note: *p<.05, **p<.01, ***p<.001.

correlation of .36 between their circulation rates. Regional differences among the sex magazines are shown in table 5.5.

The ranking of the states on the composite SMCX2 can be seen in table 5.6. Alaska has the highest circulation rate on seven of the eight sex magazines, so it is no surprise to find that Alaska leads the country on the combined index. On the average, approximately 60 pornographic magazines are purchased for every 100 adult males residing in Alaska. Inspection of the upper level of the distribution suggests that those states with the highest circulation rates are concentrated in the West. Indeed, the top five states are located in the West (Alaska, Nevada, Wyoming, Hawaii, and Oregon). And with the exception of Kansas, 9 of the 10 states with the highest circulation rates are in the West. Comparing the highest and lowest ranking states shows that approximately four times more pornography is consumed in Alaska than Mississippi. The low circulation rate for Mississippi appears to be symptomatic of the South as a whole; southern states are heavily concentrated in the bottom of the distribution.

A more precise rendering of the regional differences may be seen by examining figure 5.1, which displays a breakdown of the circulation rates of pornography by the four census regions and the nine census divisions. An analysis of variance was also computed and indicates that there are significant differences among the regions and divisions in the consumption of pornography. The region of the country with the highest circulation of pornographic magazines is the West (34 per 100 males age 15 or older), followed by the

Table 5.6

Rank Order of the States in Sex
Magazine Circulation

Rank	State	rapx20
1	Alaska	59.0
2	Nevada	49.7
3	Wyoming	40.4
4	Hawaii	33.8
5	Oregon	32.9
6	Arizona	32.3
7	Colorado	31.5
8	Kansas	29.4
9	Idaho	29.2
10	Washington	28.3
11	California	28.2
12	Montana	27.8
13	New Hampshire	27.2
14	New Mexico	26.7
15	Texas	25.3
16	Minnesota	25.1
17	Vermont	25.0
18	Oklahoma	24.8
19	Nebraska	24.4
20	Illinois	24.4
21	Georgia	23.9
22	Delaware	23.9
23	Florida	23.9
24	Michigan	23.7
25	Iowa	23.2
26	Maryland	22.9
27	South Dakota	22.9
28	Virginia	22.8
29	New Jersey	21.8
30	North Dakota	21.7
31	Ohio	21.4
32	Massachusetts	21.2
33	Indiana	21.1
34	Wisconsin	21.1
35	Utah	20.6
36	Louisiana	20.6
37	Maine	20.0
38	Connecticut	19.6
39	New York	19.2
40	Pennsylvania	18.5
41	Rhode Island	17.9
42	North Carolina	17.3
43	Alabama	17.1
44	Kentucky	17.0
45	Tennessee	16.9
46	South Carolina	16.7
47	Missouri	16.0
48	West Virginia	15.7
49	Arkansas	14.4
50	Mississippi	14.0

Note: Rate per 100 males age 15 and
older

Figure 5.1

Mean of Sex Magazine Circulation Index by Division and Region

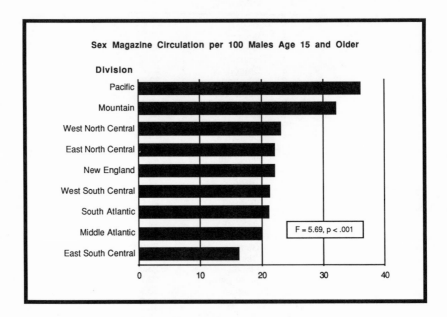

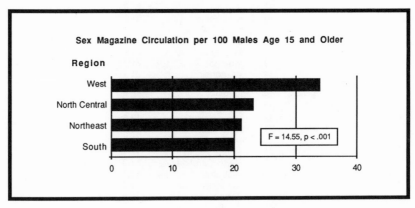

North Central (23 per 100 males age 15 or older), the Northeast (21 per 100 males age 15 or older), and the South (20 per 100 males age 15 or older). Only the western region is above the national average circulation rate of 24 per 100 adult males.

CORRELATION OF SEX MAGAZINE CIRCULATION WITH RAPE AND NONSEXUAL VIOLENT CRIME

The correlations of the SMCX2 with the average rape rate for the years 1980–82 and the 1980 rates of homicide, aggravated assault, and robbery were computed. The results show a high correlation of .64 between the SMCX2 and the rape rate. The importance of this correlation is emphasized by its comparison with the low correlations between the SMCX2 and nonsexual violence (.10 with homicide, .17 with aggravated assault, and .09 with robbery). These correlations indicate that the circulation of soft-core pornography is strongly related to the rape rate but has relatively weak relations with nonsexual violent crimes. This pattern of correlations provides evidence of the discriminate validity of the SMCX2.

The fact that the SMCX2 has a high correlation with rape lends preliminary support to the feminist theory that pornography contributes to a cultural climate conducive to rape. However, caution is advised in drawing any conclusions on the basis of this correlation because there are many other possible explanations. One possibility is that the relationship between sex magazine circulation and rape is spurious in the sense that it might reflect their association with some common third variable. For example, research shows that rapists and rape victims tend to be between the ages of 16 and 25 (Amir, 1971; Curtis, 1978; Hindelang and Davis, 1977). If sex magazines are widely read in states with a youthful population, the correlation between sex magazine circulation and rape could be due to the fact that both are related to youthfulness rather than to any causal link between pornography and rape. There are many other state characteristics that could produce a spurious association. Consequently, a multivariate analysis is used to control for several of these possibilities and is presented in chapter 8.

SUMMARY AND CONCLUSION

The issue of pornography has become a central focus of feminist theory and practice. Activists in the feminist antipornography movement claim that pornography reduces women to sex objects, promotes and maintains male dominance, and encourages acts of sexual violence against women. Catharine MacKinnon and Andrea Dworkin advance the argument that pornography victimizes women and violates their civil rights. To redress this situation,

MacKinnon and Dworkin drafted legislation that would give women a civil cause of action against those who produce and sell materials that fit their definition of pornography. The courts have ruled, though, that the legislation is unconstitutional because it violates First Amendment protections of free speech.

In addition to discussing the views of antipornography feminists, we reviewed and evaluated several definitions of pornography. Some of the limitations of these definitions include (1) the use of important dimensions of pornography (for example, violence) as constants; (2) the tendency to equate pornography with the "degradation" of women; and (3) the failure to focus on the producer's intent to sexually stimulate the viewer. In an effort to overcome these problems, we devised an alternative definition: "Pornography refers to written, pictorial, or audio visual materials that are produced for the purpose of sexual arousal." This definition shifts attention away from the effect of pornography on individual consumers and makes the *producer's intent to sexually arouse* the conceptual focus.

After presenting our definition of pornography, we then introduced the index that was constructed to assess the geographical distribution of pornography—the Sex Magazine Circulation Index (SMCX2). This index is composed of the circulation rates of the eight best-selling soft-core pornographic magazines (*Playboy, Penthouse, Hustler, Oui, Club, Chic, Genesis,* and *Gallery*). The SMCX2 measure the prevalence of pornography in each state and makes it possible to investigate the relationship between the circulation rates of pornography and the incidence of rape. State ranks and regional breakdowns of the SMCX2 were presented and indicate that more pornography is purchased in the West than any other part of the country.

A strong correlation was found between the SMCX2 and the rape rate ($r = .64$). Although this correlation is consistent with the conjectures of antipornography feminists, it would be premature to draw any conclusions on the basis of this one correlation. In the final chapter, a path analysis is presented that permits us to control for several variables that could conceivably explain the relationship between sex magazine circulation and rape.

6

SOCIAL DISORGANIZATION

Social disorganization theory was developed at the University of Chicago during the first half of the twentieth century. Although there is no single definition of social disorganization that all its practitioners adhered to, the term has generally been used to describe the conditions that undermine the ability of traditional institutions (such as the family, church, and neighborhood) to govern social behavior. Perhaps Park and Burgess (1921:785) said it best when they wrote: "All social problems turn out to be problems of social control."

The principal architects of social disorganization theory included such luminaries of American sociology as Robert Park and Ernest W. Burgess (1921), William F. Ogburn (1922), W. I. Thomas and Florian Znaniecki (1927), Frederick M. Thrasher (1927), Clifford R. Shaw and Henry D. McKay (1931), and Robert E. L. Faris and H. Warren Dunham (1939). They sought to explain differences in the rates of crime, alcoholism, vagrancy, juvenile delinquency, suicide, and mental illness by changes in the social organization of the city.

Despite the popularity of social disorganization theory over a period of three decades, criticisms of the theory since the 1950s have served to undermine its credibility among many sociologists.[1] Critics have charged that the theory is value laden, vague, circular in its explanation of social problems, and implicitly endorses existing social arrangements (Bursik, 1988; Carey, 1975; Kornhauser, 1978; Martindale, 1957; Pfohl, 1985; Wirth, 1940). Although these criticisms raise serious questions about the utility of social disorganization theory, none of them poses an insurmountable obstacle. One objective of this chapter is to rescue social disorganization theory from its critics and to

1. Kornhauser (1978:118) makes note of the paradox that while sociologists are reluctant to use the term "social disorganization" as an explanation of crime and deviance, they have not shown a similar reluctance to use the cognate term "anomie" (normlessness or without regulation). Although social disorganization and anomie have different lineages, with social disorganization theory emerging in twentieth-century American and anomie theory in late nineteenth-century France (Durkheim, 1966 [1897]), both the Chicago sociologists and Durkheim were struggling with a similar set of social concerns—the adverse consequences of urbanization, industrialization, and the breakdown of the regulative power of traditional institutions.

demonstrate that the theory can provide a conceptually rich and empirically sound explanation of crime and deviance. In order to accomplish this task we intend to (1) clarify the meaning of social disorganization, (2) delineate the causal structure underlying the theory, and (3) construct a measure of social disorganization that is conceptually and empirically independent of other variables in our analysis of rape. Toward this end, a Social Disorganization Index (SDX) was constructed. The SDX permits us to empirically assess the extent to which state-to-state differences in the level of social disorganization are associated with state-to-state differences in the incidence of rape.

THE CONCEPT OF SOCIAL DISORGANIZATION

Thomas and Znaniecki's View of Social Disorganization

Social disorganization can be understood as a breakdown in certain aspects of the organization of society (Blumer, 1937; Martindale, 1957; Mower, 1941; Wirth, 1940). In a very real sense, a prior state of social organization is a necessary precondition for social disorganization. It is therefore unfortunate, as Carey (1975) notes, that the early Chicago theorists did not explicitly define social organization. Consequently, the place to begin our discussion is with a definition of social organization. For purposes of this research, we define *social organization* as *the network of rules, roles, and institutions that regulate social behavior.* When changes in the organization of society disrupt the network of institutional controls, people are cut loose from normative constraints and nonconformity occurs. The concept of social disorganization was given its first extended treatment in Thomas and Znaniecki's (1927) investigation of *The Polish Peasant in Europe and America.*[2] The principal data for the study were 762 letters that were written between Polish immigrants in America and their families in Poland. Thomas and Znaniecki (1927:1128) defined social disorganization as "a decrease of the influence of existing social rules of behavior upon individual members of the group." This definition captured well the experience of displaced Polish immigrants, who, upon arriving in America, quickly found that rural existence had provided few guidelines to help them navigate through the buzz and confusion of urban-industrial life. Isolated from the familiar customs and constraints of family and community, yet detached from the conventions and institutional controls of the host culture, the Polish immigrant was set adrift in a sea of disorganization.

2. The five-volume edition of *The Polish Peasant in Europe and America* was originally published between 1918 and 1920. In 1927, Alfred Knopf published a new edition of the book, combining the five volumes into a two-volume set (Madge, 1962:52).

As Carey (1975) notes, Thomas and Znaniecki conceptualized social disorganization as a temporary state, not a permanent condition. They described social disorganization as one phase in the three-part process of social organization—social disorganization—reorganization. According to this view, disorganization arises when social circumstances make it impossible for institutional and informal constraints to effectively preserve the prevailing social order. Thomas and Znaniecki's (1927:1130) description of this process is worth quoting at length:

> The stability of group institutions is thus simply a dynamic equilibrium of processes of disorganization and *reorganization.* This equilibrium is disturbed when processes of disorganization can no longer be checked by any attempts to reinforce the existing rules. A period of prevalent disorganization follows which may lead to a complete dissolution of the group. More usually, however, it is counteracted and stopped before it reaches this limit by a new process of reorganization which in this case does not consist in a mere reinforcement of the decaying organization, but in a production of new schemes of behavior and new institutions better adapted to the changed demands of the group; we call this production of new schemes of behavior and new institutions *social reconstruction.*

Thomas and Znaniecki's observation that social disorganization can lead to the establishment of more constructive modes of organization is an extremely penetrating insight, and one which helps explain some of the empirical findings to be presented later. Consider, for example, the breakdown of racist organizational structures. Although institutional racism still exists in the United States, the disruption of such structures has stimulated the development of nondiscriminatory forms of organization. This aspect of social disorganization theory is often overlooked by those who focus exclusively on the adverse consequences of social disorganization.

Social Disorganization as a Macrosociological Control Theory

Kornhauser (1978) maintains that contemporary control theories of crime and deviance (for example, Hirschi, 1969) are conceptually similar to social disorganization theories. As is true of social disorganization theory, control theory focuses on the circumstances that weaken primary group[3] controls and,

---

3. A primary group refers to a small group with close personal ties. Examples of primary groups are families, clubs, gangs, and church groups.

consequently, reduce constraints against nonconformity (Hirschi, 1969; Reckless, 1973; Toby, 1957). Control theorists maintain that whether or not an individual engages in prohibited behavior depends on the strength of the individual's social bond to the collective order. Hirschi (1969:16–34) argues that individuals who have (1) close ties to family, friends, and other significant others; (2) a greater investment of time and energy in obtaining some future goal (for example, getting an education, forging a career, or building a reputation); (3) greater involvement in conventional activities (for example, athletics, studying, and working); and (4) a strong belief in the legitimacy of dominant values and norms, are likely to be constrained from engaging in illegal behavior.

One important difference between control theory and social disorganization theory is that control theory endeavors to explain why *individuals* break the law, whereas social disorganization theory seeks to explain differences between groups or communities in *rates* of lawbreaking. Shaw and McKay's (1931, 1942, 1969) classic study of the geographic distribution of delinquency in Chicago provides an early illustration of this aspect of social disorganization theory. Drawing from Burgess's (1967) concentric zone theory of urban growth, Shaw and McKay found that rates of delinquency decrease as one moves from areas close to the central business district outward to the residential and commuter districts. They also found that the high rate of delinquency persisted for decades even though the ethnic and racial groups living in those areas changed. Moreover, as members of an ethnic or racial group moved out of a high delinquency area, the rate of delinquency for that group decreased while the rate for the incoming ethnic or racial group increased.

Shaw and McKay computed zero-order correlations to ascertain what community characteristics are associated with high delinquency areas. They found that poverty, percentage decrease or increase of the population, and population heterogeneity increased the likelihood of delinquency. These findings suggest that social disorganization (as measured by poverty, population turnover, and population heterogeneity) reduces the effectiveness of institutional and informal controls, thereby releasing youths to engage in delinquent behavior.

Shaw and McKay's work can be criticized for failing to distinguish between the effects of poverty and social disorganization on rates of delinquency. Since they conceptualize poverty as an indicator of social disorganization, it is not possible to discern from their analysis whether high rates of delinquency are due to the effects of economic deprivation (poverty), the failure of social control (social disorganization), or a combination of the two. In order to avoid such confusion, a measure of social disorganization is needed that is conceptually and empirically independent of measures of impoverishment. We therefore developed the Social Disorganization Index.

THE SOCIAL DISORGANIZATION INDEX

A contribution of the present study is the construction of a Social Disorganization Index (SDX). Previous research relied on single-indicator measures of social disorganization such as migration or divorce. Single-indicator measures cause numerous problems, two of which will be mentioned here. First, social disorganization, by definition, refers to disruption of more than one aspect of society. Consequently, no single indicator can represent this process adequately. A second problem is that different studies used different indicators. This may account for the frequent inconsistencies in the findings of social disorganization research (the various studies are measuring specific facets of social disorganization and these can and probably do have different consequences). The Social Disorganization Index which we devised is intended to overcome these problems by including indicators of several aspects of social disorganization.

Construction of the Index

The SDX is a six-item scale that is designed to measure the degree of instability in society. The index includes measures of geographical mobility, divorce, lack of religious affiliation, households headed by males with no female present, female-headed households with children, and the ratio of tourists to residents in each state.

Construction of the SDX began by choosing 12 indicators that seemed to measure some aspect of social disorganization. Next, we converted these variables to rates and adjusted the outliers. The 12 items were then factor analyzed using the principal components option of SCSS (Nie et al., 1980) with varimax rotation. Six of the 12 items loaded on factor 1 and had factor loadings of .65 or better. These 6 items were retained for the index. Correlations between the indicators comprising the SDX may be found in table 6.1. Table 6.2 shows the results of a reliability analysis (Cronbach, 1970). The internal consistency reliability of the SDX is .86.

It is important to note that we do not conceptualize social disorganization as an all-or-nothing condition, but as a matter of degree. As will be shown in the discussion of state and regional differences on the SDX, the degree of social disorganization varies from state to state and region to region. Social disor-

Table 6.1

Correlation Matrix of the Social Disorganization Indicators

Indicators	1	2	3	4	5	6
1. Percent of the Population Moving from a Different State or Abroad, 1975-1980	1.00					
2. Ratio of Tourists to Residents, 1977	.69	1.00				
3. Percent Divorced of the Population, 1980	.62	.28	1.00			
4. Percent of Female Headed Families with Children under Age 18, 1980	.61	.39	.54	1.00		
5. Percent of the Population with no Religious Affiliation, 1980	.53	.31	.69	.37	1.00	
6. Nonfamilied Male Householders Per 1,000 Population, 1980	.60	.40	.60	.46	.50	1.00
Mean	14.13	11.25	6.22	68.51	49.24	38.42
Standard Deviation	6.61	6.32	1.21	4.53	11.72	7.19

Table 6.2

Reliability Analysis of the Social Disorganization Index

Indicators	Corrected Item - Total Correlations	Alpha if Item Deleted
Percent of the Population Moving from a Different State or Abroad, 1975-1980	.79	.68
Ratio of Tourists to Residents, 1977	.52	.74
Percent Divorced of the Population, 1980	.74	.78
Percent of Female Headed Families with Children under Age 18, 1980	.57	.75
Percent of the Population with no Religious Affiliation, 1980	.56	.79
Nonfamilied Male Householders Per 1,000 Population, 1980	.64	.71

Standardized Alpha Coefficient = .86

ganization should therefore be understood as something that is more-or-less rather than either-or.

Indicators Included in the Index

Each variable included in the SDX makes a contribution to the conceptualization of social disorganization. This section presents the theoretical rationale for the six social disorganization indicators.

PERCENT OF THE POPULATION MOVING FROM A DIFFERENT STATE OR ABROAD BETWEEN 1975 AND 1980. When people move to a new state or country, they leave behind a network of family and friends and must go through a period of adjustment. The loss of familiar social ties can weaken the power of social controls and stimulate nonconformity (Durkheim, 1966 [1897]; Sampson, 1987; D. A. Smith and Jarjoura, 1988; Stark, 1987). According to Faris (1955:110),

> any weakening of stability and integration has an emancipating effect on character and allows in varying degrees the development of irresponsibility, unconventionality, and disorganization. Those whose lives involve a considerable amount of mobility and who thus are forced to spend a large proportion of their time among strangers are subject to this effect. They are not controlled by an organized society to the extent that settled peoples are and are thus free to express individuality to a greater extent.

Thus, the theoretical reason for using a measure of geographical mobility as an indicator of social disorganization is that change in the residential population diminishes the sense of attachment to community norms and reduces the ability of established institutions to regulate social behavior. This can happen in at least two ways. First, in-migrants tend to lack social ties through which informal social control operates. Second, in-migrants tend to bring with them beliefs and behaviors which, to the extent that they differ from those of the established community, can undermine the legitimacy of community norms among the resident population.

Research by Shaw and McKay supports the contention that areas with highly mobile and heterogeneous populations have higher rates of lawbreaking behavior. Shaw and McKay (1931) collected data on the home addresses of juvenile delinquents in Chicago, separated the data into census tracts, and correlated the delinquency rates with a number of predictor variables. They found that the percentage increase or decrease in the population and an index of the percentage foreign born and black were significantly associated with delinquency rates.

Crutchfield, Geerken, and Gove (1982) provide additional support for the criminogenic consequences of population turnover. Multiple regression was employed using data on the 65 largest SMSAs to investigate the relationship between geographical mobility (as measured by a composite index of residential mobility and in-migration) and property and violent crime rates. They found that geographical mobility was significantly related to rates of murder, assault, rape, burglary, and larceny. Crutchfield et al. interpret these findings as indicating that population fluctuation tends to reduce social cohesion and diminish the community's ability to control crime.

Similarly, Stark et al. (1983) hypothesized that states with lower levels of social integration, as indicated by proportion born out of state, would have higher rates of crime. They tested this hypothesis by correlating state-level crime rates from the 1920s (based on convictions) with a measure of population heterogeneity (the proportion of the population born out of state, excluding foreign born) and found that forgery, larceny, burglary, rape, and robbery were all significantly associated with population heterogeneity, while homicide and assault were not.

These studies suggest that the presence of large numbers of outsiders who do not share the social ties and values of the resident population provides alternatives to those ties and values which may lead some to question the status quo.

RATIO OF TOURISTS TO RESIDENTS, 1977. People take vacations for a variety of reasons, including sightseeing, recreation, and visits to relatives and friends (E. Cohen, 1984). S. Cohen and Taylor (1978) suggest that people also take vacations to escape from the scripted roles and routines of everyday life. Faris (1955:111) characterizes the tourist as a "temporary migrant" and observes that "the folkways and mores of [the tourist's] home community lose some of their power to control him when he is away from home." Thus, the short-term release of tourists from the rules and regulations of their local communities may reduce restraints against nonconforming behavior.

Although there is a paucity of research on the criminogenic character of tourism, some empirical studies suggest that there might be a link between tourism and crime. For example, Hayner (1929) noted that hotel guests sometimes view themselves as being on a "moral holiday" and consequently indulge in the theft of hotel property. Nicholls (1976) reports that tourism fosters a number of illegal activities such as prostitution, fraud, and theft. And P. L. Pearce (1982) reviewed several studies which show that the residents of vacation areas sometimes come to resent tourists for violating local norms and may retaliate against them by swindling, robbing, or assaulting them. Regardless of whether tourists are resented or welcomed, their presence tends to introduce alien modes of thought and behavior, the very presence of which tends to undermine the presumption that local ways are best. In fact, they create an industry devoted to satisfying these tastes.

Thus, to the extent that tourism increases the number of transients and undermines normative constraints, it is an appropriate indicator of social disorganization. The tourist variable in the SDX is the number of nights spent by tourists in each state, divided by the state population. This is a measure of the ratio of tourists to residents.

PERCENT DIVORCED, 1980. Divorce constitutes a profound break in the organizational structure of one of the most important institutions of society. When families split up, family members are separated from a network of rules and roles that provided some degree of order and stability in their lives. Studies show that the weakening of familial bonds can induce feelings of apprehension, disorientation, and confusion (Goetting, 1981; Weiss, 1976). In their analysis of stressful life events, Holmes and Rahe (1967) found that divorce was rated more stressful than being given a prison sentence, enduring a personal injury or illness, and being fired from one's job. Overall, divorce was rated the second most stressful life event after the death of a spouse.

The process of disengaging from a spouse is often accompanied by anger, conflict, and great emotional turmoil (Goetting, 1981; Wallerstein and Kelly, 1980; Weiss, 1976). Even when divorce is perceived as a welcome release from an intolerable situation, both spouses experience changes that disrupt their everyday lives. For example, divorce alters the couples' relationship to their children, friends, and extended family. Routinely scheduled activities are also disrupted. Hetherington, Cox and Cox (1978) report that meals are no longer served at predictable times, children are awakened and put to sleep at inconsistent hours, household chores are left undone, and appointments are forgotten or missed.

In view of the emotional distress and disruptive consequences of divorce, it seems reasonable to infer that a concentration of divorced persons in a particular geographic area might loosen the bonds of social control and increase the likelihood of nonconforming behavior. In fact, research on the connection between marital dissolution and crime provides support for this conjecture. Studies reveal that the percentage of separated and divorced residents in an SMSA is associated with higher rates of robbery, assault, rape, and homicide (Blau and Blau, 1982; Blau and Golden, 1986; Simpson, 1985). Analyses of state-level rape rates (Baron, Straus, and Jaffee, 1988; M. D. Smith and Bennett, 1985) also show that rape increases in proportion to the percentage of separated and divorced residents of the state.

The aforementioned studies suggest that marital dissolution contributes to a context of confusion and instability that may weaken social controls against criminal violence. The percentage of the population divorced was therefore included as one of the indicators of social disorganization.

NONFAMILIED MALE HOUSEHOLDERS PER 1,000 POPULATION, 1980. Ever since Durkheim (1966 [1897]) found that suicide rates are inversely related to the degree of integration in domestic society, sociologists have investigated the potentially deleterious effects of social isolation (for example, Gove and Hughes, 1980; Henry and Short, 1954; Stack, 1982). The suggestion is that social problems (for example, suicide, crime, and mental illness) are a function of the degree to which individuals are integrated into primary groups. Since men who live alone are subject to lower levels of informal control and fewer constraints against nonconformity, we expect to find higher rates of problem behavior among men who live alone.

Research on the social and psychological consequences of different household arrangements supports the conclusion that living alone increases the likelihood of personal and social problems. Gove and Hughes (1980) analyzed data from 389 cities to investigate the effect of living alone on deaths due to suicide and alcoholism. A multivariate analysis showed that living alone was a strong predictor of both suicide and alcohol deaths. Kobrin and Hendershot (1977) used national survey data from death certificates to examine the effect of various living arrangements on mortality rates. Among nonmarried men, those who lived alone had the highest mortality rates. Kobrin and Hendershot also compared the mortality rates of men and women. They found that nonmarried men who live alone had significantly higher mortality rates than nonmarried women who live alone.

These studies suggest that solitary living poses a serious threat to the physical and mental well-being of single householders, especially men. Since men who live alone are likely to have weak domestic ties and be subject to low levels of informal control, nonfamilied male householders was used as an indicator of social disorganization.

PERCENT OF FEMALE-HEADED FAMILIES WITH CHILDREN UNDER AGE 18, 1980. Mothers without a male partner face much the same problems as were just discussed for men living without a female partner. However, they also tend to face additional problems which undermine the stability of their lives and those of their children. First, many have experienced divorce and separation. Second, the other causes of female-headed families also involve either socially disrupting or deviant behavior (for example, death of the husband and unwed motherhood). Third, most single mothers experience poverty (Gongla and Thompson, 1987; D. Pearce and McAdoo, 1981; Shortridge, 1984) and the alienation which tends to accompany poverty. Fourth, since the two-parent family is the cultural ideal in the United States (Birdwhistle, 1970), female-headed families represent a deviant family structure (Levitan and Belous, 1981; Schorr and Moen, 1979) and such women therefore tend to experience negative reactions. Finally, single mothers experience residential mobility, which, as was shown previously, is an important indicator of social disorganization. Bane and Weiss (1980) report that 75% of single mothers move within four years of their divorce and more than half of them move again shortly thereafter.

The research suggests, then, that single-mother families are less likely to become rooted in a stable residence and social network and are more apt to find themselves in alienating life circumstances. It seems reasonable to conclude that the characteristics of female-headed families contribute to a climate of social instability. We therefore included the percent of female-headed families with children as an indicator of social disorganization.

PERCENT OF THE POPULATION WITH NO RELIGIOUS AFFILIATION, 1980. Durkheim (1954 [1912]) and many others hold that religion legitimates existing norms and values and promotes social cohesion. In other words, religion functions as a mechanism of social control. If this view is correct, there should be an inverse relationship between religiosity and deviance; religious commitment should inhibit nonconformity.

Survey research on the relationship between religiosity and delinquency has turned up mixed support for this hypothesis. Hirschi and Stark (1969) investigated junior high school and high school students in Richmond, California, and found that students who attended religious services were no less likely to be delinquent than students who do not attend services. One year later, Rhodes and Reiss (1970) drew a sample of junior and senior high school students in Nashville, Tennessee, and examined the effects of religious orientation on delinquency and truancy. They found that the students with no religious affiliation had the highest rates of delinquency and truancy.

Since the publication of these two studies, subsequent survey research has also spawned contradictory findings. Burkett and White (1974) performed a replication of Hirschi and Stark's study using a sample of high school students in the Pacific Northwest. The results showed that church attendance was not significantly associated with personal or property crimes but was inversely related to the use of alcohol and marijuana. Albrecht, Chadwick, and Alcorn (1977) followed Burkett and White's lead and made a distinction between victim deviance (for example, fighting or shoplifting) and victimless deviance (for example, smoking or using alcohol) in their study of teenagers from six congregations of the Mormon Church. Their findings showed that religious commitment inhibits victimless deviance but has no effect on victim deviance.

Stark and his colleagues (Stark, Doyle, and Kent, 1980; Stark, Kent, and Doyle, 1982) have reexamined the issue of religion and delinquency and offer a plausible explanation for the inconsistent findings. They contend that the inconsistencies are a function of the "religious climates" of the communities sampled (a contextual effect). Stark and his associates tested this hypothesis using a measure of church membership and discovered that in more religious communities, devout individuals have lower rates of deviance. Conversely, in more secular communities, religious and nonreligious individuals show no differences in rates of delinquency (Stark, Kent, and Doyle, 1982). Stark, Doyle, and Kent (1980) have also used the measure of church membership in an analysis of SMSA crime rates and found that the higher the rate of church membership, the lower the rate of every major property and violent crime, including rape.

We interpret these studies as suggesting that the absence of religious affiliation weakens people's attachment to the collectivity and releases them to engage in crime and deviance. Consequently, the percent of the population not affiliated with an organized religion was included as one of the indicators in the SDX.

CAUSAL MODEL OF SOCIAL DISORGANIZATION THEORY

A frequent criticism of social disorganization theory is that it collapses cause and effect and offers a circular explanation of social problems (Carey, 1975; Kornhauser, 1978; Pfohl, 1985). Kornhauser (1978) maintains that social disorganization theorists were not always clear about the causal structure of their model and sometimes lapsed into using the predicted outcomes of social disorganization (such as crime, delinquency, and mental illness) as indictors of the phenomenon itself.[4] The equation of social disorganization with its

4. An example of a social disorganization index that hopelessly confounds indicators of disorganization with its consequences was constructed by D. M. Smith (1973). Smith's index is composed of 10 indicators that are split into three categories. The first category is "Personal Pathologies," which includes rates of suicide, alcoholism, narcotics addiction, gonorrhea, and

predicted effect made it logically impossible to estimate the extent to which the two are empirically related.

Although the Chicago theorists were not insensitive to the criticisms of circular reasoning, they seemed to have had great difficulty conceptualizing social disorganization apart from its presumed consequences. For example, in his textbook *Social Disorganization,* Robert Faris (1955) warned readers to make a clear distinction between social disorganization and social problems. As a step in that direction, Faris defined social disorganization as the erosion of social order and conceptualized social problems as "pathological conditions." Despite his stated intention, Faris failed to see that an "undesirable" change in the social order (for example, an increase in the crime rate) qualifies as both a social problem and as evidence of social disorganization. In fact, his chapter "Crime and Social Disorganization" variously describes crime, which constitutes a social problem according to his definition, as a cause, effect, and reflection of social disorganization.

Given the logical and methodological problems that have plagued social disorganization theory, we felt that it was essential to develop a theoretical model which avoids these problems. This model is shown in figure 6.1. It should be noted that figure 6.1 depicts a recursive model (all the causal arrows point in one direction and there are no reciprocal relationships or feedback loops). Although it might be argued that a feedback loop logically runs from the boxes labeled Social Problems and Social Reorganization to the box labeled Factors that Disrupt Social Stability, Weaken Social Bonds, and Undermine Social Control (social problems and social reforms could stimulate social disorganization), the data used in this study are cross-sectional and cannot be used to test a feedback model (see Skogan, 1986, for a discussion of reciprocal relationships in the investigation of crime and social disorganization).

The first box on the left in figure 6.1 contains the six indicators of social disorganization. As was previously mentioned, these indicators were selected from a larger pool of items on the basis of a principal components analysis.

---

syphilis. The second category is "Family Breakdown," which includes rates of divorce and percentage of husband-wife households. The final category is "Crime and Safety," which includes rates of violent crimes, property crimes, and motor vehicle deaths. Of the three categories, only the "Family Breakdown" indicators are consistent with the theoretical thrust of social disorganization theory (the weakening of institutional and informal controls). The other two categories, "Personal Pathologies" and "Crime and Safety," are theoretically predicted *effects* of social disorganization, not indicators of it. Since Smith equates social disorganization with criminal violence, the index cannot be used to examine the extent to which social disorganization is related to the incidence of rape.

Figure 6.1
Causal Model of Social Disorganization Theory

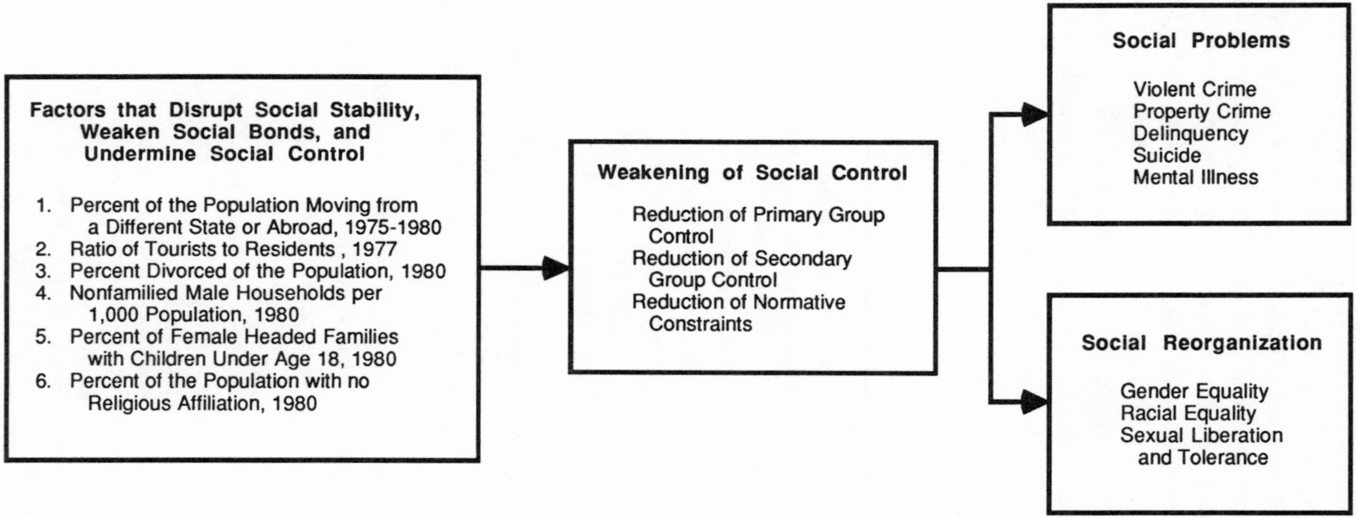

Factors that Disrupt Social Stability, Weaken Social Bonds, and Undermine Social Control

1. Percent of the Population Moving from a Different State or Abroad, 1975-1980
2. Ratio of Tourists to Residents, 1977
3. Percent Divorced of the Population, 1980
4. Nonfamilied Male Households per 1,000 Population, 1980
5. Percent of Female Headed Families with Children Under Age 18, 1980
6. Percent of the Population with no Religious Affiliation, 1980

Weakening of Social Control

Reduction of Primary Group Control
Reduction of Secondary Group Control
Reduction of Normative Constraints

Social Problems

Violent Crime
Property Crime
Delinquency
Suicide
Mental Illness

Social Reorganization

Gender Equality
Racial Equality
Sexual Liberation and Tolerance

The composite group of indicators is conceptualized as reflecting the latent construct of social disorganization. The arrow moving from the Factors that Disrupt Social Stability, Weaken Social Bonds, and Undermine Social Control to the box labeled Weakening of Social Control signifies that the composite set of social disorganization indicators are posited to undermine the efficacy of institutional controls and reduce the effectiveness of normative constraints. The arrow from the Weakening of Social Control to the boxes labeled Social Problems and Social Reorganization indicates that social problems and social reforms are the hypothesized outcomes of the failure of social control.

STATE AND REGIONAL DIFFERENCES IN SOCIAL DISORGANIZATION

The ranking of the states on the social disorganization indicators is displayed in tables 6.3(a and b). Table 6.3a shows that there are large differences among the states in the percent of the population migrating or immigrating to a state, the number of tourists visiting a state, and the percent of men and women divorced. The first column of table 6.3a indicates that, between 1975 and 1980, a larger proportion of residents moved into Nevada, Alaska, Wyoming, and Arizona than any other states. The states with the fewest number of immigrants were Pennsylvania, Michigan, Ohio, and New York.

The second column of table 6.3a shows that the states with the highest ratio of tourists to residents are Vermont, Nevada, Wyoming, and Hawaii. The lowest ratio of tourists to residents is found in Connecticut, New Jersey, Pennsylvania, and New York, suggesting that compared to the West, northeastern states have relatively fewer transients and a lower degree of social disruption. The third column of table 6.3a presents the ranking of the states in the percentage of *residents* who are divorced. Nevada has liberal residency requirements and expeditious divorce procedures, so it is not surprising to find that it has the highest proportion of divorced residents. However, Nevada is not alone among western states with a high percentage of divorcees. California, Alaska, Oregon, and Washington also have a heavy concentration of divorced residents. The states with the lowest proportion of divorces are located in the north central and northwestern sections of the country.

The first column of table 6.3b shows that the states with the highest proportion of female-headed families with children are Alaska, Idaho, Montana, Nevada, and Oregon. Western states dominate the upper level of the

Table 6.3a

Ranking of the States on the Social Disorganization Indicators

Rank	Percent of Population Moving from a Different State or Abroad, 1975-1980		Ratio of Tourists to Residents, 1977		Percent Divorced of the Population, 1980	
	State	cb15r	State	rap4r	State	sb98tr
1	Nevada	34.2	Vermont	39.7	Nevada	11.96
2	Alaska	31.4	Nevada	33.9	California	8.55
3	Wyoming	29.5	Wyoming	28.6	Alaska	8.50
4	Arizona	25.9	Hawaii	22.8	Oregon	8.32
5	Hawaii	22.7	Florida	20.7	Washington	8.14
6	Colorado	22.6	New Hampshire	15.7	Colorado	7.97
7	Florida	22.2	New Mexico	15.5	Florida	7.69
8	Idaho	21.3	Montana	15.4	Arizona	7.62
9	New Hampshire	19.4	Maine	14.8	Oklahoma	7.42
10	New Mexico	19.2	North Dakota	14.6	New Mexico	7.37
11	Oregon	18.6	Arizona	14.6	Indiana	7.03
12	Washington	18.5	Colorado	14.2	Texas	6.89
13	Utah	18.0	Idaho	14.0	Wyoming	6.86
14	Virginia	16.1	South Dakota	13.6	Ohio	6.85
15	Montana	15.9	Arkansas	13.5	Georgia	6.82
16	Vermont	15.1	Delaware	13.3	Michigan	6.78
17	Oklahoma	15.1	Minnesota	12.2	Tennessee	6.74
18	Delaware	14.6	Utah	12.2	Maine	6.57
19	Kansas	14.0	Wisconsin	11.4	Idaho	6.53
20	North Dakota	13.7	Oklahoma	11.2	Hawaii	6.50
21	Texas	13.6	South Carolina	11.2	Montana	6.49
22	California	13.2	Oregon	10.3	Missouri	6.46
23	Arkansas	13.0	Iowa	10.0	New Hampshire	6.28
24	Georgia	12.6	Alaska	9.6	Illinois	6.27
25	South Carolina	12.4	North Carolina	9.4	Kentucky	6.24
26	Maryland	12.3	Nebraska	9.4	Alabama	6.23
27	South Dakota	11.8	Missouri	9.3	Kansas	6.20
28	Maine	11.6	Virginia	9.1	Arkansas	6.01
29	Nebraska	11.5	Texas	9.1	Delaware	5.86
30	Tennessee	11.2	Washington	8.7	Vermont	5.82
31	Connecticut	11.1	Kansas	8.6	Connecticut	5.73
32	Rhode Island	10.6	Tennessee	8.4	Utah	5.71
33	North Carolina	10.6	California	8.2	Maryland	5.68
34	Missouri	10.1	Georgia	8.2	West Virginia	5.56
35	Mississippi	9.9	Michigan	7.9	Rhode Island	5.56
36	New Jersey	9.8	West Virginia	7.3	Virginia	5.42
37	Kentucky	9.7	Louisiana	7.2	Mississippi	5.38
38	Alabama	9.6	Mississippi	6.5	Massachusetts	5.21
39	Louisiana	9.5	Kentucky	6.3	Louisiana	5.15
40	West Virginia	9.0	Alabama	5.9	Nebraska	5.05
41	Massachusetts	8.7	Massachusetts	5.8	Wisconsin	5.02
42	Iowa	8.5	Illinois	5.5	Iowa	5.02
43	Minnesota	8.2	Maryland	5.4	Minnesota	5.00
44	Indiana	8.2	Rhode Island	5.3	New York	4.92
45	Illinois	7.8	Indiana	5.2	North Carolina	4.75
46	Wisconsin	7.3	Ohio	5.0	Pennsylvania	4.67
47	New York	6.5	New York	4.9	New Jersey	4.58
48	Ohio	6.3	Pennsylvania	4.8	South Carolina	4.53
49	Michigan	6.0	New Jersey	4.4	South Dakota	4.38
50	Pennsylvania	5.9	Connecticut	3.9	North Dakota	3.82

distribution in that the nine highest ranking states are located in the West. Compared to the western states, the northeastern, north central, and southern states show only small differences in the proportion of female-headed families.

The ranking of the states in no religious affiliation and nonfamilied male householders reveals great similarity to the rank-order distribution of female-

Table 6.3b

Ranking of the States on the Social Disorganization Indicators

Rank	Percent of Female Headed Families with Children Under Age 18, 1980 State	sb117r	Percent of the Population with no Religious Affiliation, 1980 State	rap7r	Nonfamilied Male Householders per 1,000 Population, 1980 State	rap5
1	Alaska	90.0	Nevada	70.7	Nevada	67.8
2	Idaho	78.2	Alaska	69.2	California	53.6
3	Montana	75.0	Washington	69.0	Colorado	53.3
4	Nevada	75.0	Hawaii	66.8	Alaska	52.3
5	Oregon	74.3	California	65.5	Washington	52.2
6	Washington	74.0	Oregon	63.9	Oregon	50.2
7	Utah	73.5	Colorado	63.4	Wyoming	49.2
8	New Mexico	73.3	Florida	61.5	Montana	45.2
9	Colorado	73.0	Arizona	60.5	Florida	43.1
10	Michigan	71.1	West Virginia	60.3	New York	42.8
11	Oklahoma	70.8	Delaware	59.8	Arizona	42.3
12	Louisiana	70.7	Maryland	59.8	North Dakota	42.2
13	Texas	70.6	Maine	59.0	Vermont	41.2
14	South Dakota	70.5	Virginia	58.2	Minnesota	41.1
15	Arizona	70.5	Michigan	57.3	Illinois	40.5
16	Georgia	70.5	Wyoming	55.9	Nebraska	40.2
17	California	70.4	New Hampshire	55.7	Kansas	39.9
18	Mississippi	70.0	Montana	55.7	New Mexico	39.3
19	Wyoming	70.0	Indiana	55.2	Massachusetts	39.3
20	Arkansas	69.6	Georgia	53.0	New Hampshire	39.2
21	Delaware	69.5	Vermont	52.2	Texas	39.1
22	Indiana	69.4	Ohio	50.5	South Dakota	38.0
23	North Dakota	69.2	New York	50.3	Idaho	38.0
24	Kansas	69.2	Idaho	49.9	Maryland	37.4
25	Hawaii	68.9	South Carolina	48.5	Iowa	37.2
26	Vermont	68.7	Kansas	46.5	Hawaii	37.2
27	South Carolina	68.7	Missouri	46.4	Michigan	37.1
28	Maryland	67.9	North Carolina	46.0	Oklahoma	37.1
29	Nebraska	67.5	Kentucky	45.8	Rhode Island	37.0
30	North Carolina	67.2	New Jersey	45.8	Virginia	36.7
31	Iowa	67.1	Tennessee	45.7	Delaware	36.7
32	Alabama	67.0	Texas	45.3	Missouri	36.7
33	Wisconsin	66.9	Mississippi	45.0	Connecticut	36.1
34	Virginia	66.6	Illinois	44.8	Ohio	36.0
35	Maine	66.6	Arkansas	43.8	Louisiana	35.5
36	New Hampshire	66.6	Louisiana	42.5	Maine	35.3
37	Illinois	66.5	Alabama	42.5	Wisconsin	34.4
38	Minnesota	66.3	Oklahoma	42.0	Pennsylvania	34.2
39	Missouri	66.2	New Mexico	40.9	Indiana	33.7
40	Ohio	66.2	Pennsylvania	39.1	New Jersey	32.5
41	Florida	66.2	Iowa	38.8	Georgia	31.9
42	Tennessee	65.5	Connecticut	38.4	North Carolina	30.7
43	Kentucky	65.1	Nebraska	36.8	Tennessee	30.2
44	New York	64.5	Wisconsin	35.4	Arkansas	29.9
45	New Jersey	62.3	Massachusetts	35.3	Alabama	28.9
46	Connecticut	61.8	Minnesota	34.9	Kentucky	28.5
47	Rhode Island	60.5	South Dakota	33.0	Utah	28.0
48	Massachusetts	59.6	North Dakota	26.1	West Virginia	28.0
49	Pennsylvania	57.8	Utah	24.8	South Carolina	27.9
50	West Virginia	57.8	Rhode Island	24.5	Mississippi	27.0

headed families with children. Western states are more heavily represented in the first decile of the distribution and only small differences exist among northeastern, north central, and southern states.

The geographical distribution of the six social disorganization indicators suggests that states in the western region have higher levels of social instability than the states in any other section of the country. This impression is con-

Table 6.4
Regional Differences on Social Disorganization
Indicators

	Regions			
Indicators	Northeast	North Central	South	West
Percent of the Population Moving from a Different State or Abroad, 1975-1980***	11.01	9.50	12.63	22.42
Ratio of Tourists to Residents, 1977	11.08	9.44	9.60	16.05
Percent Divorced of the Population, 1980***	5.48	5.66	6.02	7.73
Percent of Female Headed Families with Children under Age 18, 1980***	63.21	68.05	67.78	74.35
Percent of the Population with no Religious Affiliation, 1980**	44.78	42.14	49.98	58.17
Nonfamilied Male Householders Per 1,000 Population, 1980***	37.55	38.12	33.08	46.86

Note: *p<.05, **p<.01, ***p<.001.

firmed by table 6.4, which shows that the western region has a higher score on every indicator of social disorganization.

The state rankings on the summated Social Disorganization Index (SDX) are displayed in table 6.5. There is substantial variation among the states on this index, with scores ranging from a high of 100 to a low of 18. The state with the highest index score, and hence the highest level of social disorganization, is Nevada, followed by Alaska, Wyoming, Colorado, and Washington. Western states clearly dominate the first decile of the distribution: 9 of the 10 highest ranking states are located in the West. Conversely, the states in the Northeast are heavily concentrated at the bottom of the distribution, indicating that northeastern states have comparatively less social disorganization. Southern and north central states are scattered throughout the middle and lower half of the distribution without any pronounced or discernible pattern.

A more precise delineation of the regional differences may be found in figure 6.2. This figure presents the mean SDX scores for each of the nine divisions and regions recognized by the U.S. Census and reports the results of a one-way analysis of variance. Consistent with our comments on the state-by-state rank-order distribution, the western states have the highest average index score (75), followed by the South (44), the North Central (40), and the Northeast (37). In fact, the western region has a score that is twice as high as

Table 6.5

Rank Order of the States on the
Social Disorganization Index

Rank	State	rapx18zp
1	Nevada	100
2	Alaska	96
3	Wyoming	84
4	Colorado	83
5	Washington	80
6	Oregon	79
7	Arizona	74
8	California	73
9	Florida	72
10	Hawaii	70
11	Montana	67
12	Idaho	67
13	Vermont	64
14	New Mexico	63
15	New Hampshire	58
16	Oklahoma	54
17	Delaware	54
18	Texas	52
19	Maine	51
20	Michigan	49
21	Kansas	49
22	Georgia	49
23	Virginia	48
24	Maryland	46
25	Indiana	45
26	Arkansas	44
27	Missouri	43
28	Utah	41
29	Ohio	40
30	Illinois	40
31	Tennessee	39
32	South Dakota	39
33	Louisiana	38
34	Nebraska	38
35	North Dakota	37
36	Minnesota	36
37	South Carolina	36
38	New York	35
39	Iowa	35
40	Mississippi	34
41	Kentucky	34
42	Alabama	34
43	North Carolina	34
44	Wisconsin	32
45	Connecticut	30
46	West Virginia	29
47	Massachusetts	27
48	New Jersey	26
49	Rhode Island	25
50	Pennsylvania	18

Figure 6.2
Mean of Social Disorganization Index by Division and Region

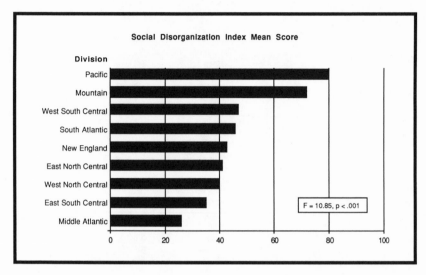

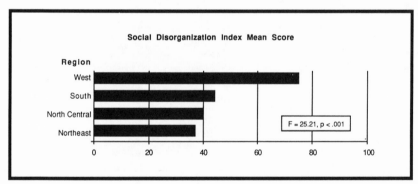

the Northeast. In contrast, the differences among the southern, north central, and northeastern regions are small, suggesting that social disorganization is fairly evenly apportioned among nonwestern regions. These findings indicate that the states in the western region have a higher level of social disorganization than any other section of the country.

SOCIAL DISORGANIZATION AND RAPE

If social disorganization diminishes the effectiveness of institutional constraints against crime and deviance, the rape rate should be higher in states that have a greater magnitude of social disorganization. This was tested in a preliminary way by running a zero-order correlation between the SDX and the average rape rate for the years 1980–82. The results indicate that the SDX is strongly related to the rape rate ($r = .68$). This finding provides preliminary support for the conjecture that the rape rate increases in proportion to the level of social disorganization. A more stringent test of this hypothesis will be reported in chapter 8.

SUMMARY AND CONCLUSION

Social disorganization theory is based on the idea that the erosion of institutional and informal forces of social control undermines social constraints and frees individuals to engage in nonconforming behavior. To the extent that social disorganization reduces social constraints against rape, we hypothesize higher rates of rape in states where social disorganization is most prevalent. To test this hypothesis, we developed a Social Disorganization Index (SDX), which measures state-to-state differences in the level of social instability.

The SDX is composed of measures of geographical mobility, divorce, lack of religious affiliation, female-headed households, nonfamilied male householders with no female present, and the ratio of tourists to residents in each state. Rank-order distributions and regional breakdowns of the six indicators and the composite index demonstrate substantial differences among the states and regions on all six measures. The states in the western region have the highest level of social disorganization, followed by the south, north central, and northeastern regions. This suggests that, on the average, western states have comparatively fewer institutional and informal restraints against criminal activity. They should therefore also have the highest rape rate, and as the rates reported in chapter 3 reveal, that is the case.

A better test of the hypothesis that social disorganization is associated with rape is the correlation between the SDX and the rape rate. We found a .68 correlation, which lends support to the conjecture that a high level of social disorganization increases the risk of rape. Although suggestive, this correlation must be viewed as tentative until examined in the context of a multivariate analysis. Such an analysis is presented in chapter 8, where the direct and indirect effects of social disorganization on rape are examined in the context of a path analysis.

7

LEGITIMATE VIOLENCE

Rape is such a heinous crime that it is difficult for most people to accept the idea that there may be covert or implicit cultural norms which encourage some men to rape. The existence of such norms was brought to public attention by members of the feminist movement (Brownmiller, 1975; Greer, 1973; Griffin, 1971; Scully and Marolla, 1985) and substantiated by research on rape myths, such as the belief that women expect or enjoy being forced to have sex (Burt, 1980; Check and Malamuth, 1983; Field, 1978).

In addition to beliefs and values which directly refer to rape, there may be other aspects of the culture which indirectly serve to increase the probability of rape. The presence of norms which legitimate nonsexual violence could be implicated in rape. This might occur if a positive evaluation of physical force in one aspect of life were to be extrapolated by part of the population to relationships between the sexes. To the extent that such extrapolations occur, violence for nonsexual and socially legitimate purposes will be associated with phenomena such as rape.

Although cultural theories of criminal violence, such as the subculture of violence theory (Wolfgang and Ferracuti, 1967) or the southern culture of violence theory (Gastil, 1971; Hackney, 1969; Messner, 1983), have attained a moderate degree of influence in the social sciences, these explanations have been the subject of considerable controversy and have not been adequately tested (Baron and Straus, 1988; Baron, Straus, and Jaffee, 1988; Loftin and Hill, 1974; Nettler, 1984). A major obstacle in testing such theories is the lack of an independent measure of the purported culture that supports crimes of violence. In order to avoid the circular reasoning of inferring cultural support for violence from high rates of violent crime, it is necessary to use a measure of cultural approval of violence that is conceptually and empirically distinct from the measure of criminal violence. As a step in that direction, this chapter describes the development of two measures of cultural support for violence. These measures will be used to test the theory that, within the United States, the large differences among states in the incidence of rape are partly the result of state-to-state differences in cultural support for nonsexual and legitimate violence.[1]

1. Despite the importance of the concept of culture to sociological analysis, there is little agreement about what it is and how it should be defined (Wallace, 1983). The aspect of culture

THE CULTURAL SPILLOVER THEORY OF CRIMINAL VIOLENCE

The theory tested in this chapter is one that we refer to as cultural spillover theory. The distinctive feature of cultural spillover theory is the idea that cultural support for rape may not be limited to beliefs and attitudes that directly condone rape and other criminal violence. There could be cultural elements which indirectly legitimate sexual violence. The central proposition of this theory is that the more a society tends to endorse the use of physical force to attain socially approved ends (such as order in the schools, crime control, and military dominance), the greater the likelihood that this legitimation of force will be generalized to other spheres of life where force is less socially approved, such as the family and relations between the sexes.

Although this concept may seem tenuous, there are a number of empirical studies which can be interpreted as supporting cultural spillover theory. Lambert, Triandis, and Wolf's (1959) study of nonliterate societies showed that societies which have a religious system in which deities are punitive tend to rely on physical punishment in child rearing. Studies of modern nations reveal that the implicit cultural support for killing inherent in war tends to be reflected in a higher murder rate (Archer and Gartner, 1984; Jensen and Baxter, 1985), a higher rate of child abuse (Shwed and Straus, 1979), and more violence in fiction (Huggins and Straus, 1980). And a natural experiment of mass media violence showed a short-term increase in the incidence of homicide following several widely publicized heavyweight boxing matches (Phillips, 1983).

Sanday's (1981) cross-cultural study of 156 tribal societies can also be interpreted as substantiating spillover effects. Sanday found strong support for an association between the level of nonsexual violence in the society (for example, whether warfare is frequent or endemic) and rape. She concluded that "where interpersonal violence is a way of life, violence frequently achieves sexual expression" (Sanday, 1981:10). This implies that rape is partly a spillover from cultural norms that permit and condone violent behavior in other areas of life.

Amir's study of rape also suggests a spillover effect. Amir found a positive correlation between arrests for rape and arrests for other crimes of violence

---

which is relevant to this chapter is the constellation of norms, values, and beliefs shared by the members of society. This is not to say that all members of society have the same degree of commitment to particular norms and values. There are person-to-person variations as well as group differences. This chapter examines differences among states in one aspect of violent cultural norms and their relationship with rates of rape.

and interprets this as showing the existence of subcultural norms approving of rape:

> Because the highest rates of the offenses studied occurred among rela-
> tively homogeneous groups, it is, therefore, assumed that these groups
> situated in a subculture, hold a particular set of conduct norms which
> emphasize and condone aggressive behavior, and have also the least
> "resistance potential" toward aggressive sexual behavior. Thus, under
> special circumstances, violence, including sexual violence toward wom-
> en, is more likely to occur. (Amir, 1971:319–320)

It should be noted that, since Amir does not provide evidence of beliefs and values which specifically approve or promote rape, his findings can just as appropriately be interpreted as supporting cultural spillover theory. In actuality, Amir's subcultural explanation of rape is not supported by the data since he did not directly investigate the extent to which violent offenders accept norms that advocate and legitimate violence. Instead, Amir *infers* the existence of such norms from their violent behavior. This is an example of the circular reasoning that has given the subculture of violence thesis its notoriety.

The controversy over the subculture of violence theory and other cultural theories of violence[2] cannot be resolved without data which directly reflect shared beliefs, values, and norms, that is, data on the relevant aspects of culture itself. The balance of this chapter describes the development of two indexes which are intended to measure cultural support for violence.

THE LEGITIMATE VIOLENCE INDEX

Conceptual Basis

The theoretical basis for selecting the indicators was the assumption that group differences in values concerning violence should be manifest in many different activities including education, recreation, and law enforcement.

2. We define violence as an act carried out with the intent of causing physical pain or injury to another person. There are many different dimensions which must be taken into account in research on violence. For example, the pain or injury of an attack can vary from little or none to death. Another critically important aspect is whether the acts are normatively legitimate as in the case of the physical punishment of a child and execution of a murderer, or illegitimate as in the case of rape or homicide. As explained elsewhere (Gelles and Straus, 1979), these critically important aspects of violence are deliberately omitted from the definition so that they can be treated as variables. This paper treats *legitimate* violence as a variable and investigates its relationship to rates of rape.

Consequently, we searched for indicators that might reflect an underlying belief in the efficacy and desirability of physical force. However, since the index was intended to test the theory that part of the explanation for criminal violence (such as rape and murder) is a diffusion or spillover from socially approved violence, indicators were restricted to violent activities that are noncriminal and socially approved.

The indicators which were selected for inclusion in the Legitimate Violence Index (LVX) have in common the fact that they describe the extent to which the population of each state has a noncriminal or socially approved involvement in violence. In some cases, this is vicarious involvement in violence (for example, readership rate for violent magazines), in other cases it is socially legitimate behaviors which involve violence or willingness to use violence (for example, National Guard enrollment rate), and in still other cases it is a collective action or product which reflects a belief in the efficacy of violence for socially desirable ends (such as, corporal punishment in the schools).

It should be noted that the indicators comprising the LVX are aggregate behaviors (such as the readership rate for violent magazines) or cultural products (such as legislation authorizing corporal punishment in the schools) rather than verbal expressions of beliefs, attitudes, and values. This roughly corresponds to Durkheim's concept of "collective representations" (Durkheim, 1954 [1912]) and is consistent with much anthropological research (Geertz, 1973) and studies in ethnomethodology (Garfinkel, 1964; Leiter, 1980). The choice of behavioral and cultural product indicators was partly based on the lack of comparative opinion survey data for states but also on the limitations of such data. Specifically, there are cultural contradictions in the evaluation of violence which make it extraordinarily difficult for people to verbalize their true beliefs and attitudes (Dibble and Straus, 1980; Greenblat, 1983). Therefore, public opinion survey data, even if they were available for states, might not accurately reflect the extent to which there are proviolence elements in American culture.

There are four conceptual points that need to be clarified before describing the indicators. First, the measure is called the Legitimate Violence Index rather than the Subculture of Violence Index because it is intended to refer to only one aspect of cultural support for violence—socially legitimate violence. Second, the term *subculture* was avoided because we do not think that what it measures is restricted to limited groups in American society. This does not discount the possibility that cultural support for violence may be relatively more characteristic of some groups and geographic areas than others. What it does suggest is that norms legitimating violence are widely diffused; therefore, the measure should be one that is widely applicable. Third, the use of *legiti-*

mate in the name of this index does not indicate our evaluation of these activities as desirable or morally acceptable but the socially acceptable character of the indicators. Finally, it was not our intention to use indicators of approval or tolerance of rape itself, and none of the indicators in the index has any manifest relation to rape. Instead, the theory we are testing asserts that there is a carryover, or diffusion, from legitimate violence to criminal violence. Hence the hypothesis is that there is a higher incidence of rape in sectors of society characterized by a high level of legitimate violence.

Types of Indicators

The indicators included in the Legitimate Violence Index are summarized below. They fall into three broad groups.

1. *Mass Media Preferences.* The mass media indicators serve two purposes. The first was to use a group of indicators that measures the extent to which a population is interested enough in violence to choose television programs and magazines with a high violence content. Two such indicators were used: the readership rate per 100,000 population of violent magazines and the Nielson ratings for the six most violent network television programs. Use of these indicators assumes that the larger the readership or audience for violence, the greater the interest or fascination with violence. The other purpose was to use a group of indicators that measures the military and veteran population in a particular geographical area.

2. *Governmental Use of Violence.* The second group of indicators is based on the idea that socially shared beliefs about the utility of violence can be expressed in laws and government actions which seek to attain socially desirable ends through the use of physical force. The indicators in this category include state legislation permitting corporal punishment in the schools, prisoners sentenced to death per 100,000 population, and executions per 100 homicide arrests.

3. *Participation in Legal or Socially Approved Violent Activities.* The third group of indicators is the rate of participation in violent but legal or socially approved activities. The indicators in this group are hunting licenses per 100,000 population, the state of origin of college football players, National Guard enrollment per 100,000 population, National Guard expenditures per capita, and lynchings per million population during the period 1882–1927.

Specific Indicators

VIOLENT TELEVISION VIEWING INDEX. Our use of violent television as an indicator is based on the large body of evidence showing that violent television encourages aggression and that aggressive persons are more attracted to violent programs (Andison, 1977; Eron, 1982; Huesmann, 1982; Parke et al., 1977). This is in sharp contrast to the catharsis theory of media violence. There has been a great deal of research designed to test the catharsis theory, almost all of which shows the opposite effect: ventilation and vicarious participation, rather than serving to work off aggression, tends to increase it (see the studies cited in Straus, 1974).

The Violent Television Viewing Index described below reflects the size of the audience in each state for the six most violent television programs on national television in the fall of 1980. The six programs were selected on the basis of ratings published by the National Coalition on Television Violence (National Coalition on Television Violence, 1981:4). The most violent programs were ascertained by counting the number of physically violent acts in each program and converting that to a rate of violent acts per hour. The six programs were "Charlie's Angels," "Enos," "Incredible Hulk," "Hart to Hart," "Dukes of Hazzard," and "Fantasy Island."

The audience size data for these programs are Nielson Index scores obtained from the A. C. Nielson Company. The Violent TV Viewing Index for each state was computed by multiplying the state's Nielson Index score for each program by the number of violent acts per hour corresponding to those programs. The index score for each state is the mean of the six products. For example, if a state had a Nielson Index score of 23 for "Charlie's Angels," the product would be the Nielson Index of 23 times 13.2 (the average number of violent acts per hour for "Charlie's Angels").[3]

The first column of table 7.1a shows the states in rank order on the Violent TV Viewing Index. As with almost all other variables we have examined, there are large differences among states, and also large regional differences. The

---

3. The Nielson Index data were obtained in collaboration with Steven Messner of the State University of New York at Albany. Messner's (1986) use of the television data and the use reported here are somewhat different: (1) Messner used the data in their original market areas (similar to Standard Metropolitan Statistical Areas). For purposes of our study, the 203 market areas were aggregated into data for 47 states. (2) Messner used the sum of the six Nielson Index scores, whereas we used a weighted average. The weighted average was obtained by multiplying the Nielson Index score by the following number of violent acts per hour: "Enos" 23.1, "Incredible Hulk" 19.2, "Hart to Hart" 15.8, "Charlie's Angels" 13.2, "Dukes Of Hazard" 11.4, "Fantasy Island" 8.2.

As noted above, we were able to compute state-level violent television viewing indexes for only 47 states. The missing states are Alaska, New Hampshire, and New Jersey. Since the television variable was the only one of the 12 indicators with missing data for these states, it seemed desirable to avoid losing these three states from the measure. To accomplish this we computed the mean score for the other states in the region where each of these states was located and substituted that score for the missing values.

Table 7.1a

Ranking of the States on the Legitimate Violence Indicators

	Violent Television Viewing Index		Violent Magazine Circulation Index		NATIONAL GUARD Enrollment		NATIONAL GUARD Expenditures	
Rank	State	cv16a	State	xvmc	State	v474r	State	v475r
1	South Carolina	226	Alaska	5.29	Vermont	7.35	Alaska	47.5
2	Louisiana	223	Wyoming	2.33	Alaska	6.81	Hawaii	31.5
3	Georgia	208	Nevada	1.56	Wyoming	5.90	Wyoming	30.5
4	North Carolina	206	Hawaii	1.05	Alabama	5.87	Idaho	28.2
5	Montana	200	Kansas	0.74	South Dakota	5.83	Vermont	28.1
6	Tennessee	199	Idaho	0.72	Delaware	5.67	Delaware	28.0
7	West Virginia	189	Arizona	0.69	Hawaii	5.64	South Dakota	26.6
8	Alabama	186	Colorado	0.67	Mississippi	5.52	Montana	25.2
9	Mississippi	185	Montana	0.52	Arkansas	5.22	Mississippi	23.9
10	Kentucky	185	Washington	0.34	North Dakota	4.98	North Dakota	22.5
11	Wyoming	179	Oregon	0.33	Utah	4.64	Nevada	22.4
12	Idaho	179	Texas	0.27	Idaho	4.45	Alabama	17.9
13	Arkansas	173	North Dakota	0.25	Rhode Island	3.99	Rhode Island	17.8
14	Maryland	171	New Mexico	0.24	Montana	3.85	Maine	17.7
15	Illinois	170	California	0.17	South Dakota	3.83	Utah	16.8
16	Ohio	169	South Dakota	0.06	Maine	3.74	Arkansas	16.1
17	Texas	167	New Hampshire	0.04	Oklahoma	3.65	New Mexico	16.0
18	Oklahoma	166	Virginia	0.03	New Mexico	3.42	Kansas	15.0
19	South Dakota	165	Delaware	-0.07	New Hampshire	3.41	New Hampshire	14.9
20	Wisconsin	164	Vermont	-0.14	Tennessee	3.25	Arizona	13.9
21	Indiana	163	Maine	-0.18	Oregon	3.22	Oklahoma	13.2
22	Virginia	163	Georgia	-0.22	Nevada	3.11	Oregon	13.1
23	New Mexico	162	Louisiana	-0.24	Kansas	3.30	Iowa	12.4
24	Missouri	160	Nebraska	-0.32	Nebraska	2.96	Nebraska	12.4
25	Kansas	160	Michigan	-0.34	Iowa	2.89	Tennessee	12.0
26	Utah	159	Iowa	-0.42	Minnesota	2.72	West Virginia	11.8
27	Delaware	158	Maryland	-0.43	Indiana	2.58	South Carolina	11.6
28	North Dakota	155	Utah	-0.43	West Virginia	2.58	Minnesota	11.0
29	Florida	154	Illinois	-0.46	Louisiana	2.47	Colorado	10.5
30	Colorado	153	Ohio	-0.47	Georgia	2.45	Georgia	10.0
31	Michigan	153	Indiana	-0.47	Missouri	2.30	Missouri	9.7
32	Iowa	153	Florida	-0.48	Arizona	2.29	Washington	9.6
33	Minnesota	152	North Carolina	-0.50	North Carolina	2.29	Massachusetts	9.2
34	Maine	149	Kentucky	-0.50	Wisconsin	2.26	Indiana	8.4
35	Vermont	146	Wisconsin	-0.51	Connecticut	2.21	Louisiana	8.2
36	Pennsylvania	139	Arkansas	-0.54	Massachusetts	2.17	Connecticut	8.1
37	New York	139	West Virginia	-0.55	New Jersey	2.09	Wisconsin	7.8
38	Nebraska	135	Pennsylvania	-0.55	Washington	1.99	New Jersey	7.6
39	Oregon	133	South Carolina	-0.55	Kentucky	1.87	Michigan	7.4
40	Connecticut	132	Missouri	-0.58	Maryland	1.81	Maryland	6.6
41	Washington	131	Connecticut	-0.60	Ohio	1.72	Kentucky	6.6
42	Nevada	125	Alabama	-0.69	Pennsylvania	1.62	Ohio	6.5
43	California	118	Tennessee	-0.70	Colorado	1.59	North Carolina	6.4
44	Massachusetts	116	Minnesota	-0.70	Virginia	1.57	Texas	6.0
45	Hawaii	115	New York	-0.73	Texas	1.51	Virginia	6.0
46	Arizona	109	Massachusetts	-0.83	New York	1.32	Pennsylvania	5.9
47	Rhode Island	108	Mississippi	-0.83	Michigan	1.26	California	5.0
48	Alaska	Missing	New Jersey	-0.91	Florida	1.19	New York	4.6
49	New Hampshire	Missing	Rhode Island	-1.06	California	1.09	Florida	3.8
50	New Jersey	Missing	Oklahoma	Missing	Illinois	0.97	Illinois	3.8

first row of table 7.2 shows that the southern states have by far the highest audience for these programs (the regional average is 185 for the 17 southern states). The region with the smallest audience for violent television is the Northeast, where the regional average is 133. The differences among regions are statistically significant, as indicted by the three asterisks below the label for this variable.

VIOLENT MAGAZINE CIRCULATION INDEX. The data used to construct the Violent Magazine Circulation Index were obtained from the Audit Bureau of Circulation (ABC). The ABC is an independent nonprofit organization which

Table 7.1b
Ranking of the States on the Legitimate Violence Indicators

Rank	Football Player Production State	cv53	Hunting Licenses Issued Per 100,000 Population State	cv49er	Corporal Punishment Permission Index State	xvcp1	Lynchings Per Million Population State	v1829r
1	Texas	2.01	Wyoming	324	New Mexico	9	Florida	520
2	Louisiana	1.90	Montana	232	North Carolina	8	Wyoming	445
3	Mississippi	1.77	Idaho	230	Nevada	8	Montana	366
4	Montana	1.68	Vermont	209	Vermont	7	Mississippi	361
5	Idaho	1.68	Utah	188	Colorado	7	Arizona	295
6	Ohio	1.48	South Dakota	182	North Dakota	7	Louisiana	247
7	North Dakota	1.38	Maine	180	Delaware	6	Georgia	247
8	Georgia	1.29	Alaska	163	Texas	6	Arkansas	238
9	Florida	1.25	Wisconsin	148	Oregon	6	New Mexico	194
10	South Dakota	1.19	Oregon	147	New York	6	Alabama	194
11	Virginia	1.16	Arkansas	141	Florida	6	Oklahoma	178
12	Oregon	1.12	West Virginia	141	Illinois	6	Texas	175
13	Pennsylvania	1.12	North Dakota	138	Virginia	6	Nevada	139
14	Oklahoma	1.10	Minnesota	120	Minnesota	5	Tennessee	132
15	Hawaii	1.08	Tennessee	108	Ohio	5	Idaho	130
16	Alaska	1.08	Mississippi	104	Washington	5	South Carolina	129
17	California	1.05	Pennsylvania	102	Georgia	5	Colorado	126
18	South Dakota	1.04	Michigan	101	Michigan	5	Kentucky	108
19	Massachusetts	1.03	Nebraska	98	Arkansas	5	South Dakota	59
20	Utah	1.00	Oklahoma	98	Oklahoma	4	Virginia	58
21	Illinois	0.99	New Mexico	97	Montana	4	West Virginia	56
22	Washington	0.98	Missouri	93	California	4	Nebraska	54
23	Kansas	0.98	Louisiana	89	Louisiana	4	Washington	54
24	Arizona	0.97	Iowa	89	Pennsylvania	4	North Carolina	52
25	Tennessee	0.97	Kansas	88	South Dakota	4	Oregon	48
26	Kentucky	0.96	Colorado	87	South Carolina	3	Missouri	37
27	Arkansas	0.91	Washington	86	Hawaii	3	Kansas	37
28	New Jersey	0.89	Kentucky	82	Arizona	2	North Dakota	34
29	Indiana	0.88	Virginia	80	Nebraska	2	California	33
30	Iowa	0.81	New Hampshire	80	Connecticut	2	Utah	28
31	New Hampshire	0.80	Arizona	71	Alabama	2	Maryland	22
32	Alabama	0.79	Alabama	70	Utah	1	Indiana	20
33	Nebraska	0.77	Georgia	68	Kentucky	1	Iowa	8
34	North Carolina	0.74	Texas	64	Wyoming	1	Illinois	6
35	Colorado	0.74	South Carolina	64	New Hampshire	1	Ohio	6
36	Connecticut	0.74	Indiana	62	Indiana	1	Delaware	5
37	Wyoming	0.73	Nevada	61	Kansas	1	Minnesota	5
38	West Virginia	0.72	North Carolina	58	Iowa	1	Michigan	3
39	Michigan	0.70	Ohio	44	Missouri	1	Wisconsin	2
40	Minnesota	0.70	Delaware	41	Mississippi	1	Maine	1
41	Vermont	0.63	New York	40	Tennessee	1	Pennsylvania	1
42	Maryland	0.59	Maryland	36	Idaho	1	Connecticut	1
43	Missouri	0.57	Illinois	30	West Virginia	1	New Jersey	0
44	Rhode Island	0.55	Connecticut	26	Wisconsin	1	New York	0
45	New Mexico	0.53	Florida	25	Alaska	1	Vermont	0
46	Wisconsin	0.52	New Jersey	23	Rhode Island	1	Rhode Island	0
47	Delaware	0.51	California	22	Maine	1	New Hampshire	0
48	Nevada	0.50	Massachusetts	19	Massachusetts	0	Massachusetts	0
49	Maine	0.47	Rhode Island	13	New Jersey	0	Alaska	0
50	New York	0.38	Hawaii	11	Maryland	0	Hawaii	0

audits and certifies magazine sales. The ABC "blue book" gives the number of copies sold in each state for more than 400 magazines. We selected magazines whose content or readership, in our judgment, reflected a high level of violence: *Easy Riders, Guns and Ammo, Heavy Metal,* and *Shooting Times.* In addition, we used the combined circulation of the *Army, Air Force,* and *Navy Times* (the ABC groups the three) because, even though the content of these magazines does not depict violence, they represent a readership who are or were engaged in an occupation that epitomizes violence.

The circulation rates for these five magazines were factor analyzed using

Table 7.1c

Ranking of the States on the Legitimate Violence Indicators

| | PRISONERS UNDER SENTENCE OF DEATH | | | | EXECUTIONS PER 100 HOMICIDE ARRESTS | | | |
| | Per 100,000 White Population | | Per 100,000 Black Population | | 1940-1959 | | 1960-1978 | |
Rank	State	z266r2	State	z267r2	State	cv59	State	cv60
1	Georgia	21.1	Utah	100.0	Nevada	100.0	Utah	5.45
2	Florida	15.5	Arizona	75.0	Vermont	76.3	Kansas	5.29
3	Alabama	15.4	Montana	50.0	Utah	69.7	Arkansas	5.25
4	Mississippi	14.2	Nevada	37.5	Georgia	42.8	Wyoming	4.96
5	Nebraska	7.1	Oklahoma	33.8	Connecticut	42.7	Iowa	4.11
6	Delaware	6.2	Nebraska	31.5	New York	39.0	Mississippi	4.04
7	Illinois	6.0	Florida	19.3	South Carolina	37.1	Colorado	3.92
8	Arkansas	5.8	Georgia	11.4	Arkansas	36.6	Nevada	3.70
9	Oklahoma	5.3	Delaware	10.5	Oregon	35.1	Oklahoma	3.42
10	Utah	5.0	Texas	7.7	North Carolina	34.7	Arizona	2.77
11	Louisiana	4.4	Arkansas	6.3	Arizona	33.4	South Carolina	2.48
12	Texas	4.0	Mississippi	4.9	Maryland	32.8	Texas	2.39
13	Indiana	3.4	Alabama	4.1	California	32.7	Georgia	2.31
14	Montana	3.3	Tennessee	3.7	Mississippi	32.2	California	1.76
15	Virginia	3.2	Kentucky	3.5	Florida	31.1	Virginia	1.63
16	Arizona	2.9	South Carolina	3.3	Washington	31.0	Florida	1.60
17	South Carolina	2.6	California	1.9	Colorado	30.6	Washington	1.46
18	North Carolina	2.0	Louisiana	1.7	Louisiana	30.3	Connecticut	1.23
19	Tennessee	1.6	Virginia	1.5	New Jersey	25.7	Alabama	1.15
20	Missouri	1.3	North Carolina	1.4	Ohio	25.2	Ohio	1.15
21	Pennsylvania	1.2	Indiana	1.3	Pennsylvania	23.8	New Mexico	1.11
22	California	0.3	Illinois	1.0	Iowa	23.0	Missouri	1.08
23	South Dakota	0.0	Missouri	0.7	Delaware	21.7	Oregon	1.03
24	Kentucky	0.0	Pennsylvania	0.5	Texas	20.9	New Jersey	0.88
25	Washington	0.0	Maryland	0.4	Virginia	20.2	New York	0.74
26	West Virginia	0.0	Idaho	0.0	Idaho	19.5	Pennsylvania	0.55
27	Kansas	0.0	Wyoming	0.0	Kentucky	18.6	Indiana	0.38
28	North Dakota	0.0	Washington	0.0	Kansas	18.0	Kentucky	0.37
29	Colorado	0.0	West Virginia	0.0	Alaska	17.4	Maryland	0.30
30	Idaho	0.0	Colorado	0.0	Wyoming	17.0	Tennessee	0.27
31	Maryland	0.0	North Dakota	0.0	West Virginia	16.9	Louisiana	0.25
32	Nevada	0.0	Oregon	0.0	Oklahoma	16.5	Illinois	0.22
33	Iowa	0.0	Kansas	0.0	Massachusetts	15.8	North Carolina	0.19
34	New Mexico	0.0	New Mexico	0.0	Nebraska	15.3	Idaho	0.00
35	Wyoming	0.0	South Dakota	0.0	Tennessee	13.4	Nebraska	0.00
36	Ohio	0.0	Ohio	0.0	New Mexico	12.7	Massachusetts	0.00
37	Minnesota	0.0	Minnesota	0.0	South Dakota	10.2	West Virginia	0.00
38	Michigan	0.0	Michigan	0.0	Missouri	9.3	South Dakota	0.00
39	Wisconsin	0.0	Wisconsin	0.0	Indiana	6.7	Delaware	0.00
40	Maine	0.0	Maine	0.0	Illinois	6.6	Vermont	0.00
41	Oregon	0.0	Iowa	0.0	Montana	4.8	Montana	0.00
42	Connecticut	0.0	Connecticut	0.0	North Dakota	0.0	North Dakota	0.00
43	New Jersey	0.0	New Jersey	0.0	Wisconsin	0.0	Wisconsin	0.00
44	New York	0.0	New York	0.0	Michigan	0.0	Michigan	0.00
45	Vermont	0.0	Vermont	0.0	Rhode Island	0.0	Rhode Island	0.00
46	Rhode Island	0.0	Rhode Island	0.0	New Hampshire	0.0	New Hampshire	0.00
47	New Hampshire	0.0	New Hampshire	0.0	Maine	0.0	Maine	0.00
48	Massachusetts	0.0	Massachusetts	0.0	Alaska	0.0	Alaska	0.00
49	Alaska	0.0	Alaska	0.0	Hawaii	0.0	Hawaii	0.00
50	Hawaii	0.0	Hawaii	0.0	Minnesota	0.0	Minnesota	0.00

the SCSS (Nie et al., 1980) principal components extraction method. This analysis revealed one factor which accounted for 73% of the state-to-state variation in the circulation rates. The Violent Magazine Circulation Index was computed using the SCSS factor score option, which weights each item by its factor score coefficient.

The second column of table 7.1a shows the rank-order distribution of the states on the Violent Magazine Circulation Index. The state and regional rankings are presented in the form of Z scores. Z scores have a mean of zero and a standard deviation of one. Alaska and western states generally tend to be

Table 7.2

Regional Differences on Legitimate Violence Indicators

Indicators	Northeast	North Central	South	West
Violent Television Viewing Index, 1980***	133.0	158.0	185.0	147.0
Violent Magazine Circulation Index, 1979***	-.6	-.3	-.4	1.0
National Guard Enrollment Per 1,000 Population, 1976	3.1	2.8	3.2	3.7
National Guard Expenditures Per Capita, 1976*	12.7	12.0	12.0	20.8
State of Origin of NCAA Football Players, 1972	.7	.9	1.1	1.0
Hunting Licenses Issued Per 100,000 Population, 1980	77.5	99.9	79.7	132.8
Corporal Punishment Permission Index, 1979	2.3	3.3	3.7	4.0
Persons Lynched Per Million Population, 1882-1927***	.5	23.1	173.8	140.0
Whites Sentenced to Death Per 100,000 White Homicide Arrests, 1980 ***	.1	1.5	6.4	.9
Blacks Sentenced to Death Per 100,000 Black Homicide Arrests, 1980***	.1	2.9	7.1	36.0
Ratio of Execution Rate to Homicide Rate, 1940-1959	24.8	9.6	26.5	29.8
Ratio of Execution Rate to Homicide Rate, 1960-1978	.4	1.0	1.6	2.0

Note: * p < .05, ** p < .01, *** p < .001.

at the top of the distribution. This is also indicated by the regional comparisons in table 7.2, which shows that the West has the highest score, and the Northeast the lowest.

NATIONAL GUARD EXPENDITURE AND ENROLLMENT. These items were included in the Legitimate Violence Index on the assumption that the level of state expenditures on the National Guard, and the popularity of participation in the National Guard, may reflect a belief in the efficacy of physical force. The data were obtained from the Statistical Abstract of the United States and transformed to per capita expenditures and to enrollment per 100,000 population. Considering the fact that National Guard expenditures are largely paid for by the federal government, the magnitude of the differences among states shown in the third and fourth columns of table 7.1a is especially remarkable. We take it as indicating that those states which have a military orientation somehow manage to manipulate the federal grants system in a way which supports that orientation.

FOOTBALL PLAYER PRODUCTION. Football is among the most violent of American sports. According to the National Collegiate Athletic Association (NCAA), in the 44-year period between 1931 and 1975 there were 821 deaths and over 400 serious injuries directly linked to playing football (Atyeo, 1979). In a preliminary study of the relationship between normative supports for violence and violent crime, Messner (1980:3) hypothesized that "groups adhering to values relatively supportive of violent behavior will be more predisposed to football . . . than groups with value preferences less compatible with violent behavior." Messner tested this idea using data collected by Rooney (1975) on the state in which college football players attended high school. This variable was treated by Messner as an indicator of the state's cultural approval of violence. Messner found a positive correlation ($r = .25$) between football player production and the homicide rate. Both the theoretical reasoning and the evidence cited led us to consider including football player production as one of the items in the LVX.

Rooney computed a ratio of NCAA college football players to the population of each state. He then divided the ratio for each state by the national ratio. The resulting scores indicate how far each state is above or below the U.S. average. The state rankings on this measure are presented in the first column of table 7.1b and show that the top ranking state (Texas) has a score of 2.01, which means that Texas produced double the national average of college football players. The bottom ranking state was New York, with a score of 0.38. This indicates that New York had a rate that was one-third of the U.S. average of high school football players who went on to play NCAA football.

HUNTING LICENSES PER 1,000 POPULATION. People may hunt for the outdoor experience, to augment their food supply, or because it is a challenge. But in addition to these aspects of the sport, it is possible that a major attraction of hunting is the killing itself. To the extent that this is the case, wide popular participation in hunting indicates a satisfaction with, or at least a fascination with, killing. We therefore decided to include a measure of the extensiveness of participation in hunting. The fact that there are much greater opportunities to hunt in Montana as compared to Rhode Island does not necessarily invalidate the measure. Rather, it helps explain why there is more hunting in Montana. But regardless of the causes, the fact is that in Rhode Island few people hunt and display guns in the windows of pickup trucks, whereas many do in Montana.

Although data on hunting licenses sold in each state are readily available, most states do not report separate figures for licenses sold to residents and nonresidents. However, states do report the number of hunting tags (a permit to shoot a specific type of animal) sold to residents and nonresidents. We computed the ratio of the resident to nonresident hunting tags to estimate the proportion of hunting done by residents. The total number of hunting licenses was then multiplied by this proportion to estimate the number of licenses issued to residents of the state. Finally, the estimated number of hunting licenses was divided by the state population to obtain a rate per 100,000 population.

Because of the vast differences in the degree of urbanization of the states, it should not be surprising that table 7.1b shows a rate of hunting licenses which is 20 to 30 times greater for the high ranking states than for the low ranking states. Western states seem to predominate at the top of this list as they did at the top of the Violent Magazine Circulation Index, and this is also shown in table 7.2. However, the differences among regions are not statistically significant because there is considerable variation within each region.

CORPORAL PUNISHMENT PERMISSION INDEX. Laws permitting the use of physical punishment by teachers can be regarded as one of the clearest examples of cultural approval of violence. There are large differences among the states in the extent to which such punishment is permitted. Only a few states have an outright prohibition on the use of physical punishment by teachers or other school officials. Most states permit it under certain circumstances.

The Corporal Punishment Permission Index gives each state a score for the number of circumstances specified by law under which school authorities have the right to hit children. The more circumstances in which teachers and principals are permitted to use corporal punishment, the higher the score on the index. As can be seen from the third column of table 7.1b, the range is from zero (under no circumstances) to nine such circumstances.

LYNCHINGS. An estimated 4,951 lynchings occurred during the period 1882–1972, or about 100 per year. While most victims were black and most lynchings occurred in the South, almost every state had lynchings: there were 9 in Minnesota, 6 in Wisconsin, and 41 in Wyoming. Moreover, 29% of the persons lynched during this period were white. Despite the number and symbolic importance of lynching and the fact that it is, by definition, a group activity, two questions concerning the use of lynchings in each state as an indicator of legitimate violence need to be addressed.

First is the question of whether lynching reflects deviance rather than a cultural norm. Historians of lynching hold that, although illegal, lynching nonetheless reflects the dominant groups and culture. Brown (1979:31), for example, describes lynching as "an integral part of the post-Reconstruction system of white supremacy." He goes on the point out that, on the western frontier, lynch law and vigilante actions were "dominated by social conservatives who desired to establish order and stability in newly settled areas" (Brown 1979:32).

The second question concerns the relevance for contemporary society of events which occurred 50 or more years ago. We take these events as an indicator of one aspect of the historical legacy of violence of particular states and regions. We assume that the greater the frequency with which lynchings occurred, the greater the probability that a tradition of violence became embedded in the culture of that state or region.

RATIO OF EXECUTIONS TO HOMICIDES, 1940–59 AND 1960–78. The frequency of capital punishment can be viewed as an indicator of the extent to which the population of a state believes that this most violent of all punishments is morally acceptable. To the extent that this assumption is correct, the death penalty epitomizes the culturally legitimate use of violence. For this reason, and because relatively dependable data are available, we decided to include both contemporary and historical indicators of the use of capital punishment. The contemporary measure uses the number of prisoners currently under sentence of death, rather than the actual number of executions, because U.S. Supreme Court rulings have severely limited the number of executions since 1969. The historical measure is based on the number of persons actually executed during the period 1940–59.

The use of capital punishment as an indicator of approval of violence conflicts with the belief that it is a deterrent to murder. Research on this issue is equivocal (Blumstein, Cohen, and Nagin, 1978). Our view is that rather than acting as a deterrent, capital punishment provides a model for violent behavior. This is one of many examples of acts and social policies whose effects are the opposite of those intended. For example, even parents who rarely use physical punishment tend to do so if their child strikes them. But, in addition to teaching that hitting a parent is a serious transgression, it also tends to teach that the way to deal with serious transgressions is to use physical force (Straus, Gelles, and Steinmetz, 1980).

Table 7.1c gives the ranking of the states with respect to the four indicators of the use of capital punishment. The third column shows the number of executions per 100 persons arrested for murder during the 1940s and 1950s. This was a period in American history in which executions flourished (Bowers, 1984). The reliance on execution during this period can be grasped by comparing the rates for 1940–59 with those for 1960–78 in the fourth column. The 1940–59 rate for New York, for example, was 53 times greater than the 1960–78 rate. The rate for Georgia was 18 times greater in 1940–59 than during the subsequent period (42.8 versus 2.3).

Although there was a tendency during the 1940–59 period for the southern states to have a high ratio of executions to arrests, the important regional difference in table 7.2 is the relatively low rate of executions in the north central states. The southern states were not significantly different from the other regions at this point in history. They may have had more homicides but, with the exception of the north central states, they did not execute a larger proportion of murderers than did other regions. In fact, during this period, a number of northeastern states had very high rates of execution; Vermont and Connecticut, for example, ranked second and fifth.

The drastic reduction in the use of capital punishment which, as Bowers (1984) points out, occurred before the Supreme Court's Furman decision was accompanied by a change in the relative position of the states and regions.[4] Northeastern states disappeared from the top of the postwar ranking, and the South, but especially the West, clearly began to stand out as the most capital punishment prone regions. At every period, however, there are extremely large differences among states in each of the indicators of capital punishment.

RATIO OF DEATH SENTENCES TO HOMICIDE ARRESTS, BY RACE. Our first approach to constructing capital punishment indicators was to compute rates per 100,000 population. However, this method is not adequate because, as defenders of the death penalty argue, capital punishment is largely a response to

4. The Furman decision invalidated all capital punishment laws then in existence and caused a moratorium on executions until the states devised new statutes which met the standards set forth in the Furman decision.

violent crime. The number of executions or death sentences is a function of the legal code, customary practices, and the number of capital crimes committed. To take this into account, we computed rates using capital punishment as the numerator and the number of arrests for homicide as the denominator.

For the recent period in which there have been few executions, the proclivity to execute seemed to be better indexed by the number of death sentences rather than the number of actual executions. We therefore used the ratio of death sentences to persons arrested for murder in 1980 as the final two indicators in the index. Since death sentences are confounded with the size of the black population in each state, that variable was taken into account by using race-specific rate and computing race-specific ratios of death sentences to homicide arrests.

Indexing Method and Reliability

After carrying out the indexing procedures described in appendix A, we summed and standardized the 12 indicators described above to create the Legitimate Violence Index. We then computed the internal consistency reliability of the index (Cronbach, 1970). The results show that the LVX has an alpha coefficient of .72. Table 7.3 displays the scale items, the item-to-total correlations, and the alpha coefficient if a particular item were to be deleted. A correlation matrix of the legitimate violence indicators is presented in table 7.4. The ranking of each state on the LVX is given in table 7.5.

State and Regional Differences in Legitimate Violence

Inspection of table 7.5 shows that there are substantial differences among states in legitimate violence. The state in which legitimate violence is most prevalent, and presumably most strongly built into the culture, is a western state, Wyoming. In fact, four of the top five states on the LVX are in the West. However, Mississippi and Georgia are included in the top five, and southern states tend to have generally high index scores, even though not as high as the scores of the western states. Examining the states arrayed at the bottom of table 7.5 suggests that northeastern states tend to have the lowest level of legitimate violence.

The regional differences are more clearly shown by figure 7.1, which also presents the results of a one-way analysis of variance (ANOVA). The ANOVA revealed a statistically significant difference among the four census regions in legitimate violence. The western region has the highest average index score. Nonetheless, there is only a small difference between the western region (65)

Table 7.3

Reliability Analysis of the Legitimate Violence Index

Indicators	Corrected Item - Total Correlation	Alpha if Item Deleted
Violent Television Viewing Index, 1980	.38	.38
Violent Magazine Circulation Index, 1979	.11	.36
National Guard Enrollment Per 1,000 Population, 1976	.24	.36
National Guard Expenditures Per Capita, 1976	.15	.36
State of Origin of NCAA Football Players, 1972	.44	.36
Hunting Licenses Issued Per 100,000 Population, 1980	.36	.28
Corporal Punishment Permission Index, 1979	-.01	.36
Persons Lynched Per Million Population, 1882-1927	.47	.14
Whites Sentenced to Death Per 100,000 White Homicide Arrests, 1980	.41	.36
Blacks Sentenced to Death Per 100,000 Black Homicide Arrests, 1980	.20	.35
Ratio of Execution Rate to Homicide Rate, 1940-1959	.02	.36
Ratio of Execution Rate to Homicide Rate, 1960-1978	.22	.36

Standardized Alpha Coefficient = .72

and the states in the southern region (56). The two areas of the country with the weakest support for legitimate violence are the north central (40) and northeastern (32) states. Turning to the divisional breakdown in figure 7.1, we see that there are even larger differences among the states on the Legitimate Violence Index. One particularly interesting finding from the divisional breakdown is that the Pacific states (California, Hawaii, Oregon, Washington, and Alaska) are below the national average in the approval of violence; thus, the Mountain states (Arizona, Colorado, Idaho, Montana, Nevada, New Mexico, Utah, and Wyoming) are responsible for the primacy of the western region in legitimate violence.

Correlation of the LVX with Rape

In the first section of this chapter ("The Cultural Spillover Theory of Violence") it was conjectured that increases in the level of legitimate violence would be accompanied by increases in the rape rate. This was tested in a preliminary way by correlating the LVX with the average rape rate for the

Table 7.4

Correlation Matrix of the Legitimate Violence Indicators

Indicators	1	2	3	4	5	6	7	8	9	10	11	12
1. Violent Television Viewing Index, 1980	1.00											
2. Violent Magazine Circulation Index, 1979	-.15	1.00										
3. National Guard Enrollment Per 1,000 Population, 1976	.10	.23	1.00									
4. National Guard Expenditures Per Capita, 1976	-.04	.51	.90	1.00								
5. State of Origin of NCAA Football Players, 1972	.37	.08	-.02	.02	1.00							
6. Hunting Licenses Issued Per 100,000 Population, 1980	.28	.40	.51	.54	.08	1.00						
7. Corporal Punishment Permission Index, 1979	-.02	.20	-.09	-.06	.04	-.13	1.00					
8. Persons Lynched Per Million Population, 1882-1927	.40	.31	.15	.18	.43	.27	.07	1.00				
9. Whites Sentenced to Death Per 100,000 White Homicide Arrests, 1980	.34	-.23	.09	-.05	.31	-.16	.05	.55	1.00			
10. Blacks Sentenced to Death Per 100,000 Black Homicide Arrests, 1980	-.03	.45	.21	.37	.22	.49	-.16	.34	.07	1.00		
11. Ratio of Execution Rate to Homicide Rate, 1940-1959	-.05	.16	.09	.04	-.05	-.02	.29	.12	.13	.29	1.00	
12. Ratio of Execution Rate to Homicide Rate, 1960-1978	.03	.34	.11	.09	.08	.15	-.04	.37	.19	.30	.46	1.00
Mean	1610.96	-.11	3.13	13.79	.97	98.52	3.59	102.23	2.77	12.69	24.07	1.37
Standard Deviation	285.57	.67	1.60	7.96	.39	66.16	2.55	129.71	4.85	25.21	20.35	1.70

Table 7.5

Ranking of the States on the
Legitimate Violence Index

Rank	State	xcv12zp
1	Wyoming	98
2	Montana	87
3	Mississippi	85
4	Idaho	83
5	Utah	83
6	Georgia	78
7	Nevada	77
8	Arkansas	74
9	Vermont	71
10	Louisiana	66
11	Alaska	64
12	Florida	63
13	Alabama	62
14	Oklahoma	62
15	Texas	61
16	Arizona	60
17	South Carolina	60
18	South Dakota	59
19	North Dakota	57
20	Oregon	56
21	Delaware	54
22	New Mexico	54
23	Colorado	54
24	Kansas	52
25	North Carolina	47
26	Virginia	47
27	Washington	45
28	Hawaii	45
29	Tennessee	44
30	Nebraska	42
31	Iowa	41
32	Ohio	41
33	West Virginia	38
34	Kentucky	36
35	Pennsylvania	35
36	Maine	34
37	Illinois	34
38	California	33
39	Minnesota	32
40	Indiana	31
41	Missouri	30
42	New Hampshire	30
43	Connecticut	29
44	Michigan	29
45	Wisconsin	27
46	New York	27
47	Maryland	26
48	New Jersey	22
49	Massachusetts	19
50	Rhode Island	18

Figure 7.1

Legitimate Violence Index by Division and Region

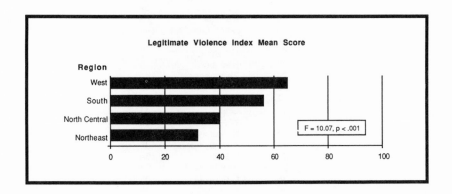

period 1980–82. The results showed a positive association of .22. Although this correlation is in the predicted direction, the LVX did not evidence a greater than chance association with the rape rate.

These findings fail to confirm the hypothesis that rape increases in proportion to increments in the level of legitimate violence. Nonetheless, it is best to remain cautious when interpreting bivariate correlations because any number of variables could be suppressing or masking the association of legitimate violence with rape. In the final chapter, multivariate analysis will be employed to control for the effects of several possible confounding variables.

THE VIOLENCE APPROVAL INDEX

Since the Legitimate Violence Index is a new and unvalidated measure, a test
of the cultural spillover theory using the LVX might result in no support for
the theory because the theory is incorrect or possibly because the measure is
not valid. Consequently, it is desirable to test the theory with an alternative
measure. We therefore developed a second indicator of cultural support for
violence: the Violence Approval Index (VAX).

The VAX differs fundamentally from the Legitimate Violence Index
(LVX) because it is based on directly expressed attitudes regarding the circumstances under which it is appropriate to use physical force and, specifically, on the percentage of persons in each state who endorsed the use of violence
under each circumstance. This measure has the disadvantage, as noted above,
of being dependent on self-report data. Nonetheless, it has the advantage of
being a direct measure of shared beliefs, and therefore of the norms and
values of society (Wallace, 1983; R. M. Williams, 1970). If we find parallel
results using a measure based on attitudinal data, it will enhance confidence in
the validity of the cultural spillover theory and also in the validity of both the
Legitimate Violence Index and the Violence Approval Index. Thus, we expect
to find a significant relationship between the VAX and the LVX, although not
a perfect correlation. Moreover, since the attitudes expressed in the VAX are
directly related to the social approval of violence, the VAX is expected to be
related to rape in the same way, and for the same reasons, as the LVX.

It should be emphasized that, even though the VAX was constructed by
aggregating individual attitudes, it is a measure of the extent to which the
population of each state *shares* these views and is therefore intended as a
measure of social norms and values which characterize the culture of each
state. The VAX cannot be used to make inferences about the relationship
between an individual's attitudes and his propensity to commit a rape. Rather,
we are interested in establishing whether cultural support for nonsexual and
socially approved forms of violence contributes to a social climate that increases the risk of rape.

Construction of the Violence Approval Index

The Violence Approval Index (VAX) is based on 14 questions from the
General Social Survey (GSS), which deals with attitudes toward the use of
violence and force that were reported in surveys from 1972 to 1984 (Davis and
Smith, 1985). For each of the individual items included in the index we

computed the percentage of respondents in each state who indicated approval of the use of violence in their response to the questions. The 14 questions can be grouped into three categories.

MILITARISM, EXECUTIONS, AND GUNS. The three items in this group are the percentage of respondents in each state who support greater military spending, support the death penalty, and oppose gun permits. For example, 29% of the respondents opposed gun permits, but these percentages ranged from 8.4% in Maryland to 64% in Mississippi.

APPROVAL OF PUNCHING ADULT MALE STRANGER. Six of the items are based on questions asking whether the respondent approves of punching an adult male stranger under a variety of different circumstances. For instance, 10% of the respondents would approve of punching a man who was drunk and bumped into someone else on the street.

APPROVAL OF POLICE STRIKING AN ADULT MALE CITIZEN. The remaining 5 questions ask respondents whether they would approve of a policeman striking an adult male citizen under a number of different conditions. Twenty-three percent of the respondents, for example, approved if a man said vulgar and obscene things to a policeman.

The VAX score for each state was obtained by summing the 14 percentages and dividing by 14. This yields the mean percentage of approval. We interpret this score as an indicator of the extent of social approval for violence. The alpha reliability coefficient for the Violence Approval Index is .68.

The Violence Approval Index, like the Legitimate Violence Index, was found to have a low and nonsignificant correlation ($r = .17$) with the incidence of rape. However, as we observed in discussing this result for the Legitimate Violence Index, this relationship could change when other variables are included in the model, as will be done when we specify and test an integrated model in the next chapter.

VALIDITY OF THE TWO MEASURES OF CULTURAL SUPPORT FOR VIOLENCE

The two measures of cultural support for violence are, to the best of our knowledge, unique. Consequently, it is not possible to estimate the concurrent validity of these measures by correlating them with an established measure of known validity. However, the regional rankings and the correlation between the Legitimate Violence Index and the Violence Approval Index are relevant. It is reasonable to expect that if each is a valid measure they will have comparable regional distributions and a moderate positive correlation. In fact, this is what was found. A regional breakdown indicates that the states have the same regional rankings on the VAX and the LVX. The West registered the highest score on both indexes, followed by the South, the North Central, and the Northeast. As expected, the correlation between the LVX and the VAX is .40. These results can be taken as evidence of the validity of both measures of cultural support for violence.

One can, of course, regard a correlation of .40 as indicating low validity, especially since there is no established convention concerning what size coefficient is necessary for validation. However, because the average size of published validity coefficients seems to be less than .40, we regard this as evidence of concurrent validity.[5] This interpretation is further reinforced by the fact that the two measures use entirely different data: attitudes in the case of the Violence Approval Index and laws and behavior in the case of the Legitimate Violence Index. For example, the Violence Approval Index uses the percent of respondents in each state who favor increased military spending, and the Legitimate Violence Index uses a parallel behavioral measure— the enrollment in the National Guard per 1,000 population. Since one of these measures is based on "objective" data and the other on self-reported attitudes, the correlation suggests the validity of both measures. Finally, the fact that both measures have a similar low correlation with the incidence of rape also suggests that they measure a similar domain.

Although the VAX provides an additional method of testing the cultural

5. It is remarkable that there are no established standards for judging concurrent validity coefficients. This is most clearly the case in our own discipline (sociology). In fact, sociological research rarely presents any evidence of validity for the instruments used. Sociologists place great importance on the representativeness of the sample and seem to assume implicitly that if the sample is representative, the measure is valid. The situation is almost the opposite in psychology. Relative to sociologists, psychologists pay much more attention to the validity of the measures and seem to assume implicitly that if the measure is valid, the sample is not crucial.

Even in psychology, an answer to the question of how large a coefficient is needed for an instrument to be considered valid is elusive. Inspection of several psychometrics texts revealed that almost none gives numerical figures, nor does the *Standards for Educational and Psychological Tests and Manuals* published by the American Psychological Association. Perhaps the reason is that the assessment of validity is a complex issue that is best approached multidimensionally (see, e.g., Brindberg and Kidder, 1982; Campbell and Fiske, 1959). Nevertheless, some numerical frame of reference can be helpful. Cronback (1970) is one of the few authors who provides this. In a table entitled Illustrative Validity Coefficients (table 5.3), Cronbach includes 18 coefficients for widely used tests and subtests. Our tabulation of these coefficients shows that they range from .08 to .77, with a mean of .37. However, as Cronbach points out, "it is unusual for a validity coefficient to rise above 0.60."

spillover theory, it has certain disadvantages and we therefore regard it as a supplemental test. First, the sample design for the General Social Survey is intended to provide a nationally or regionally representative sample rather than a representative sample for each state. Second, even though we used the cumulative file of approximately 15,000 cases, the number of respondents per state is low for the smaller states. Third, the sample for the General Social Survey includes 40 rather than all 50 states. For these reasons, despite the excellence of the General Social Survey at the individual level, findings based on state-aggregated GSS data must be regarded as highly tentative.

SUMMARY AND CONCLUSION

Cultural spillover theory attributes the high rate of violent crime in certain states to a diffusion or carryover of socially approved forms of violence into contexts and relationships in which the use of violence is considered illegiti-mate or illegal. Since rape is a crime of violence, rape rates should be higher in states where violent cultural norms are strongest. An empirical test of this proposition requires a measure of cultural support for violence that is inde-pendent of measures of criminal violence. Without such a measure it would not be possible to determine whether the magnitude of socially approved violence is related to the incidence of rape. We therefore developed two measures of cultural support for violence which we call the Legitimate Vio-lence Index and the Violence Approval Index.

The Legitimate Violence Index (LVX) is composed of 12 indicators of noncriminal and culturally legitimate forms of violence. The LVX includes the audience for mass media violence, laws permitting corporal punishment in schools, violent sports, military expenditures, and the use of capital punish-ment. Each of the 12 indicators showed substantial state-to-state variation, as did the composite index. States in the western and southern regions registered the highest average index scores, suggesting that there is relatively greater cultural support for violence in these two sections of the country. This seems to reflect the frontier heritage of the West, the history of slavery and military tradition of the South, and the rural nature of both regions.

To provide an additional test of the theoretical approach linking the social approval of violence to rape, we replicated the analysis with the Violence Approval Index (VAX). The VAX is based on the percent of the population who gave proviolence responses to 14 attitude questions, such as opposition to restrictions on the purchase of handguns and endorsement of the death penalty.

To take a step toward testing cultural spillover theory, we correlated both measures of cultural support for violence with the average rape rate for the years 1980–82. The correlations were low ($r = .22$ and $.17$) and not statistically significant. Although these correlations are in the hypothesized direction, they are not high enough to support the theory that state-to-state differences in the rape are due to differences in cultural support for violence. However, bivariate correlations are not an adequate test of the cultural spillover theory. Consequently, the relationship of these two measures with the rape rate is further explored in chapter 8, where a structural model is specified and path analysis is used to investigate the direct and indirect effects of the LVX and VAX on rape.

Part III

AN INTEGRATED THEORY AND ITS IMPLICATIONS

8

TOWARD AN INTEGRATED
THEORY OF RAPE

The preceding chapters have examined a number of theories that might explain the large differences among U.S. states in the incidence of rape. We paid particular attention to gender inequality, pornography, social disorganization, and culturally legitimate violence. Up to this point, each of these theories was examined as a discrete explanation of rape; however, we view them as complementary parts of a more comprehensive theory. In this chapter we put the pieces together, first in the form of a theoretical model which includes all the variables discussed up to this point, second in the form of an empirical test of this model using path analysis. The path model we tested specifies the direct and indirect linkages among the variables representing the four theories and their hypothetical effects on rape. The path analysis also includes several other variables that might account for the differences among states in the incidence of rape, such as the age structure of the population, economic inequality, urbanization, and the sex ratio.

THE THEORETICAL MODEL

Figure 8.1 presents the hypothesized relationships in our theoretical model. The variables are logically structured so that those to the left are presumed to be causally antecedent to those on the right. The single-headed arrows signify the direction of influence from one variable to another, and the plus (+) and minus (−) signs denote whether the hypothesized relationships between social disorganization, legitimate violence, sex magazine circulation, gender equality and rape, are positive or negative.

The data were analyzed using path analysis. Path analysis is a technique for estimating the effects of several interrelated variables in a causal model. The advantage of path analysis over ordinary multiple regression is that path analysis allows us to estimate both the direct and the indirect effects on rates of rape whereas multiple regression permits an estimate of the direct effects only. For example, the arrow connecting social disorganization to the rape rate

Figure 8.1

Theoretical Model of Variables Antecedent to Rape

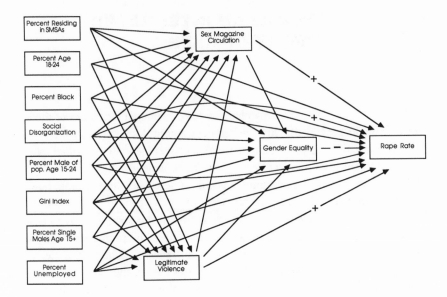

signifies that social disorganization is hypothesized to influence the rape rate
directly. At the same time, social disorganization is hypothesized to influence
the rape rate indirectly through its effects on legitimate violence, sex magazine
circulation, and gender equality. This is denoted by the arrows linking social
disorganization to legitimate violence, sex magazine circulation, and gender
equality, which in turn have arrows connecting them directly to the rape rate.
Thus, path analysis furnishes valuable information about empirical linkages
among the predictor variables and provides a comprehensive test of the determinants of rape.

The core of the theoretical model can be summarized in the form of the
following four hypotheses, although much more is specified in the diagram:

H1: The lower the level of gender equality, the higher the rape rate.

H2: The higher the circulation rate of sexually explicit magazines, the
higher the rape rate.

H3: The higher the level of social disorganization, the higher the rape
rate.

H4: The higher the level of legitimate violence, the higher the rape rate.

Causal linkages among the four explanatory variables are discussed in the
following section.

Theoretical Integration

An integrated theory of rape needs to be more than a collection of discrete causal links. Ideally, it is based on some underlying principle or principles that not only account for the relationships of the independent variables to rape, but also account for the relationships of the independent variables to one another. Therefore, the links among the causal variables need to be specified and explained.[1]

SOCIAL DISORGANIZATION AND CULTURAL SUPPORT FOR VIOLENCE. There is a large amount of evidence indicating that social disorganization is associated with higher crime rates and with violent crime in particular (see chapter 6). Presumably, this is because the social control processes which serve to limit crime are weaker under conditions of social disorganization. Consistent with this reasoning, Wolfgang and Ferracuti (1967) suggest that patterns of social disorganization may contribute to normative support for violence. However, they do not provide empirical data supporting that proposition. We believe they are correct and that the link between social disorganization and normative support for violence can be explained by the cultural spillover theory, discussed in chapter 7. Cultural spillover theory is based on the proposition that the use of violence for socially legitimate purposes tends to spill over to the use of violence for criminal purposes. Here we argue that the carryover from one sphere to another also goes in the opposite direction. For example, a society confronted with a high level of violent crime may turn to capital punishment (legitimate violence) as a way of controlling the crime rate. Thus, our theory posits the following causal sequence. Social disorganization engenders criminal violence, which in turn engenders the use of socially sanctioned violence against criminals (what we call legitimate violence). We therefore predict a significant relationship between social disorganization and cultural support for violence.

SOCIAL DISORGANIZATION AND PORNOGRAPHY. Social disorganization is expected to increase the circulation of sexually explicit magazines. This hypothesis is based on Tiryakian's (1981) insightful discussion of sexual anomie.

1. While the intramodel relations in figure 8.1 are based on theoretical and empirical considerations, a word of caution is in order. Since some of the causal linkages are between variables with no clear temporal priority, other causal sequences are also possible. For example, while social disorganization is presumed to affect cultural support for violence, it could be also argued that cultural support for violence contributes to social disorganization. Furthermore, sex magazine circulation is given causal priority over gender inequality, but an argument could be made that gender inequality influences the circulation of sex magazines. These and other model specifications should be analyzed in future research.

According to Tiryakian, conditions that undermine the efficacy of institutional controls may loosen norms guiding sexual conduct and weaken the regulatory power of sexual taboos. Therefore, a breakdown of conservative norms regarding sex could engender a cultural climate that is more favorable to the consumption of pornography.

SOCIAL DISORGANIZATION AND GENDER EQUALITY. Ever since Durkheim's (1964 [1897]) classic work on suicide, sociologists have emphasized the negative consequences of social disorganization. Although there is much evidence to support this view (for example, Blau and Blau, 1982; Crutchfield, Geerken, and Gove, 1982; M. D. Smith and Bennett, 1985), there is reason to believe that social disorganization can have positive effects as well. As was noted in chapter 6, a breakdown of outmoded organizational structures can lead to the development of more modern forms of social organization. Consequently, conditions that disrupt the established moral norms and institutions could foster the development of more egalitarian norms and institutions. Consistent with this line of reasoning, we predict that social disorganization increases gender equality.

CULTURAL SUPPORT FOR VIOLENCE AND PORNOGRAPHY. Research indicates that physical violence is rarely present in pornography (Malamuth and Spinner, 1980; Scott, 1985; Scott and Cuvelier, 1987). We think this is because consumers of pornography are primarily interested in sex. Accordingly, there is little reason to anticipate that cultural support for violence would influence men to buy pornography magazines. On the other hand, some authors claim that, regardless of the amount of physical violence depicted, pornography expresses a hostile and contemptuous attitude toward women (Barry, 1979, Dworkin, 1979; Lederer, 1980; S. J. McCarthy, 1980; Stoller, 1976). If these writers are correct, we would expect to find that the greater the cultural legitimation of violence, the greater the sale of pornographic materials.

CULTURAL SUPPORT FOR VIOLENCE AND GENDER INEQUALITY. Anthropological research on the genesis of gender inequality suggests that cultural support for violence is inimical to the status of women (Chafetz, 1984; Quinn, 1977). Divale and Harris (1976) argue that warfare contributes to a "male supremacist complex" because in militaristic societies men monopolize the more valued fighting roles, while women are designated roles that are comparatively less important. Sanday's (1981) analysis of tribal societies showed that war was endemic in or chronic in 82% of the male-dominant societies as compared to 50% of the egalitarian societies. Reiss (1986) also analyzed data on tribal societies and found an inverse relationship between the degree of interpersonal violence and the status of women. These findings suggest that cultural support for violence diminishes gender equality.

PORNOGRAPHY AND GENDER INEQUALITY. Feminist critiques of pornography allege that pornography is a direct cause of gender inequality (Dworkin, 1985; Dworkin and MacKinnon, 1988; MacKinnon, 1984). Support for this argument comes from Zillmann and Bryant's (1982, 1984) study of the effects of massive exposure to nonviolent pornography on attitudes toward women. This study showed that men exposed to a large number of sexually explicit films over a period of time were less favorable to gender equality. Therefore, if pornography fosters the belief that women do not deserve equal rights, it is possible that the widespread availability of sexually explicit magazines might lead to discriminatory practices against women.

Other Antecedents of Rape

The model presented in figure 8.1 was constructed to permit us to explore several relationships besides those specified in the theoretical integration. Consequently, indicators of the demographic and economic structure of the states, which were introduced in chapter 3, are included in the analysis to examine these alternatives to the four theories tested and to control for spurious relationships. The variables are as follows:

Percent of the population residing in SMSAs, 1980
Percent of the population black, 1980
Percent of the population age 18–24, 1980
Percent male of the population age 15–24, 1980
Gini Index of economic inequality, 1979
Percent single of males age 15 and older, 1979
Percent of the population unemployed, 1980

TEST OF THE THEORETICAL MODEL

The model shown in figure 8.1 was analyzed using ordinary least squares regression with backward elimination (Asher, 1983; Duncan, 1975).[2] We first estimated all the direct paths depicted in figure 8.1. Then we used the theory trimming method (Heis, 1969) to eliminate the direct paths that were not

2. See appendix C for the methodological analyses carried out to determine if the assumptions required for using multiple regression were satisfied.

statistically significant at the .05 level, and reestimated the equations in the
reduced model. The results are shown in table 8.1 and figure 8.2.

Interpretation of Table 8.1

UNSTANDARDIZED REGRESSION COEFFICIENTS. Table 8.1 presents the unstandardized regression coefficients for all the variables in the reduced model.
The correlations used to compute table 8.1 and figure 8.2 are given in appendix B.

The interpretation of the regression coefficients in table 8.1 can be illustrated by reference to the next to the last column of the table. This column
shows the unstandardized regression coefficients for the variables significantly related to the rape rate. These coefficients are estimates of the average
change in the rape rate that is associated with each change of one unit in the
independent variables. For example, the regression coefficient of 2.834 for
the Gini Index indicates that for each change of one point in the level of
economic inequality (as measured by the Gini Index) there is an average
increase of 2.8 rapes per 100,000 population, if we control for the other
variables in the equation. Similarly, the regression coefficient of 1.422 of the
Percent Unemployed indicates that a 1% rise in the proportion of the population unemployed is associated with an average increase of 1.4 rapes per
100,000 population, if we control for the other variables in the equation. And
the regression coefficient of −.166 for the Gender Equality Index indicates
that a one-point increase in the level of gender equality is associated with an
average *decrease* of .17 rapes per 100,000 population, if we control for the other
variables in the equation.

STANDARD ERRORS. The standard errors in table 8.1 indicate the confidence
interval for each regression coefficient in the table. Confidence intervals
provide a range of scores within which we can be reasonably confident that the
true regression coefficient falls (J. Cohen and P. Cohen, 1983).

The meaning of the standard error can be illustrated using the regression
coefficients and the standard errors for the variables related to the rape rate in
the right-hand columns of table 8.1. The first row shows that the Gini Index
of income inequality has a regression coefficient of 2.834 and a standard error
of .622. The confidence interval around the Gini Index regression coefficient
can be computed by subtracting the standard error of .622 from the regression
coefficient of 2.834 to determine the lower bound of the confidence interval,
and by adding the standard error to the regression coefficient to get the upper
end of the confidence interval, as follows: $2.834 - .662 = 2.172$, and $2.834 + .622 = 3.456$. Therefore, the confidence interval ranges from 2.172 to 3.456.

Table 8.1

Unstandardized Regression Coefficients and Standard Errors

Variables	Legitimate Violence		Sex Magazine Circulation		Gender Equality		Rape Rate	
	Regression Coefficient	Standard Error	Regression Coefficient	Standard Error	Regression Coefficient	Standard Error	Regression Coefficient	Standard Error
Gini Index, 1979			-1.224	.303	-3.013	1.095	2.834	.622
Legitimate Violence, 1882-1980					-.522	.110		
Social Disorganization, 1977-1980	.484	.097	.279	.032	.727	.110	.299	.085
Percent Black, 1980	.734	.203						
Percent Single Male Age 15+, 1979	-2.232	.835						
Percent Age 18-24, 1980	6.746	2.732						
Percent Residing in SMSAs, 1980	-3.45	.090					.366	.039
Percent Male of Population Age 15-24, 1980			1.942	.564				
Percent Unemployed, 1980							1.422	.562
Gender Equality, 1977-1983							-.166	.060
Sex Magazine Circulation, 1979							1.050	.209

Note: All of the coefficients are significant at p < .02.

This means that the true unstandardized regression coefficient for the Gini Index falls between 2.172 and 3.456. The same procedure can be used to compute the confidence intervals for the other regression coefficients in table 8.1.

Path Coefficients

Figure 8.2 displays the path coefficients for the variables in the reduced model. Path coefficients indicate the degree of association between two variables. Thus, the higher the path coefficient, the stronger the relationship. The interpretation of path coefficients is similar to the interpretation of unstandardized regression coefficients, with the exception that path coefficients are expressed in terms of standard deviation units rather than the real units of measurement.[3] For example, each increase of one standard deviation in the proportion of the population residing in Standard Metropolitan Statistical Areas is associated with a .531 standard deviation change in the rape rate, if we control for the other variables in the equation. And each increase of one standard deviation in the level of gender equality is associated with a −.230 change in the rape rate, if we control for the other variables in the equation.[4]

Direct Effects on Rape

The path coefficients in figure 8.2 confirm three of the four hypotheses. They show that (1) social disorganization is positively related to the rape rate, (2) sex magazine circulation is positively related to the rape rate, and (3) gender equality is inversely related to the rape rate. Figure 8.2 does not show a direct path from the box labeled Legitimate Violence to the box labeled Rape Rate,

3. The standard deviation provides a measure of how far each state's score on any of the variables deviates from the average or mean score for all the states. The means and standard deviations of the variables in figure 8.1 are in the last two rows of appendix B.

A key advantage of expressing the regression coefficients in standard deviation units (as path coefficients) is that it permits us to evaluate the *relative* importance of each variable. Relative importance cannot be evaluated using the unstandardized coefficients because each coefficient is expressed in different units of measurement. Consequently, the balance of this chapter will focus on the path coefficients.

4. The residuals or error terms are symbolized by the letters T, V, W, and U. Each regression equation has a residual term attached to it. The residuals symbolize the universe of independent variables that are not included in the causal model. Residuals are calculated by computing the square root of $R^2 - 1$ (Pedhazur, 1982). Thus, the residuals provide a measure of the unexplained variation in the dependent variables.

because this relationship was not statistically significant. Thus, the hypothesis that legitimate violence directly influences the rape rate was not confirmed.[5]

5. Some of the coefficients in figure 8.2 are different from those reported in our earlier studies of rape (Baron and Straus, 1984; Baron, Straus, and Jaffee, 1988). Those studies employed different model specifications and somewhat different measures of four key variables used in the present study (gender equality, sex magazine circulation, social disorganization, and rape). Since different models and measures were used, the resulting coefficients are somewhat different. Notwithstanding the two differences discussed forthwith, the coefficients reported in our earlier studies and those reported in figure 8.2 lead to parallel conclusions.

First, in the present study we found a negative association between gender equality and rape, whereas in an earlier study we found a positive association (Baron and Straus, 1984). There could be several reasons for this difference. One possible explanation is methodological. The discrepant findings could be attributed to the differences in the variable used to measure gender equality in each of the two studies. In the earlier study, gender equality was measured with the Status of Women Index (SWX), which is composed of 22 indicators and covers *four* dimensions of equality between women and men: economic, political, legal, and educational. In contrast, gender equality was measured in the present study with the Gender Equality Index (GEX), which is composed of 24 indicators and covers *three* dimensions of equality between women and men: economic, political, and legal. Another difference between the SWX and the GEX is that the GEX incorporates a number of indicators not included in the SWX (e.g., percent of female households with incomes above the poverty level, percent of small business loan money lent to women, statutes that permit warrantless arrest based on probable cause in domestic violence cases, and statutes that provide funds for family violence shelters or established standards for shelter operations). Moreover, the earlier study was based on a population of 51 states (the District of Columbia was treated as a state) and 1979 rape data, whereas the present study was based on a population of 50 states (District of Columbia was not included in the analysis) and a three-year average rape rate for the period 1980–82.

Another possible explanation for the discrepant effects of gender equality is that the findings reflect a historical shift in the relationship between gender equality and rape. This might be explained by the temporal differences in the data used to measure gender equality and rape in each of the two studies. In the earlier study, the SWX was based on data for the years 1970–79 and the rape rate was based on 1979 data. In the present study, the GEX was based on data for the years 1979–83 and the rape rate was based on data averaged for the three-year period between 1980 and 1982. We interpreted the positive association between the SWX and rape during the 1970–79 period as reflecting a backlash against women and the women's movement (Baron and Straus, 1984:206), whereas the negative association between the GEX and rape during the 1979–83 period seems to suggest that gender equality effects rape through the low valuation of women. Although both these processes undoubtedly occur (rape as a means of putting women "back in their place," and rape as an expression of the low valuation of women), it appears that the latter process is predominant in the current period. As plausible as this explanation may be, we are reluctant to make a strong case in support of it because of the aforementioned methodological differences between the two studies.

The other finding that differs from our previous research involves the effect of legitimate violence on rape. In an earlier study, we found a positive association between the Legitimate Violence Index (LVX) and the rape rate (Baron, Straus, and Jaffee, 1988), whereas in the present study we failed to find a significant association between the LVX and rape. The most likely

Figure 8.2
Reduced Model of Variables Antecedent to Rape

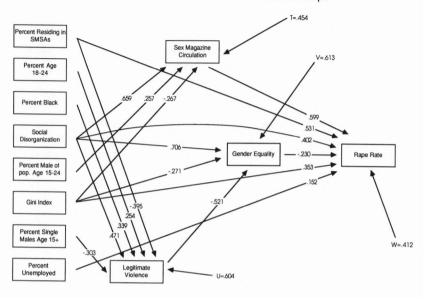

Note: Correlations among the exogenous variables are reported in appendix B.

These findings indicate that the rape rate increases in proportion to the level of instability and disorganization in society. Moreover, as one goes from states with low sex magazine circulation rates to states with high circulation rates, there is a concurrent increase in the incidence of rape. In addition, there is a significant tendency for the rape rate to decrease as the status of women increases.

Three of the control variables are also significantly related to rape. Figure 8.2 shows that the percent of the population residing in SMSAs, the Gini Index of income inequality, and percent of the population unemployed all have positive direct effects on the rape rate. This pattern of associations suggests that the combination of urbanism, economic inequality, and unem-

explanation for this discrepancy is that the present study used a more adequately specified model than the earlier study (see chapter 2 for a discussion on specification error). For instance, neither the Sex Magazine Circulation Index (SMCX2) nor the Social Disorganization Index (SDX) was included in the previous study. However, as appendix B of the present study shows, both the SMCX2 and the SDX are strongly correlated with the rape rate and moderately correlated with the LVX. Consequently, when we regressed the rape rate on legitimate violence and partialled out the effects of sex magazine circulation and social disorganization, legitimate violence did not emerge as a significant predictor of rape.

ployment constitutes a mixture of societal characteristics that increases the likelihood of rape.

Since the path coefficients in figure 8.2 are standardized, the size of the coefficients can be used to evaluate the relative importance of individual predictor variables. A comparison of the coefficients on the paths leading directly to the box labeled Rape Rate reveals that the circulation of sex magazines (.599) and the level of urbanization (.531) are more strongly related to the incidence of rape than is the degree of social disorganization (.402). However, social disorganization is more influential in the prediction of rape than the magnitude of economic inequality (.353), unemployment (.152), and gender equality ($-.230$). The combined effect of the six variables directly related to the rape rate accounts for 83% of the state-to-state variation in rates of rape ($F = 40.93, p < .001$).[6] Thus, our model accounts for almost all the differences among states in the incidence of rape.

Indirect Effects on Rape

The indirect paths in figure 8.2 show that some of the independent variables have both direct and indirect associations with rape, and some are related to rape only indirectly through their effect on the variables directly related to the rape rate.

SEX MAGAZINE CIRCULATION. Three of the variables in figure 8.2 are significantly related to the circulation of sex magazines: social disorganization (.659), the ratio of males to females (.257), and economic inequality ($-.267$). Since these three variables directly influence the circulation rate of sex magazines, they are indirectly related to the rape rate.

The tendency for sex magazine circulation to be higher in states with a higher level of social disorganization is consistent with Tiryakian's (1981) argument that a breakdown of conservative norms regarding sex can result in a more sexually liberal atmosphere—including increased consumption of pornography. The finding that more sex magazines are purchased in states where a larger proportion of men reside is not surprising since almost all the magazines comprising the Sex Magazine Circulation Index are consumed by men. Even *Playboy*, which aims at the broadest market, claims only a 10% female

6. The finding that 83% of the variation in rape is accounted for by the 6 variables directly related to the rape rate is based on a statistic known as the coefficient of determination (R^2), which varies on a scale from 0 to 1. The reported R^2 of .83 means that 83% of the variation in state rape rates can be explained by a linear combination of the proportion of the population residing in SMSAs, social disorganization, gender inequality, sex magazine circulation, economic inequality, and percent of the population unemployed.

readership. And the negative relationship between economic inequality and the sales of sex magazines is probably due to the fact that impoverishment reduces the consumption of all magazines.

STATUS OF WOMEN. The path coefficients in figure 8.2 show that gender equality is affected by social disorganization (.706), economic inequality (−.271), and legitimate violence (−.521). That is to say, in states with a *high* level of social disorganization, a *low* level of legitimate violence, and *less* economic inequality, there is *greater* gender equality. Thus, in addition to any direct effects on rape, social disorganization, economic inequality, and legitimate violence affect rape indirectly through their direct influence on the level of gender equality.

The finding that gender equality tends to increase as social disorganization increases is consistent with the causal model presented in chapter 6. The model postulates that social disorganization can have constructive and beneficial effects, especially where disadvantaged groups stand to gain from fundamental changes in the social organization of society. In this case, the findings suggest that social disorganization has contributed to equality between men and women by disturbing the system of gender stratification that keeps women in a subordinate position.

The indirect effect of legitimate violence on rape, through its negative effect on gender equality, is consistent with research on tribal societies which shows that the status of women is lower in more violent societies (Divale and Harris, 1976; Reiss, 1986; Sanday, 1981). Our findings suggest that this process applies not only to tribal societies but also to modern industrial societies.

Figure 8.2 also shows that the Gini Index affects rape indirectly through its inverse relationship to gender equality. The indirect effect indicates that in states with greater economic inequality, the status of women is lower, and where the status of women is lower, the rape rate tends to be higher. This highlights the underlying importance of economic constellations in understanding state-to-state differences in gender equality and rape (see Blumberg, 1984, for a discussion of the economic basis of gender stratification).

Methodological Analyses

Several additional analyses were undertaken to investigate various threats to the validity (T. D. Cook and Campbell, 1979) of the findings just reported, including controls for outliers, reporting effects, confounding with southernness and westernness, climatic effects, and interaction effects. The results of these analyses are presented in appendix C. Neither these analyses nor the methodological analyses reported in our earlier study of state-to-state differences in rape (Baron and Straus, 1984) suggest any modifications of the results just presented.

THE SOCIAL ORIGINS OF RAPE

The results provide support for three of the four macrosociological theories of rape included in the integrated model: (1) the theory that gender inequality contributes to rape, (2) the theory that pornography provides ideational support for rape, and (3) the theory that rape is a function of the level of social disorganization in society. We did not find support for the theory that rape is a direct function of a spillover from aspects of society in which violence is culturally approved, although we did find indirect support for this theory. We also found that the more economic inequality, unemployment, and urbanization in a state, the higher the rape rate. Each of these findings deserves further discussion, but we will devote the most attention to pornography because we regard those findings as the most problematic.

Gender Inequality

Our finding that the lower the status of women relative to men, the higher the rape rate is consistent with feminist theory and suggests that gender inequality contributes to a social climate that is conducive to violence against women (Brownmiller, 1975; Clark and Lewis, 1977; Russell, 1984). We believe that this relationship exists because, in a male-dominated society, rape both reflects the low valuation of women and contributes to their subordinate position in the gender stratification system.

Pornography

Our finding that the higher the circulation rate of sex magazines, the higher the rape rate is consistent with the theory that pornography contributes to a cultural climate favorable toward violence against women. Although this is a plausible interpretation, correlations of this type can be produced by many circumstances even when there is no cause-effect relationship. A cause-effect relationship is, at best, only one of several interpretations of the findings. This caveat also applies to the findings for gender equality and social disorganization. However, in the case of pornography, greater skepticism is needed because a causal interpretation is inconsistent with a large body of empirical evidence.

There are three bodies of evidence which cast doubt on the idea that the association between sex magazines circulation and rape represents a cause-effect relationship. First, as mentioned in chapter 1, experimental studies demonstrate that exposure to extremely graphic but nonviolent pornography *diminishes* aggression against women (Donnerstein, Linz, and Penrod, 1987). Second, a time series analysis of the United States, Denmark, Sweden, and West Germany showed either no increase or a decrease in the rape rate in the years following the legalization and wide increase in the circulation of pornographic materials (Kutchinsky, 1988). Third, we found that the circulation rate of the women's magazine *Playgirl* is also highly correlated with the rape rate ($r = .68$). Since it is unlikely that female readership of sex magazines contributes directly to rape, the relationship is probably due to confounding with an unmeasured third variable.

In view of the evidence summarized in the preceding paragraph, we are extremely hesitant to interpret our findings as reflecting a cause-effect relationship between pornography and rape. A more likely possibility, in our opinion, is that the correlation between the circulation of sexually explicit magazines and the rape rate is due to the presence of a hypermasculine or macho culture pattern (Mosher and Anderson, 1986; Parsons, 1947; Toby, 1966). This cultural pattern might include such traits as normative support for violence, the use of physical force to settle quarrels, belief in male supremacy, endorsement of rape myths, and approval of sexual coercion. A greater magnitude of this cultural orientation in some states than in others could influence men both to purchase more pornography and to commit rape. If this is the case, the relationship between pornography and rape would be a spurious consequence of their shared association with hypermasculinity.[7]

A partial test of the spurious correlation proposition was conducted using the Violence Approval Index (VAX) for 40 states, presented in chapter 7. When the Violence Approval Index is introduced into the regression analysis, the relationship between sex magazine circulation and rape vanishes. This finding supports the view that the correlation between pornography and rape reflects confounding with an underlying variable such as hypermasculinity.[8]

7. Feinberg (1985) comes to a similar conclusion in his theoretical discussion of pornography. Feinberg posits that correlations between pornography and rape can probably be explained by what he calls the "cult of macho."

8. This interpretation is further supported by certain correlations. These include correlations of .44 with percentage of the population in the high violence age group of 18–24, .46 with

The combination of three bodies of empirical evidence which are inconsistent with the idea that pornography causes rape, and our finding that the effect of sex magazine circulation on rape is reduced to a level of nonsignificance when the Violence Approval Index is added to the Analysis, lead us to believe that the significant relationship between sex magazine circulation and rape reflects an underlying third variable rather than a causal relationship between pornography and rape.

Social Disorganization

The effect of social disorganization on rape cuts in two directions. On the one hand, social disorganization can have serious adverse consequences. This is shown by the finding that social disorganization is related to rape directly. Consequently, in the context of a sexist and violent society, a low level of social integration and social control contributes to a high incidence of rape. On the other hand, social disorganization can have positive effects. This is suggested by the finding that social disorganization contributes indirectly to *reducing* rape through its relationship with gender equality. As we suggested in chapter 6, it seems that social disorganization tends to erode traditional norms and practices, including traditional patterns of domination and subordination. The reduction in gender inequality, in turn, contributes to a reduction in the rape rate.

Legitimate Violence

Contrary to expectation, we did not find a direct relationship between legitimate violence and rape. Nevertheless, legitimate violence is related to rape indirectly through its inverse relationship with gender equality. The fact that the status of women is lower in states that have high levels of legitimate violence indicates that women are devalued in more violent societies. These findings are in accord with cross-cultural research, which shows that women are assigned subservient roles in societies marked by relatively high levels of violence.

---

percentage of males in the population, .40 with the Legitimate Violence Index, .45 with the Social Disorganization Index, and .50 with the Sex Magazine Circulation Index. However, there are also reasons for regarding the Violence Approval Index with caution. First, the data are restricted to 40 states. Second, there are a number of anomalous associations, such as a negative correlation ($r = -.41$) with the percentage of single males, and a low correlation between the VAX and the 1980–82 rape rate ($r = .17$). Third, the increased standard error resulting from the additional variable and the reduced sample size could produce unstable regression coefficients.

Urbanism, Economic Inequality, and Unemployment

The direct effect of urbanism on rape is consistent with research that reports high rates of violent crime in urban areas (Friday, 1983). One explanation for this association is that urban areas provide greater opportunities for criminal violence, including violence against women (Brownmiller, 1975; L. Cohen, Kluegel, and Land, 1981).

The significant relationships of unemployment and economic inequality to rape are consistent with research which shows that a disproportionate number of both victims and perpetrators are likely to come from groups with low socioeconomic status (Amir, 1971; Curtis, 1975; Rabkin, 1979; Schwendinger and Schwendinger, 1983). These findings might be explained by the high levels of resentment and hostility that are generated by status inequalities (Nettler, 1984). Because the "good provider role" has historically been an integral component of the masculine identity, circumstances which make it difficult to fulfill that role, such as unemployment, poverty, and economic inequality, could produce a climate of antagonism and resentment, some of which is directed against women. As Curtis (1975) argues, rape may be a way for some men to assert their masculinity in the absence of viable avenues of economic success.

Policy Implications

Although the theoretical model that we developed to explain the differences among states in the incidence of rape provides a remarkably good fit to the data, it is important to exercise caution in interpreting the findings. Since the model was tested using cross-sectional data, the results must be interpreted as being consistent with the theories tested by the model rather than proving them. This caution is especially important in regard to the policy implications of the pornography-rape linkage because censorship is a widely advocated policy (see Brownmiller, 1975; Dworkin, 1985; Dworkin and MacKinnon, 1988; MacKinnon, 1984; Russell, 1977). In our opinion, prohibiting sexually explicit materials would be a mistake because censorship threatens the freedom of all citizens and feminists in particular (Baron, 1987; Duggan, Hunter, and Vance, 1985; Lynn, 1986b). Aside from the threat to freedom of expression, the research reviewed in previous sections leads us to doubt that pornography is a cause of rape. Rather, we believe that the fundamental causes of rape are to be found in sexism, economic inequality, and social disorganization, not in pornography, no matter how explicit and impersonal the sexual content. Social policy designed to reduce rape should focus on these underlying causes rather than on pornography. These issues are discussed more fully in the following section.

RESTRICTING PORNOGRAPHY AS A RAPE REDUCTION POLICY

Ironically, proposals to regulate pornography have become virtually the only publicly debated approach to reducing rape. This is unfortunate because the scientific evidence does not support the proposition that prohibiting pornography is an effective way to deal with rape. Moreover, censorship threatens the free speech rights of feminists and other groups that frequently challenge conservative norms and values. Despite this, there are reasons that antipornography groups are not likely to be persuaded by our conclusion that the restriction of pornography is a misguided and ineffectual strategy for the reduction of rape.

First, our findings do not provide incontrovertible support for this conclusion. However, we base this conclusion only in part on our own data. The conclusions about pornography follow primarily from the empirical research of other investigators (see p. 186).

Second, and more important, the views of antipornography feminists and political conservatives do not depend on scientific evidence. They reflect differences in lifestyle and values which are taken as given rather than being based on scientific evidence. Indeed, to suggest that these moral values should be influenced by science is itself anathema to many who wish to ban pornography. In all likelihood, there is no body of empirical evidence that would convince antipornography groups that efforts to reduce rape by restricting pornography are misplaced. This is because the central issue for antipornography activists is not really rape but the perceived offensiveness of pornography.

To a considerable extent, the antipornography movement has become a symbolic crusade (Baron, 1987; Gusfield, 1963; Kirkpatrick and Zurcher, 1984; Zurcher and Kirkpatrick, 1976). As such, right-wing opponents of pornography have used the antipornography crusade to champion a way of life based on traditional values, sexual abstinence, and the exaltation of traditional gender roles. At the same time, feminist opponents of pornography have used the antipornography movement as a platform to extol the virtues of a separate women's culture, celebrate the innate moral superiority of women, and denounce the degrading nature of heterosexual sex.

However, not all of those who are inclined to favor restricting pornography fall into these two categories. Indeed, we believe that the issue is one that is subject to reconsideration by the majority of those who are now uneasy about permitting pornographic materials to be sold. Given this assumption and the importance of the issue, we believe it is necessary to delineate the reasons that censorship is undesirable.

Problems with Censorship

THREAT TO CIVIL LIBERTIES. Censorship of unconventional or offensive sexual depictions paves the way for the prohibition of controversial or unpopular political ideas, including feminist ideas, and helps to establish a social climate in which censorship is morally acceptable. As Small (1985:8) notes:

> If the state can ban pornography because it "causes" violence against women, it can also ban *The Wretched of the Earth* because it causes revolution, *Gay Community News* because it causes homosexuality, *Steal This Book* because it causes thievery, and *The Feminine Mystique* because it causes divorce. When speech is abridged in order to prevent crime, the precedent is set for censoring any book, magazine, or film documentary that encourages civil disobedience or draft resistance, suggests herbal remedies unapproved by the F.D.A., explains home birth techniques, or approves gay or lesbian sex.

This is not a remote possibility, especially as it affects feminists and gays (Valverde and Weir, 1985). For example, the Attorney General's Commission on Pornography (1986) recommended that the criminal justice system give high priority to prosecuting "degrading" pornography. It certainly gives one pause to consider that the police, prosecutors, and judges who enforce obscenity laws are not likely to distinguish between feminist and antifeminist pornography in their effort to regulate sexual images that they find "degrading."

FINDINGS CONTRARY TO THE SCIENTIFIC EVIDENCE. The weight of scientific evidence is that pornography without violent content, no matter how impersonal, does *not* increase aggression against women (Donnerstein, Linz, and Penrod, 1987). As indicated previously, the two most dependable types of studies, laboratory experimental studies and time series studies exhibit no relationship between pornography and sexual aggression (see chapter 1 and "The Social Origins of Rape" in this chapter). Of course, there are aggressive and violent people who will use sex as a means of expressing aggression (Groth, 1979), but there is no evidence that images of sex cause such violence.

VIOLENCE, NOT SEX, IS THE REAL PROBLEM. Empirical research indicates that *violence*, with or without sexual content, promotes aggressive behavior (Donnerstein, Linz, and Penrod, 1987). Thus, if anything is to be regulated, it should be depictions of violence. However, there is no call for censoring high violence movies such as *Rambo*, *The Texas Chain Saw Massacre*, and *Friday the 13th*, or high violence magazines like *Soldier of Fortune* and *True Detective*. Nevertheless, even if portrayals of violence do promote actual violence, censorship is the wrong approach because, as already mentioned, it constitutes a threat to civil liberties. And more important, censorship does not deal with the root causes of rape.

PORNOGRAPHY IS LESS VIOLENT THAN OTHER MEDIA. Of the few studies that have investigated the amount of violence in pornography, all indicate that there is *much less* violence in sexually explicit media than in nonsexual media (Dietz, Harry, and Hazelwood, 1986; Malamuth and Spinner, 1980; Scott, 1985). This is because most pornography is so single-mindedly focused on sex, which is the reason why most people buy it. If people want to view violence, they can simply switch on their television set or go to their local video store and rent any one of a number of slasher films that show one brutal murder after another (Linz, Donnerstein, and Penrod, 1984).

PORNOGRAPHY IS NO MORE SEXIST THAN OTHER MEDIA. There is no evidence that sexism, in the sense of portraying women in passive and subordinate roles, is any more common in pornography than in other mass media depictions of women (Goffman, 1979; Russ, 1985). Steele (1985) maintains that sexist portrayals of women prevail throughout the mass media and are not limited to pornography. She therefore criticizes antipornography crusaders for privileging pornography over other, more insidious sexist imagery, like that found in advertisements, romance novels, and women's magazines. Thus, pornography is more a symptom of sexism than a cause of it.

DIVERSION OF ATTENTION, ENERGY, AND MONEY. If public funds are to be spent on activities to produce a nonviolent and nonsexist society, there is a long list of programs, services, and social changes of much greater importance than the regulation of pornography. Some of these will be outlined in the section "Primary Prevention of Rape."

Mitigating the Effects of Sexually Violent Media

The arguments against censorship do not mean that there are no problems with pornography and that nothing should be done, only that censorship is not the way to address the problem of rape.

Even those who are against censorship of *nonviolent* pornography may feel differently about *violent* pornography.[9] Experimental research indicates that exposure to pornography with violent content (for example, films depicting rape in a positive light) increases aggressive behavior (Donnerstein, Linz, and Penrod, 1987). On the basis of these findings, it might be argued that sexually violent movies and magazines encourage men to rape and should therefore be banned. However, censorship is an extreme and unnecessary measure, and one which, as history attests, has not succeeded in eliminating pornography (Bristow, 1977; Kendrick, 1987; Marcus, 1974).

Experimental studies suggest that the most efficacious way to deal with the negative effects of violent pornography is through educational programs that dispel myths about sexual violence (Linz et al., 1986). Research by Check and Malamuth showed that subjects who were exposed to a rape depiction (which portrayed the victim as ultimately enjoying the assault) *and* were later told of the true horror of rape during the debriefing, were subsequently found to give less endorsement to rape myths than a control group (Check and Malamuth, 1984; Malamuth and Check, 1984). These findings corroborate the results of a debriefing follow-up study by Donnerstein and Berkowitz (1981), in which the subjects were exposed to either a film depicting rape or a nonsexual film. The subjects who were exposed to a rape depiction *and* debriefed were significantly less likely to endorse rape myths than the control group, who had not seen the rape film.

These studies indicate that when subjects are exposed to sexually violent materials and subsequently debriefed, they learn how to identify rape myths and develop a more realistic understanding of the meaning and consequences of rape. This suggests that the solution to violent pornography is not censorship but the construction of competing sexual images and ideas. Sex education programs could play an instrumental role in this process by teaching young men and women accurate information about sex and dispelling erroneous beliefs about rape. However, sex education in the sense just mentioned, valuable as it is, must be part of a larger process of restructuring gender roles and many other aspects of society. If, as the present research indicates, the high incidence of rape grows out of the very structure of American society, a focus on individuals and their beliefs must necessarily be only part of the overall effort. The larger effort, as outlined in the next section, involves restructuring fundamental aspects of American society.

9. Although there are no reliable national figures on the availability of violent pornography, Winick's (1985) content analysis of all the magazines ($N = 430$) at a New York City adult bookstore indicates that fewer than 5% of the magazines depicted violence.

PRIMARY PREVENTION OF RAPE

The question we set out to investigate is why women are in much greater danger of being raped in some U.S. states than in others. Since the question refers to differences among units of society, the investigation focused on theories which refer to characteristics of society rather than on theories which refer to characteristics of rapists.

The findings indicate that the combination of sexism, social disorganization, unemployment, economic inequality, and the alienating conditions of urban life constitutes a mix of societal characteristics that precipitates rape. To the extent that this interpretation is correct, it recommends social policies directed toward mitigating the conditions that make rape more likely to occur.

Although we have no illusions that rape can be totally eliminated, the low incidence rates that characterize some states and several countries suggest that high rape rates can be reduced. Efforts to reduce rape by treating individual rapists, reducing the opportunities for rape through neighborhood crime watches, increased use of safety precautions, and self-defense courses for women are all appropriate remedies (Lavrakas, 1985). However, they are essentially stopgap measures which help thwart rapes, not prevention in the sense of primary prevention (Kessler and Albee, 1975).

Primary Prevention

The concept of primary prevention is borrowed from the fields of public health and mental health. In a paraphrase of a definition from Caplan (1964), we argue that primary prevention of rape involves lowering its incidence by counteracting harmful circumstances *before they have had a chance to produce rape*. Primary prevention does not seek to prevent a specific person from committing rape; instead, it seeks to reduce the risk for a whole population. The outcome envisioned as a result of primary prevention is that, although some individuals will continue to rape, their number will be reduced.

Primary prevention therefore requires policies aimed at reducing the root causes of rape. These policies affect every aspect of social behavior ranging from how male and female children are socialized to huge military expenditures that legitimate violence in society. What follows is by no means a comprehensive list, but it suggests that there are many important and practical steps which can be taken to reduce rape.

- We can construct a society in which women have equal rights with men in all spheres of life. Passage of an equal rights amendment is one step in that direction. Another important step is to eliminate the gender gap in income, which results from the lower wage rates in "female occupations" compared to "male occupations," despite the same level of training and skill. This can be remedied by adopting the principle of equal pay for jobs of comparable worth. The policies of the Scandinavian countries, particularly Sweden, indicate that much can be accomplished along these lines in only a few decades.

• The demoralizing and brutalizing conditions of poverty and economic inequality can and should be eradicated. Again, the virtual elimination of poverty in northern European countries, which have a lower level of overall wealth per capita, indicates that this is not a pie-in-the-sky goal.

• The alienation and stress of urban life can be reduced by strengthening family and community ties and creating new neighborhood-based institutions which provide the social support and social control of traditional institutions without their stultifying conservatism.

• Male gender roles, in both sexual and nonsexual relationships, can be restructured to emphasize warmth, equality, and supportiveness rather than aloofness, dominance, and violence. The slow but measurable progress made in this direction in the past two decades provides a basis for believing that this is a feasible national goal.

In our opinion, the major obstacle standing in the way of primary prevention of rape lies in the fact that there are powerful segments of society with a vested interest in preserving a social system that generates a high rape rate. Policies favoring full employment and the elimination of poverty are regarded as too expensive, not just in government expenditures but in the higher wage rates that such programs imply. Similarly, proposals to ensure gender equality are regarded as a threat to both the family and the system of gender stratification that keeps women in a subordinate position. We suspect that the indignation of Attorney General Meese regarding pornography is not so much a reflection of his sexual concerns as it is his political and economic concerns.

The changes that we listed, in addition to their potential for reducing the rape rate, may also help to counteract other forms of criminal violence. In fact, some of the same social conditions that influence the rape rate also influence the homicide rate. Our analysis of state-to-state differences in homicide showed that the homicide rate tends to increase in proportion to increases in urbanization, impoverishment, economic inequality, social disorganization, and cultural support for noncriminal violence (Baron and Straus, 1988). Thus, three aspects of the social origins of rape—urbanization, economic inequality, and social disorganization—also seem to be at the root of high homicide rates. If so, rape may be part of a more general pattern of violence in society and subject to some of the same determinants. Thus, if we attend to these determinants, we are likely to see social changes that will have a wide variety of positive repercussions throughout American society.

APPENDIX A

METHODS USED TO COMPUTE AND STANDARDIZE INDEXES

The following steps were employed to compute each of the main indexes used to test the theories investigated in this study: the Legitimate Violence Index, the Gender Equality Index, the Sex Magazine Circulation Index, the Social Disorganization Index, and the Violence Approval Index.

Data Cleaning

Before we actually computed each of the indexes, the descriptive statistics for each of the indicators were checked to identify outliers, missing data, and unequal variances among the indicators. When problems were discovered, the procedures listed below were followed.

SUBSTITUTIONS FOR MISSING VALUES. If only a single indicator was missing for a state, it seemed best to avoid losing that state from the study because of one missing item in one index. Consequently, we substituted an estimated value for the missing observation. In most cases, the value substituted was the mean of the other states in the region. However, in a few instances other methods were used.

OUTLIERS. The frequency distributions for all items were inspected to locate outliers. Outliers refer to extreme scores. When an outlier was located, it was replaced by a less extreme value in order to prevent that one indicator from having an overwhelming influence on the index score for a state. For example, the circulation rate of sex magazines in Alaska is considerably higher than the circulation rate in the next highest state, Nevada. Similarly, Nevada's circulation rate is much higher than Wyoming, which follows it in the state ranks. Consequently, for purposes of computing the score of Alaska and Nevada on the Sex Magazine Circulation Index, the rates of Alaska and Nevada were adjusted by assigning them values just higher than the preceding states.

Two criteria were used to define outliers: (1) a value that is one or more standard deviations above or below the next value, and (2) a value that is more than 2.5 standard deviations from the mean for all states. All values that met both these criteria were replaced by a value slightly higher or lower than the value for the next state. Thus, the rates for Alaska and Nevada were recoded before transforming the circulation rates to Z scores. The rate for Alaska was changed from 59.01 to 44.00 and Nevada was changed from 49.75 to 42.00. However, the tables displaying the states in rank order according to a specific indicator show the distribution of the states before the adjustment.

Standardization of the Indicators

A last step before actually computing each index was to convert the component indicators to Z scores. This procedure was followed in order to create an index in which each of the components contributes equally to the overall index. If the raw score versions had been added together, some indicators would contribute much more than others because they have larger means and standard deviations. Since Z scoring transforms the items so that they all have the same mean (zero) and the same standard deviation (one), the use of Z-scored indicators result in an index which gives each indicator approximately the same weight in the overall index.

Indexing Method and Standardization

Each index was created by summing the Z-scored versions of the indicators. For certain indexes, this was accomplished as part of the factor analysis. The SCSS factor analysis procedure standardizes the items before outputting a factor-weighted index. We also carried out a further transformation—a modification of the Z scores, called the ZP score (Straus, 1980).

ZP scores, like T scores, are an attempt to avoid some of the difficulty with Z scores experienced by readers who lack a detailed knowledge of statistics. As in the case of the Z score, the ZP score transformation creates a variable in which the units have a known meaning (deviation units from the mean). However, ZP scoring includes an additional transformation designed to avoid negative numbers. These transform the Z score into a score with a mean of 50, a standard deviation of 20, and a range of 0 to 100. Zero is assigned to cases which are 2.5 or more standard deviations below the mean, and 100 is the ZP score for cases which are 2.5 or more standard deviations above the mean.

The interpretation of ZP scores can focus on either the fact that each change of one ZP score point is a change of 1% of the 0 to 100 score range, or focus on the fact that each change of 20 ZP score points is a change of one standard deviation. Thus, statistically trained readers can interpret ZP scores in terms of standard deviations units, and other readers can interpret ZP scores as showing the percentage of the maximum score.

Reliability

The SPSS reliability program was used to analyze the internal consistency reliability of each index. The reliability program computes a variety of statistics, including information on the contribution of each indicator to the overall index and the alpha coefficient of reliability. In the case of the Gender Equality Index, we used item analysis statistics as a means of refining the index (see chapter 4 on the Gender Equality Index for specifics).

APPENDIX B

CORRELATION MATRIX

Appendix B
Correlation Matrix of Variables in Model 8.1

Variables	1	2	3	4	5	6	7	8	9	10	11	12
1. Rape Rate, 1980-1982	1.00											
2. Sex Magazine Circulation, 1979	.64***	1.00										
3. Gender Equality, 1977-1983	.23	.56***	1.00									
4. Legitimate Violence, 1882-1980	.22	.33*	-.26*	1.00								
5. Social Disorganization, 1975-1980	.68***	.83***	.51***	.48***	1.00							
6. Percent Residing in SMSAs, 1980	.36**	-.05	.19	-.54***	-.09	1.00						
7. Gini Index, 1979	.09	-.39**	-.55***	.28*	-.19	-.18	1.00					
8. Percent Black, 1980	.15	-.39**	-.55***	.10	-.32*	.19	.61***	1.00				
9. Percent Age 18-24, 1980	.14	.35**	.00	.29*	.23	-.17	-.10	-.10	1.00			
10. Percent Male of Population Age 15-24, 1980	.38**	.58***	.31*	.23	.49***	-.14	-.01	-.12	.53***	1.00		
11. Percent Single Males Age 15+, 1979	.09	.15	.32*	-.42**	-.06	.39**	-.26*	-.05	.35**	.22	1.00	
12. Percent Unemployed, 1980	17	-.01	.08	-.11	.03	-.02	.12	.06	-.23	-.12	-.07	1.00
Mean	31.66	24.49	50.00	50.04	49.82	61.37	34.48	9.14	13.46	50.45	29.30	6.38
Standard Deviation	14.47	8.25	20.01	19.96	19.45	22.85	1.81	9.22	.75	1.09	2.60	1.55

Note: * p < .05, ** p < .01, *** p < .001.

APPENDIX C

METHODOLOGICAL ANALYSES

In addition to the substantive analyses reported in the chapters 3–8, we carried out several methodological tests to investigate a number of threats to the validity of those analyses.

Regression Assumptions

Before proceeding with the regression analysis reported in chapter 8, the data were inspected for violation of the assumptions required for multiple regression, including departures from linearity, multicollinearity, and outliers.

LINEARITY. This factor was examined by plotting the decile version of each exogenous variable against each endogenous variable. The test of linearity provided by the breakdown procedure indicated that only the joint distribution of the percentage of blacks and the Legitimate Violence Index deviated significantly from linearity. However, a comparison of two separate regressions of the Legitimate Violence Index on the percentage of blacks and the other control variables, one using the linear equation and the other using a squared term, yielded similar results. As a result, the linear equation was retained and employed in the analysis.

MULTICOLLINEARITY. The zero-order correlations of all the variables in the model (see appendix B) were examined for any excessively high coefficients that might suggest a problem with multicollinearity. None of the variables in the model showed a pattern of correlations indicative of multicollinearity.

OUTLIERS. Inspection of the regression diagnostics showed a high value of Cooks D statistic for Alaska and Nevada on the Sex Magazine Circulation Index (SMCX2), and for Alaska on the rape rate. We therefore replicated the regression of the rape rate on the full model after adjusting the outliers. The outliers were adjusted by assigning scores to the extreme cases that were approximately 2.5 standard deviations above the mean, thereby enabling us to moderate the influence of states with extreme scores without changing their relative ranking.

The replication entailed two regression analyses. In each replication, adjusted versions of the variables were used instead of the unadjusted versions. In the first, the rape rate was regressed on the full model with the exception that the adjusted SMCX2 was used. In the second, the adjusted rape rate was regressed on the adjusted SMCX2 and the other variables in the model. In each regression, the results were comparable to the original model. The results of the first replication showed that all the variables significantly associated with rape in the original regression were significantly related at

.07 or better in the reanalysis. In the second replication, the same set of independent variables emerged as significant predictors of the rape rate, but the magnitude of the path coefficients differed for those in figure 8.2. The path coefficient of the Social Disorganization Index (SDX) increased from .402 to .593, whereas the path coefficient of the SMCX2 decreased from .599 to .382. These differences notwithstanding, the replications provide evidence that the results reported in the reduced model are relatively stable.

Controls for Reporting Error

A major assumption of this study is that the large differences among states in rapes reported to the police reflect, for the most part, differences in the true incidence of rape. However, there are grounds for believing that some of the variation among states may be due to coverage of the UCR system, expenditures for law enforcement, and the willingness of women to report rather than actual differences among the states.

COVERAGE OF THE UCR. The participation of local police departments in the UCR system is voluntary. When the system started in the 1930s, only a limited number of urban police departments participated. By 1970, 97% of the population living in metropolitan areas were served by police departments that participated in the UCR system; 88% of the population in other cities, and 79% of the rural population. By 1980, the figures had increased to 98, 96, and 94%, respectively. However, these averages conceal the fact that, even in 1980, some states had a low percentage of their population covered. For example, only 53% of the rural areas of Mississippi and 63% of the rural areas of Missouri were covered by the UCR system in 1980.

To the extent that the percent covered is an indicator of police commitment to keeping accurate records and efficiency in recording crime, we would expect it to be correlated with the rape rate because states with a high level of commitment are likely to be successful in registering more of the crimes which actually occur. In order to test this possibility, we computed the correlation between the percent of each state's population included in the UCR reporting system and the rape rate (Baron and Straus, 1984). Separate correlations were computed for metropolitan areas, other cities, and rural areas in 1970 and 1980. If percent covered reflects police commitment, and if police commitment is what accounts for state-to-state differences in rates of rape, all these correlations should be positive and statistically significant. Instead, there was a mixture of low positive and low negative coefficients, none of which was significant. It is unlikely, then, that the findings are confounded by UCR coverage.

EXPENDITURES FOR LAW ENFORCEMENT. An additional factor that might influence the number of rapes that come to the attention of the police is state-to-state differences in the resources allocated for police protection. States with larger budgets for law enforcement can hire more police and utilize more efficient and precise methods of tabulating crime. Consequently, high rates of rape could reflect state differences in the level of police effectiveness rather than real differences in the incidence of rape.

In order to test this, police expenditure per capita for 1980 was correlated with the average rape rate for the years 1980–82. A correlation of .52 was found. However, when the regression of the rape rate on the full model was replicated with the addition of police expenditures to the equation, the results showed that, after we controlled for the other variables in the model, police expenditure was not significantly associated with the rape rate.

Propensity to Report Rape

Another possible source of reporting error might be state-to-state differences in the willingness of women to report rape to the police. Since feminists have been actively involved in the antirape movement and have struggled for changes in existing rape laws, we surmised that feminist organizations and ideology would encourage women to report their victimization to the police. If we assume that this is true, it might be expected that states with a higher level of feminist sentiment would have higher rates of reported rape. Consequently, we searched for indicators that might serve as proxies for the level of feminist sentiment. We investigated four such measures: (1) the number of rape crisis centers per 100,000 females, 1979; (2) the number of battered women's shelters per 100,000 females, 1980; (3) membership in the National Organization for Women per 100,000 females, 1979; and (4) the circulation of *Ms.* magazine per 100,000 females for the March issue, 1979.

THE NUMBER OF RAPE CRISIS CENTERS, 1980. The inclusion of rape crisis centers was based on the assumption that, in addition to providing services to their clients, these organizations also make efforts to change police practices and to create a climate of opinion that could increase the number of victims who report a rape to the police. Rape crisis centers may give women greater hope of securing justice, or at least of being treated humanely, and may encourage rape victims to report their victimization to the police. Because many of these services are a product of the women's movement (Kalmuss and Strauss, 1983), the availability of rape crisis services is also an indirect indicator of feminist consciousness.

We obtained the number of rape crisis services in each state by counting the number of services listed for each state in the National Directory of Rape Prevention and Treatment Resources, published by the National Center for the Prevention and Control of Rape (1981). The number of services in each state was converted to a rate per 100,000 females. Substantial differences were found among the states in the availability of rape crisis services. It ranged from a low of 1.5 per 100,000 females to a high of 46.9 per 100,000 females, with a mean of 8.6 and a standard deviation of 7.8. Thus, there is more than enough state-to-state variation to use in correlations and multiple regression.

Our analysis revealed a correlation of .22 between the availability of rape crisis services and the average rape rate for the years 1980–82. Although this association is not statistically significant, there may be a slight tendency for state differences in the UCR rape rate to be influenced by state differences in willingness of women to report this crime to the police. However, as with most correlational evidence, other interpretations are also possible. For example, the results could reflect some unidentified measurement error, or the causal direction could go the other way (states with a high incidence of rape could have more rape crisis services because of a greater need for such services). To further explore this relationship, we replicated the regression of rape on the full model with rape crisis centers added to the equation. The results showed that rape crisis centers are not significantly associated with rape net of the other variables in the equation.

NUMBER OF BATTERED WOMEN SHELTERS, 1980. A central priority of the battered women's movement has been the establishment of shelters or safe houses for abused women and their children. Shelters offer women a safe place to live and, depending on the budget of particular shelters, may provide such services as legal aid, therapy, and victim advocacy. An important organizational goal of feminist-run shelters is to empower the victims of abuse. This is closely tied to the notion of self-help, whereby abused women are encouraged to make decisions for themselves and to limit their dependence on spouses and professionals in the helping industry (Schechter, 1982). Since shelters advocate that women assert their legal rights, it is possible that shelters contribute to a cultural climate that encourages women to report rape to the police.

The data on battered women shelters come from *The Spouse Abuse Yellow Pages* (Back and During, 1981) and the Center for Women's Policy Studies 1980 publication "Programs Providing Services to Battered Women." The number of shelters in each state was transformed into a rate per 100,000 females. The state with the fewest number of shelters is Louisiana, which has less than one shelter per 100,000 females. Conversely, Alaska has more shelters than any other state with almost five shelters per 100,000 females. The correlation between the number of shelters and the average rape rate for the 1980–82 period is .08. A more rigorous test was performed by entering the measure of wife abuse shelters into the regression of rape on the full model. However, the results showed that the availability of wife abuse services is not significantly related to the rape rate.

MEMBERSHIP IN THE NATIONAL ORGANIZATION FOR WOMEN, 1980. The National Organization for Women (NOW) has been in existence since 1966 and continues to be a leading advocate of services for victimized women. Since rape has been an issue that NOW has focused on for several years, including emphasis on women's legal rights, states with a larger membership in NOW might appear to have a higher incidence of rape because more of the rapes occurring in these states are reported than in other states.

The data on NOW membership come from its national headquarters in Washington, D.C. The membership figure for each state was converted to a rate per 100,000 females. There is substantial variation among the states in NOW membership. Wyoming had the lowest membership rate with 130 members per 100,000 women, whereas California had the highest rate of 22,880 members per 100,000 women. The association between NOW membership and the average rape rate for the years 1980–82 is low and not statistically significant ($r = .18$). Despite the low coefficient, the positive directionality suggests that there might be a tendency for the rape rate to be influenced by the level of feminist organizations in the states. To investigate this possibility, we replicated the regression of the full model on the rape rate with the addition of NOW membership to the equation. The results showed that membership in NOW does not significantly affect state-to-state differences in reported rapes.

CIRCULATION RATE OF MS. MAGAZINE FOR THE MARCH 1979 ISSUE. Printed material provides important ideological support for any social movement. One of the first mass-circulated feminist magazines was *Ms.*, which began publication in 1972. Although *Ms.* has a predominantly middle-class readership, it addresses a wide variety of feminist issues, including violence against women. Since *Ms.* magazine is the most well known and widely read feminist publication (*Ms.* has the highest circulation rate of any feminist journal or magazine), we decided to use it as a measure of feminist sentiment within each state.

The data on the number of copies of *Ms.* sold for the March issue of 1979 were obtained from the Audit Bureau of Circulation (ABC). The ABC reports the combined newsstand and subscription sales for each state. This figure was then transformed to a rate per 100,000 females. We found extensive state differences in *Ms.* circulation rates, ranging from 51 copies per 100,000 females in Ohio to a high of 970 copies per 100,000 females in Alaska. The correlation between the circulation rate of *Ms.* and the average rape rate for the period 1980–82 is .35 ($p < .01$). Consequently, women may be more willing to report rape in states that have a greater feminist sentiment.

This was further tested by entering the measure of *Ms.* circulation rates into a regression analysis of the rape rate on the overall model. The results indicated that the circulation of *Ms.* magazine does significantly affect reported rapes, independent of the other variables in the model. This finding suggests that some fraction of the state variation in rape may be attributed to differences in the willingness of women to report. However, since the other measures of feminist sentiment are not significantly related to rape, it seems that reporting effects play a minimal role in accounting for state-to-state differences in the UCR rape rate.

SEXUAL LIBERALISM, 1972–84. Another factor that might influence the willingness of women to report a rape to the police is the degree of sexual liberalism. Although rape victims everywhere are reluctant to report because they may fear reprisals, feel stigmatized, or may be accused of instigating the rape, we think that victims may be less likely to report a rape in some states than others. For example, it is possible that a victim would be more reluctant to report rape to the police and risk stigmatization by friends and family in a more rural state like North Dakota than in a state like California, where there is greater anonymity and a more liberal sexual climate. Consequently, we correlated a measure of sexual liberalism and the average rape rate for the years 1980–82.

The Sexual Liberalism Index (SLX) is composed of 22 items from the General Social Survey which address such issues as attitudes toward premarital and extramarital intercourse, homosexuality, abortion, birth control, sex education, and pornography (for details see Jaffee and Straus, 1987). All the items were entered into a principal components analysis and loaded on one factor. The alpha coefficient of reliability for the composite index is .96.

Since the SLX was constructed by aggregating individual survey responses, there were not enough data to justify assigning scores to 10 states. As a result, only 40 states are included in the SLX. This is a sufficient number of cases to perform a correlation analysis, but the results can no longer be interpreted as representative of all 50 states. The zero-order correlation between the SLX and the rape rate is .23. This association is not statistically significant, but it does suggest that rates of rape have a slight tendency to increase in more sexually liberal states. However, this relationship did not hold up in a multivariate analysis of the 1980 rape rate (Jaffee and Straus, 1987). It is unlikely, then, that sexual liberalism has an appreciable effect on the willingness of women to report rape to the police.

Possible Confounding Variables: Southernness, Westernness, and Illegitimate Opportunities

In addition to the variables included in the path model, there are many others that could conceivably explain the differences among states in the incidence of rape. Theory and research on the precursors of violent crime suggest that the rape rate might be influenced by such factors as a southern culture of violence, the frontier tradition of western states, and the expansion of opportunities for criminal violence. In order to test these alternative explanations, three more replications of the rape rate on the full model were performed.

SOUTHERNNESS. It has been recognized for many years that southern states have high rates of criminal violence relative to states in other regions of the country. This has been attributed to a southern culture of violence (Gastil, 1971; Hackney, 1969; Huff-Corzine, Corzine, and Moore, 1986; Messner, 1983; Rosenfeld, 1986). It is suggested that the southern legacy of violence has become embedded in the culture of southern states and is now a major source of violent crime (Reed, 1977).

Although the research on the southern culture of violence has focused on explaining homicide and assault it is possible that many of the same conditions that increase the likelihood of nonsexual violence may be implicated in rape (see Blau and Blau, 1982, for an application of the southern culture of violence thesis to rape). The influence of southernness on rates of rape was examined by including a Confederate South dummy variable in the analysis (1 = Confederate states, 0 = Nonsouthern states). The Confederate South variable is composed of the 11 southern states that seceded from the union between the years 1860 and 1861. The replication entailed a regression of the rape rate on the full model with the addition of the Confederate South variable. The results showed that the Confederate South is not significantly associated with rape. Consequently, we have no reason to believe that southernness confounds the results reported in the trimmed model.

WESTERNNESS. Although the South has the highest rate of homicide, there are reasons for regarding the West as the most violence-prone region. Although the western region has a somewhat lower murder rate than the South, it has a higher rate for the other three major violent crimes (rape, robbery, and aggravated assault). Moreover, the fact that the western states have both the highest rate of rapes known to the police, plus the highest score on the Legitimate Violence Index and the Sex Magazine Circulation Index, raises the possibility that our findings are really a "western effect." To test this, we created a dummy variable in which the 13 western states (as defined by the Census Bureau) were coded 1 and all other states as 0. The regression analysis was then replicated with the addition of this variable. The results revealed that, when we take into account the other variables in the model, westernness is not significantly associated with rape.

ILLEGITIMATE OPPORTUNITIES. For quite some time, researchers have noted monthly variations in rates of criminal violence (Amir, 1971:71–86). The UCR indicates that the rape rate is highest during the summer months and lowest during the winter. This raises the possibility that opportunities to rape may increase during warm weather months because people are more likely to participate in activities that could possibly increase the risk of sexual assault. Following this logic, we might expect that women living in states with relatively warm temperatures during the winter months are in greater danger of being raped than women living in less temperate states.

This idea was tested by including a measure of the average temperature during the winter of 1980 in a regression of the rape rate on the full model. It is interesting that there is substantial variation among states on this measure, with the warmest winter states being Hawaii, Florida, Louisiana, and Texas, and the coldest winter states being Alaska, North Dakota, and Minnesota. However, the results of the regression analysis showed that warm winters are not significantly associated with the rape rate.

Interaction Effects

Laboratory experimental studies of pornography and aggressive behavior have shown that exposing previously angered men to pornography results in increased aggressiveness toward women, but only if the sexual depictions are combined with acts of physical violence (Donnerstein, Linz, and Penrod, 1987). Perhaps a similar process also operates at the societal level. To find this out, we explored the possibility that the link between sex magazine circulation and the incidence of rape exists only in states that have a high rate of legitimate violence.

This hypothesis was tested by constructing two different interaction terms and inserting them in separate regressions of the rape rate on the full model. One interaction term was obtained by dichotomizing the Legitimate Violence Index (LVX) at the median, constructing a dummy variable (1 = scores above the median, 0 = scores below the median), and multiplying the dummy variable by the SMCX2. The other interaction term was derived by simply multiplying the SMCX2 by the LVX. The two regression analyses showed that neither interaction term significantly influences the rape rate.

Summary

Our attempts to discover spurious relationships have not been very successful despite approaching the issue from several perspectives and with a variety of measures. Consequently, the findings presented in chapter 8 continue to provide the best estimates of the state-level determinants of rape.

APPENDIX D

REFERENCES TO DATA SOURCES

Sources for Variables Used in Chapter 2

Variable	Variable Label and Source Document	Year
ckf29	Rapes Known to the Police per 100,000 Population	
	Bureau of Justice Statistics. 1981. *Sourcebook of Criminal Justice Statistics—1980.* Washington, D.C.: U.S. Government Printing Office.	1980
Ncs1t	National Crime Survey Rape Rate: Largest Ten States per 100,000 Females	1974
	National Crime Survey. 1974. Microfilm of rape data for the ten largest states. The data were obtained from the Criminal Justice Archive and Information Network (CJAIN), Institute for Social Research, University of Michigan, Ann Arbor, Michigan.	
blk80	Percent of the Population Black	1980
	Bureau of the Census. 1982. *State and Metropolitan Area Data Book.* Washington, D.C.: U.S. Government Printing Office.	

Sources for Variables Used in Chapter 3

Variable	Variable Label and Source Document	Year
v1085	Rapes Known to the Police: State Rates per 100,000 Population	1960
	Federal Bureau of Investigation. 1960. *Uniform Crime Reports.* Washington, D.C.: U.S. Government Printing office.	
v1095	Rapes Known to the Police: State Rates per 100,000 Population	1970
	Federal Bureau of Investigation. 1970. *Uniform Crime Reports.* Washington, D.C.: U.S. Government Printing Office.	
ckf29	Rapes Known to the Police: State Rates per 100,000 Population	1980
ckf25r	Rapes Known to the Police: Standard Metropolitan Statistical Area Rates per 100,000 Population	1980
ckf26r	Rapes Known to the Police: Other Cities Rates per 100,000 Population	1980
ckf27r	Rapes Known to the Police: Rural Area Rates per 100,000 Population	1980

Bureau of Justice Statistics. 1981. *Sourcebook of Criminal Justice Statistics—1980*. Washington, D.C.: U.S. Government Printing Office.

met80	Percent of the Population Residing in Standard Metropolitan Statistical Areas	1980
blk80	Percent of the Population Black	1980
c78s	Ratio of Males to Females Age 15–24	1980
yng80	Percent of the Population Age 18–24	1980
pov80	Percent of the Population below Poverty Level Income	1980

Bureau of the Census. 1982. *State and Metropolitan Area Data Book*. Washington, D.C.: U.S. Government Printing Office.

gini79fx   Gini Index of Income Inequality

Bureau of the Census. 1979. "Provisional Estimates   1979
of Social, Economic, and Housing Characteristics
of States and Selected Metropolitan Areas."
(Publication No. PHC80-S1-1). Washington,
D.C.: U.S. Government Printing Office.

cp62r   Percent Single of the Male Population Age 15 and   1979
           Older

Bureau of the Census. 1982. "Provisional Estimates
of Social, Economic, and Housing Characteristics,
1980." (Census of Population and Housing
Document No. PHC80-S1-1). Washington, D.C.:
U.S. Government Printing Office.

cb107r   Percent of the Civilian Labor Force Unemployed   1980

Bureau of the Census. 1983. *County and City Data Book*. Washington, D.C.: U.S. Government Printing Office.

rap3   Rapes Known to the Police: State Rates per 100,000
           Population   1980–82

Bureau of Justice Statistics. 1981. *Sourcebook of Criminal Justice Statistics—1980*. Washington, D.C.: U.S. Government Printing Office.

Bureau of Justice Statistics. 1982. *Sourcebook of Criminal Justice Statistics—1981*. Washington, D.C.: U.S. Government Printing Office.

Bureau of Justice Statistics. 1983. *Sourcebook of Criminal Justice Statistics—1982*. Washington, D.C.: U.S. Government Printing Office.

Sources for Variables Used in Chapter 4

Variable	*Variable Label and Source Document*	*Year*
swre1	Percent of Women Relative to Men in the Civilian Labor Force	1982

swre2   Percent of Women Relative to Men in Professional and
           Technical Occupations   1982
swre3   Percent of Women Relative to Men Who Are Managers
           and Administrators in Nonfarm Occupations   1982
swre4   Percent of Women Who Are Employed Relative to Men
           Who Are Employed   1982
              Bureau of Labor Statistics. 1982. *Geographic Profile of*
              Employment and Unemployment: Estimates for States.
              Washington, D.C.: U.S. Government Printing
              Office.
swre5   Median Income of Female Workers Relative to the
           Median Income of Male Workers   1979
              Bureau of the Census. 1980. *Census of Population:*
              General and Social Economic Characteristics.
              Washington, D.C.: U.S. Government Printing
              Office.
swre6   Percent of Small Business Association Loans Given to
           Women Relative to Percent Given to Men   1977
swre7   Percent of Small Business Association Loan Money
           Lent to Women Relative to Percent Lent to Men   1977
              Task Force on Women Business Owners. 1978. *The*
              Battle Line: Unequal Enterprise in America.
              Washington, D.C.: U.S. Government Printing
              Office.
swre8   Percent of Female-Headed Families above Poverty
           Level Relative to Male-Headed Families above Poverty
           Level   1979
              Bureau of the Census. 1982. *State and Metropolitan*
              Area Data Book. Washington, D.C.: U.S.
              Government Printing Office.
swxe2   Economic Gender Equality Subindex   1977–82
              = (Swre1 + Swre3 + Swre4 + Swre5 + Swre6 + Swre7
              + Swre8)/7
swrp1   Percent of U.S. Congress Members Who Are Women
           Relative to Percent Who Are Men   1983
swrp2   Percent of State Senate Members Who Are Women
           Relative to Percent Who Are Men   1983
swrp3   Percent of State House Members Who Are Women
           Relative to Percent Who Are Men   1983
              Center for the American Woman and Politics. 1984.
              National Information Bank on Women in Public Office.
              New Brunswick, N.J.: Eagleton Institute of Politics,
              Rutgers University.

swrp4	Percent of Major Trial and Appellate Court Judges	
	Who Are Women Relative to Percent Who Are Men	1979
	Bureau of the Census. 1982. *Statistical Abstract of the*	
	United States, 103rd Edition. Washington, D.C.:	
	U.S. Government Printing Office.	
swrp5	Percent of Mayors Who Are Women Relative to Percent	
	Who Are Men	1983
swrp6	Percent of Governing Board Members Who Are	
	Women Relative to Percent Who Are Men	1983
	Center for the American Woman and Politics. 1983.	
	Women in Elective Office County and Municipal. New	
	Brunswick, N.J.: Eagleton Institute of Politics,	
	Rutgers University.	
swxp2b	Political Gender Equality Subindex	
	$= (\text{Swrp2m} + \text{Swrp3m} + \text{Swrp5m} + \text{Swrp6m})/4$	1979–83
swl1	State-Passed Fair Employment Practices Act	1980
swl2	Women May File Lawsuit Personally under Fair	
	Employment Practices Act	1980
swl3	State-Passed Equal Pay Laws	1980
swl4	Women May File Lawsuit Personally under Equal Pay	
	Laws	1980
swl5	Sex Discrimination Law in the Area of Public	
	Accommodations	1980
swl6	Sex Discrimination Law in the Area of Housing	1980
swl7	Sex Discrimination Law in the Area of Financing	1980
swl8	Sex Discrimination Law in the Area of Education	1980
swl9	State Requires Wife to Change Her Name at Marriage	1980
swl10	Statutes Provide for Civil Injunction Relief for Victims	
	of Abuse	1980
swl11	Statutes Provide Temporary Injunction Relief during	
	Divorce, Separation, or Custody Proceedings	1980
swl12	Statutes That Define the Physical Abuse of a Family or	
	Household Member as a Criminal Offense	1980
swl13	Statutes That Permit Warrantless Arrest Based on	
	Probable Cause in Domestic Violence Cases	1980
swl14	Statute That Requires Data Collection and Reporting	
	of Family Violence by Agencies That Serve These	
	Families	1980
swl15	Statutes That Provide Funds for Family Violence	
	Shelters or Established Standards for Shelter	
	Operations	1980
swxl2	Legal Gender Equality Subindex	1980
	$= ((\text{Swl1} + \text{Swl2} + \text{Swl3} + \text{Swl4} + \text{Swl5} +$	

	Swl6+SWl7+Swl8+Swl10+Swl12+	
	Swl13+Swl14+Swl15)/ 13)*100	
	Ross, Susan Keller, and Ann Barcher. 1983. *The Rights of Women: The Basic ACLU Guide to a Woman's Rights.* New York: Bantam Books.	
swx2zb	Gender Equality Index	1977–83
	= (swxe2+swxp2b+swxl2)/3	
z251	Percent of the Population Residing in Standard Metropolitan Statistical Areas	1978
	Bureau of the Census. 1980. *Statistical Abstract of the United States.* Washington, D.C.: U.S. Government Printing Office.	
ea8	Median Age	1980
	Bureau of the Census. 1980. *Census of the Population: General Population Characteristics*, Vol. 1, Part 1. Washington, D.C.: U.S. Government Printing Office.	
cp274	Median Income	1978
	Bureau of the Census. 1982. "Provisional Estimate of Social, Economic, and Housing Characteristics, 1980." Census of Population and Housing Document No. PHC80-S1-1. Washington, D.C.: U.S. Government Printing Office.	
z94r3	Number of National Organization for Women Groups per 100,000 Population	1980
	National Organization for Women. 1980. Data obtained from a staff member at the NOW National Office in Washington, D.C.	
rap3	Rapes Known to the Police: State Rates per 100,000 Population	1980–82
	Bureau of Justice Statistics. 1981. *Sourcebook of Criminal Justice Statistics—1980.* Washington, D.C.: U.S. Government Printing Office.	
	Bureau of Justice Statistics. 1982. *Sourcebook of Criminal Justice Statistics—1981.* Washington, D.C.: U.S. Government Printing Office.	
	Bureau of Justice Statistics. 1983. *Sourcebook of Criminal Justice Statistics—1982.* Washington, D.C.: U.S. Government Printing Office.	
xgs2a	Violence Approval Index	1972–84
	See the references to data source for chapter 7.	

Variable	*GSS Question*	*Response*	*Variable Label*
gs57t1	183	1	Have been punched or beaten by another person

gs58t1	183a	1	Have been punched or beaten as a child
gs58t2	183a	2	Have been punched or beaten as an adult
gs58ts	183a	3	Have been punched or beaten as a child and as an adult
gs59t*	183b	*	Have been punched or beaten two or more times
gs60t1	184	1	Have been threatened with a gun or shot at
gs61t3	184a	3	Have been threatened with a gun or shot at as a child and an adult
gs62t2	184b	2	Have been threatened with a gun or shot at two or more times
gs88t1	191	1	Have gun or revolvers in home
gs89t1	191aa	1	Have handgun in home
gs90t1	191ab	1	Have shotgun in home
gs91t1	191ac	1	Have rifle in home
gs93t**	193a	**	Respondent or spouse hunts
gs94t1	193b	1	Other household member hunts

* Scored if either gs59t2 or gs59t3 is positive.

** Scored if either gs93t1, gs93t2, or gs93t3 is positive.

xgs3a   Violent Behavior Index   1972–84

$$= (gs57t1 + gs58t1 + gs58t2 + gs58t3 + gs59t* + gs60t1 + gs61t3 + gs62t2 + gs88t1 + gs89t1 + gs90t1 + gs91t1 + gs93t** + gs94t1)/14$$

Davis, James A., and Tom Smith. 1985. *General Social Surveys, 1972–1984: Cumulative Codebook*: National Opinion Research Center: University of Chicago.

Variable	GSS Question	Response	Variable Label
gs28t5	127g	5	Gender role is least important quality for a child
gs33t2	157	2	Disagree that women should care for home while men run the country
gs34t1	158	1	Approve of women working outside the home
gs35t1	159	1	Would vote for a woman president
gs36t2	160	2	Disagree that men are better suited emotionally for politics than women

xgs4a   Nontraditional Sex Role Attitudes   1972–83

$$= (gs28t5 + gs33t2 + gs34t1 + gs35t1 + gs36t2)/5$$

Davis, James A., and Tom Smith. 1985. *General Social Surveys, 1972–1984: Cumulative Codebook*. National Opinion Research Center: University of Chicago.

Variable	GSS Question	Response	Variable Label
gs15t1	77a	1	Homosexuals should be allowed to speak in your community
gs16t1	77b	4	Homosexuals should be allowed to teach in college
gs17t2	77c	2	Books favoring homosexuality should not be removed from the public library
gs37t1	162a	1	Abortion is OK if there is a serious defect in baby
gs38t1	162b	1	Abortion is OK if no more children are wanted
gs39t1	162c	1	Abortion is OK is woman's health is endangered
gs40t1	162d	1	Abortion if OK if more children cannot be afforded
gs41t1	162e	1	Abortion is OK if raped
gs42t1	162f	1	Abortion is OK if not married
gs43t1	162g	1	Abortion is Ok for any reason
gs45t1	170b	1	In favor of birth control information for teens
gs46t1	171	1	In favor of sex education in school
gs48t4	174	4	Sex before marriage is not wrong at all
gs50t4	176	4	Homosexual sexual relations are not wrong at all
gs51t1	177a	1	Pornography provides information about sex
gs52t1	177b	1	Pornography leads to breakdown of morals
gs53t2	177c	2	Pornography does not lead to rape
gs54t1	177d	1	Pornography provides a sexual outlet
gs55t3	178	3	Opposed to restrictive laws regarding pornography
gs56t1	179	1	Have seen an x-rated movie in last year
xgsla	Sexual Liberalism Index		1972–84

$$= (gs15t1 + gs16t1 + gs17t2 + gs37t1 + gs38t1 + gs39t1 + gs40t1 + gs41t1 + gs42t1 + gs43t1 + gs45t1 + gs46t1 + gs48t4 + gs50t4 + gs51t1 + gs52t1 + gs53t2 + gs54t1 + gs55t3 + gs56t1)/20$$

Davis, James A., and Tom Smith. 1985. *General Social Surveys, 1972–1984: Cumulative Codebook.* National Opinion Research Center: University of Chicago.

Sources for Variables Used in Chapter 5

Variable	Variable Label and Source Document	Year
ma239r	Circulation of *Playboy* per 100 Males Age 15 and Older	1979
ma151r2	Circulation of *Hustler* per 100 Males Age 15 and Older	1979
ma411r2	Circulation of *Penthouse* per 100 Males Age 15 and Older	1979
ma59r2	Circulation of *Chic* per 100 Males Age 15 and Older	1979
ma66r2	Circulation of *Club* per 100 Males Age 15 and Older	1979
ma123r2	Circulation of *Gallery* per 100 Males Age 15 and Older	1979
ma125r2	Circulation of *Genesis* per 100 Males Age 15 and Older	1979
ma225r2	Circulation of *Oui* per 100 Males Age 15 and Older	1979
rapx20	Sex Magazine Circulation Index	1979

$$\text{rapx20} = (\text{ma239r2} + \text{ma151r2} + \text{ma411r2} + \text{ma59r2} + \text{ma66r2} + \text{ma123r2} + \text{ma125r2} + \text{ma225r2})/8$$

Audit Bureau of Circulation. 1979. *Blue Book of Publisher's Statements of Average Paid Circulation for Six Months Ending June 30, 1979.* Chicago: Audit Bureau of Circulation.

rap3	Rapes Known to the Police: State Rates per 100,000 Population	1980–82

Bureau of Justice Statistics. 1981. *Sourcebook of Criminal Justice Statistics—1980.* Washington, D.C.: U.S. Government Printing Office.

Bureau of Justice Statistics. 1982. *Sourcebook of Criminal Justice Statistics—1981.* Washington, D.C.: U.S. Government Printing Office.

Bureau of Justice Statistics. 1983. *Sourcebook of Criminal Justice Statistics—1983.* Washington, D.C.: U.S. Government Printing Office.

ckf24	Homicides Known to the Police: State Rates per 100,000 Population	1980
ckf34	Robberies Known to the Police: State Rates per 100,000 Population	1980
ckf39	Aggravated Assaults Known to the Police: State Rates per 100,000 Population	1980

Bureau of Justice Statistics. 1980. *Sourcebook of Criminal Justice Statistics—1980.* Washington, D.C.: U.S. Government Printing Office.

Sources for Variables Used in Chapter 6

Variable	Variable Label and Source Document	Year
cb15r	Percent of the Population Moving from a Different State or Abroad	1975–80

	Bureau of the Census. 1984. *County and City Data Book, 1983*. Washington, D.C.: U.S. Government Printing Office.	
rap4r	Ratio of Tourists to Residents	1977
	Bureau of the Census. 1977. "National Travel Survey: Travel During 1977." Washington, D.C.: U.S. Government Printing Office.	
sb98tr	Percent of the Population Divorced	1980
sb117r	Percent of Female-Headed Families with Children under Age 18	1980
	Bureau of the Census. 1982. *State and Metropolitan Area Data Book*. Washington, D.C.: U.S. Government Printing Office.	
rap7r	Percent of the Population with No Religious Affiliation	1980
	Quinn, Bernard, Herman Anderson, Martin Bradley, Paul Goetting, and Peggy Shriver. 1982. *Church and Church Membership in the United States, 1980*. Atlanta, Ga.: Glenmary Research Center.	
rap5	Nonfamilied Male Householders per 1,000 Population	1980
	Data provided by Rodney Stark, Department of Sociology, University of Washington, Seattle, Washington.	
Rapx18	Social Disorganization Index (Factor Weighted) $= ((cb15r^* .24) + (sb98tr^* .23) + (rap5^* .22) + (rap7r^* .20) + (sb117r^* .20) + (rap4r^* .18))$ transformed to a Z score	1977–80
rap3	Rapes Known to the Police: State Rates per 100,000 Population	1980–82
	Bureau of Justice Statistics. 1981. *Sourcebook of Criminal Justice Statistics—1980*. Washington, D.C.: U.S. Government Printing Office.	
	Bureau of Justice Statistics. 1982. *Sourcebook of Criminal Justice Statistics—1981*. Washington, D.C.: U.S. Government Printing Office.	
	Bureau of Justice Statistics. 1983. *Sourcebook of Criminal Justice Statistics—1982*. Washington, D.C.: U.S. Government Printing Office.	

Sources for Variables Used in Chapter 7

Variable	Variable Label and Source Document	Year
cv16a	Violent Television Viewing Index	1980
	A. C. Nielson Company. 1980. "Network Programs by Designated Market Area, Average Weekly Audience Estimates," October 30 to November 26.	

xvmc	Violent Magazine Circulation Index	1979
	Audit Bureau of Circulation. 1979. *Blue Book of*	
	Publisher's Statements of Average Paid Circulation for	
	Six Months Ending June 30, 1979. Chicago: Audit	
	Bureau of Circulation.	
v474r	National Guard Enrollment per 1,000 Population	1976
v475r	National Guard Enrollment per Capita	1976
	Bureau of the Census. 1977. *Statistical Abstract of the*	
	United States. Washington, D.C.: U.S. Government	
	Printing Office.	
c53	State of Origin of NCAA Football Players	1972
	Rooney, John F. 1975. "Sports From a Geographical	
	Perspective." Pp. 51–115 in *Sport and Social Order:*	
	Contributions to the Sociology of Sport, edited by	
	Donald W. Ball and John W. Loy. Reading, Mass.	
cv49er	Hunting Licenses Issued per 100,000 Population	1980
	U.S. Fish and Wildlife Service. 1980. *Federal Aid to*	
	Fish and Wildlife Restoration. Washington, D.C.:	
	U.S. Department of the Interior.	
xcp1	Corporal Punishment Permission Index	1979
	Friedman, Robert H., and Irwin A. Hyman. 1979.	
	"Corporal Punishment in the Schools: A	
	Descriptive Survey of State Regulations." In	
	Corporal Punishment in American Education: Readings	
	in History, Practice and Alternatives, edited by Irwin	
	Hyman and James H. Wise. Philadelphia, Pa.:	
	Temple University Press.	
v1829r	Persons Lynched per Million Population	1882–1927
	White, Walter. 1929. *Rope and Faggot.* New York:	
	A. A. Knopf.	
z266r2	Whites Sentenced to Death per 100,000 White	
	Homicide Arrests	1980
z267r2	Blacks Sentenced to Death per 100,000 Black	
	Homicide Arrests	1980
	Bureau of Justice Statistics. 1981. *Sourcebook of*	
	Criminal Justice Statistics—1980. Washington,	
	D.C.: U.S. Government Printing Office.	
cv59	Ratio of Execution Rate to Homicide Rate	1940–59
	Grove, Robert D., and Alice M. Hetzel. 1968. *Vital*	
	Statistics Rates in the United States, 1940–1960.	
	Washington, D.C.: U.S. Government Printing	
	Office.	
cv60	Ratio of Execution Rate to Homicide Rate	1960–78

Bureau of the Census. 1960–1978. *Statistical Abstract of the United States*. Washington, D.C.: U.S. Government Printing Office.

xcv12	Legitimate Violence Index (Factor Weighted)	1882–1980

$$= ((v475rlz^*.95) + (v474rz^*.86) + (cv49erl^*.74) + (xvmclz^*.69) + (cv16amz^*.05) + (v1829rlz^*.19) + (z266r2z^*-.17) + (cv53z^*.07) + (cv60z^*.03) + (cv59z^*-.06) + (z267r2z^*.37) \text{transformed to a } Z \text{ score}$$

rap3	Rapes Known to the Police: State Rates per 100,000 Population	1980–82

Bureau of Justice Statistics. 1981. *Sourcebook of Criminal Justice Statistics—1980*. Washington, D.C.: U.S. Government Printing Office.

Bureau of Justice Statistics. 1982. *Sourcebook of Criminal Justice Statistics—1981*. Washington, D.C.: U.S. Government Printing Office.

Bureau of Justice Statistics. 1983. *Sourcebook of Criminal Justice Statistics—1982*. Washington, D.C.: U.S. Government Printing Office.

Variable	*GSS Question*	*Response*	*Variable Label*
gs14t1	68i	1	Spending too little on military
gs18t1	79	1	In favor of death penalty for murder
gs19t2	80	2	Oppose requiring gun permits
gs69t1	185	1	OK for a man to punch an adult male
gs70t1	185ra	1	OK for a man to hit a protester with opposing views
gs71t1	185rb	1	OK for a man to hit a drunk who bumped into him and wife
gs72t1	185rc	1	OK for a man to hit someone who hits your child
gs73t1	185rd	1	OK for a man to hit a male if male beat a woman
gs74t1	185re	1	OK for a man to hit a male if he is breaking in
gs80t1	186r	1	OK for police to strike an adult male
gs81t1	186ra	1	OK for police to hit a male saying obscene things to police
gs82t1	186rb	1	OK for police to hit a murder suspect
gs83t1	186rc	1	OK for police to hit male attempting to escape
gs84t1	186rd	1	OK for police to hit male attacking police with his fists

xgs2a   Violence Approval Index   1972–84

$$= (gs14t1 + gs18t1 + gs19t2 + gs69t1 + gs70t1 +$$
$$gs71t1 + gs72t1 + gs73t1 + gs74t1 + gs80t1 + gs81t1 +$$
$$gs82t1 + gs83t1 + gs84t1)/14$$

Davis, James A., and Tom Smith. 1985. *General Social Surveys, 1972–1984: Cumulative Codebook.* National Opinion Research Center: University of Chicago.

Sources for Variables Used in Chapter 8

Variable	Variable Label and Source Document	Year
met80	Percent of the Population Residing in Standard Metropolitan Statistical Areas	1980
blk80	Percent of the Population Black	1980
c78s	Ratio of Males to Females Age 15–24	1980
yng80	Percent of the Population Age 18–24	1980
pov80	Percent of the Population below Poverty Level Income	1980

               Bureau of the Census. 1982. *State and Metropolitan Area Data Book.* Washington, D.C.: U.S. Government Printing Office.

gini79fx	Gini Index of Income Inequality	1979

               Bureau of the Census. 1979. "Provisional Estimates of Social, Economic, and Housing Characteristics of States and Selected Metropolitan Areas." (Publication No. PHC80-81). Washington, D.C.: U.S. Government Printing Office.

cp62r	Percent Single of the Male Population Age 15 and Older	1979

               Bureau of the Census. 1982. "Provisional Estimates of Social, Economic, and Housing Characteristics, 1980." (Census of Population and Housing Document No. PHC80-S1-1). Washington, D.C.: U.S. Government Printing Office.

cb107r	Percent of the Civilian Labor Force Unemployed	1980

               Bureau of the Census. 1981. *County and City Data Book.* Washington, D.C.: U.S. Government Printing Office.

swx2zb	Gender Equality Index	1977–83

               See the references to data sources for chapter 4.

Rapx20	Sex Magazine Circulation Index	1979

               See the references to data sources for chapter 5.

rapx18	Social Disorganization Index	1977–80

               See the references to data sources for chapter 6.

xcv12   Legitimate Violence Index   1882–1980
             See the references to data sources for chapter 7.
xgs2a   Violence Approval Index   1972–84
             See the references to data sources for chapter 7.
rap3   Rapes Known to the Police: State Rates per 100,000
             Population   1980–82
             Bureau of Justice Statistics. 1981. *Sourcebook of
             Criminal Justice Statistics—1980*. Washington,
             D.C.: U.S. Government Printing Office.
             Bureau of Justice Statistics. 1982. *Sourcebook of
             Criminal Justice Statistics—1981*. Washington,
             D.C.: U.S. Government Printing Office.
             Bureau of Justice Statistics. 1983. *Sourcebook of
             Criminal Justice Statistics—1982*. Washington,
             D.C.: U.S. Government Printing Office.

Sources for Variables Used in Appendix C

Variable	Variable Label and Source Document	Year
met80	Percent of the Population Residing in Standard Metropolitan Statistical Areas	1980
blk80	Percent of the Population Black	1980
c78s	Ratio of Males to Females Age 15–24	1980
yng80	Percent of the Population Age 18–24	1980
pov80	Percent of the Population below Poverty Level Income	1980

             Bureau of the Census. 1982. *State and Metropolitcan
             Area Data Book*. Washington, D.C.: U.S.
             Government Printing Office.
gini79fx   Gini Index of Income Inequality   1979
             Bureau of the Census. 1979. "Provisional Estimates
             of Social, Economic, and Housing Characteristics
             of States and Selected Metropolitan Areas."
             (Publication No. PHC80-S1-1). Washington,
             D.C.: U.S. Government Printing Office.
cp62r   Percent Single of the Male Population Age 15 and
             Older   1979
             Bureau of the Census. 1982. "Provisional Estimates
             of Social, Economic, and Housing Characteristics,
             1980." (Census of Population and Housing
             Document No. PHC80-S1-1). Washington, D.C.:
             U.S. Government Printing Office.
cb107r   Percent of the Civilian Labor Force Unemployed   1980
             Bureau of the Census. 1983. *County and City Data
             Book*. Washington, D.C.: U.S. Government
             Printing Office.

swx2zb   Gender Equality Index   1977–83
          See the references to data sources for chapter 4.
Rapx20   Sex Magazine Circulation Index   1979
          See the references to data sources for chapter 5.
rapx18   Social Disorganization Index   1977–80
          See the references to data sources for chapter 6.
xcv12   Legitimate Violence Index   1882–1980
          See the references to data sources for chapter 7.
xgs2a   Violence Approval Index   1972–84
          See the references to data sources for chapter 7.
rap3   Rapes Known to the Police: State Rates per 100,000
          Population   1980–82
          Bureau of Justice Statistics. 1981. *Sourcebook of
              Criminal Justice Statistics—1980.* Washington,
              D.C.: U.S. Government Printing Office.
          Bureau of Justice Statistics. 1982. *Sourcebook of
              Criminal Justice Statistics—1981.* Washington,
              D.C.: U.S. Government Printing Office.
          Bureau of Justice Statistics. 1983. *Sourcebook of
              Criminal Justice Statistics—1982.* Washington,
              D.C.: U.S. Government Printing Office.
rap2r   Police Expenditures: State Rates per Capita   1980
          Bureau of Justice Statistics. 1984. *Sourcebook of
              Criminal Justice Statistics—1983.* Washington,
              D.C.: U.S. Government Printing Office.
v1c   Confederate South Dummy Variable   1861–65
          1 = states in the Confederacy, 0 = all other states
          Faulkner, H. U. 1957. *American Political and Social
              History.* 7th ed. New York: Appleton-Century-
              Crofts.
ckz1   Percentage of Departments Covered by the UCR:
          Standard Metropolitan Statistical Areas   1970
ckz2   Percentage of Departments Covered by the UCR:
          Other Cities   1970
ckz3   Percentage of Departments Covered by the UCR: Rural
          Areas   1970
          Federal Bureau of Investigation. 1971. *Uniform Crime
              Reports.* Washington, D.C.: U.S. Government
              Printing Office.
ckfx1   Percentage of Departments Covered by the UCR:
          Standard Metropolitan Statistical Areas   1980
ckfx2   Percentage of Departments Covered by the UCR:
          Other Cities   1980

ckfx3   Percentage of Departments Covered by the UCR: Rural
            Areas   1980
                Federal Bureau of Investigation. 1981. *Uniform Crime
                Reports. Washington, D.C.: U.S. Government
                Printing Office.
West   Western Region Dummy Variable
                1 = states in the western region, 0 = all other states
v2342   Mean Warm Winter States
                Bureau of the Census. 1980. *Statistical Abstract of the
                United States*, 101st ed. Washington, D.C.: U.S.
                Government Printing Office.
z241rl   Rape Crisis Center for the Prevention and Control of
            Rape. 1981. *National Directory: Rape Prevention and
            Treatment and Resources*. Rockville, Md.: National
            Institute of Mental Health, DHHS Publication No.
            (ADM) 81-1008.
z91rl   Wife Abuse Shelters per 100,000 Females   1980
                Back, Susan, and Linda During. 1981. *Spouse Abuse
                Yellow Pages*. Denver: University of Denver.
z94r1l   Number of National Organization for Women Members
            per 100,000 females   1980
                National Organization for Women. 1980. Data
                obtained from a staff member at the NOW
                National Office in Washington, D.C.
ma202rl   Circulation Rate of the March 1979 Issue of *Ms.*
            magazine per 100,000 females   1979
                Audit Bureau of Circulation. 1979. *Blue Book of
                Publisher's Statements of Average Paid Circulation for
                Six Months Ending June 30, 1979*. Chicago: Audit
                Bureau of Circulation.
xgs1a   Sexual Liberalism Index   1972–84
                See the references to data sources for chapter 4.

REFERENCES

Adamec, Connie Stark, and Robert E. Adamec. 1981. "Aggression by Men Against Women: Adaptation or Abberation." *International Journal of Women's Studies* 5:1–21.

Albrecht, Stan L., Bruce A. Chadwick, and David S. Alcorn. 1977. "Religiousity and Deviance: Application of an Attitude-Behavior Contingent Consistency Model." *Journal for the Scientific Study of Religion* 16:263–274.

American Booksellers, Inc. v. Hudnut, 771 F.2d 323 (7th Cir. 1985), aff'd 106 S.Ct. 1172 (1986).

American Heritage Dictionary of the English Language, 1976. Boston: Houghton Mifflin.

Amir, Menachem. 1971. *Patterns in Forcible Rape.* Chicago: University of Chicago Press.

Andison, F. S. 1977. "TV Violence and Viewer Aggression: A Cumulation of Study Results." *Public Opinion Quarterly* 41:314–331.

Andrews, Alice. 1981. "The State of Women in the Americas." *Journal of Cultural Geography* 2:27–44.

Aneshensel, Carol, Ralph R. Fredrichs, and Virginia A. Clark. 1981. "Family Roles and Sex Differences in Depression." *Journal of Health and Social Behavior* 22:379–393.

Archer, Dane, and Rosemary Gartner. 1984. *Violence and Crime in Cross-National Perspective.* New Haven: Yale University Press.

Asher, Herbert B. 1983. *Causal Modeling.* 2nd ed. Sage University Paper series on Quantitative Applications in the Social Sciences, series no. 07–003. Beverly Hills, Calif.: Sage.

Attorney General's Commission on Pornography. 1986. *Final Report of the Attorney General's Commission on Pornography.* Washington, D.C.: United States Department of Justice.

Atyeo, Don. 1979. *Violence in Sports.* New York: Van Nostrand Reinhold.

Back, Susan M., and Linda During. 1981. *Spouse Abuse Yellow Pages.* Denver: University of Denver.

Bailey, William C. 1984. "Poverty, Inequality, and City Homicide Rates." *Criminology* 22:531–550.

Bane, Mary Jo, and Robert S. Weiss. 1980. "Alone Together: The World of Single-Parent Families." *American Demographics* 2, 5:11–15, 48.

Barnett, Rosiland C., and Grace K. Baruch. 1985. "Women's Involvement in Multiple Roles, and Psychological Distress." *Journal of Personality and Social Psychology* 49:135–145.

Baron, Larry. 1987. "Pornography and its Discontents: Immoral, Inviolate, or Inconclusive?" *Society* (July/August):6–12.

Baron, Larry, and Murray A. Straus. 1983. "Conceptual and Ethical Problems in Research on Pornography." Paper presented at the 1983 Annual Meeting of the Society for the Study of Social Problems.

Baron, Larry, and Murray A. Straus. 1984. "Sexual Stratification, Pornography, and Rape in the United States. Pp. 185–209 in *Pornography and Sexual Aggression*, ed. Neil M. Malamuth and Edward Donnerstein. New York: Academic Press.

Baron, Larry, and Murray A. Straus. 1987. "Four Theories of Rape: A Macrosociological Analysis." *Social Problems*, 34:467–488.

Baron, Larry, and Murray A. Straus. 1988. "Cultural and Economic Sources of Homicide in the United States." *Sociological Quarterly*, 29:371–392.

Baron, Larry, Murray A. Straus, and David Jaffee. 1988. "Legitimate Violence, Violent Attitudes, and Rape: A Test of the Cultural Spillover Theory." Pp. 79–110 in *Human Sexual Aggression: Current Perspectives*, ed. Robert A. Prentky and Vernon L. Quinsey. New York: New York Academy of Sciences.

Benson, Rebecca. 1986. "Pornography and the First Amendment: *American Booksellers v. Hudnut.*" *Harvard Women's Law Journal* 9:153–172.

Barry, Kathleen. 1979. *Female Sexual Slavery.* Englewood Cliffs, N.J.: Prentice-Hall.

Berns, Walter. 1971. "Pornography and Democracy." *The Public Interest* 22:3–24.

Bianchi, Suzanne M., and Daphne Spain. 1983. *American Women: Three Decades of Change.* Washington, D.C.: U.S. Department of Commerce, Bureau of the Census.

Birdwhistell, Ray L. 1970. "The Idealized Model of the American Family." *Social Work* (April):195–198.

Blalock, Hubert M. 1979. "Measurement and Conceptualization Problems: The Major Obstacle to Integrating Theory and Research." *American Sociological Review* 44:881–894.

Blau, Judith R., and Peter M. Blau. 1982. "The Cost of Inequality: Metropolitan Structure and Violent Crime." *American Sociological Review* 47:114–128.

Blau, Peter M., and Reid M. Golden. 1986. "Metropolitan Structure and Criminal Violence." *Sociological Quarterly* 27:15–26.

Blumberg, Rae Lesser. 1978. *Stratification: Socioeconomic and Sexual Inequality.* Dubuque, Iowa: Wm. C. Brown.

Blumberg, Rae Lesser. 1984. "The General Theory of Gender Stratification." Pp. 23–101 in *Sociological Theory*, edited by Randall Collins. San Francisco: Jossey-Bass.

Blumer, Herbert. 1937. "Social Disorganization and Individual Disorganization." *American Journal of Sociology* 42:871–877.

Blumstein, Alfred, Jacqueline Cohen, and Daniel Nagin, eds. 1980. *Deterrence and Incapacitation: Estimating the Effects of Criminal Sanctions on Crime Rates.* Washington, D.C.: National Academy of Science.

Bolen, Kenneth A., and Sally Ward. 1980. "Ratio Variables in Aggregate Data Analysis: Their Uses, Problems and Alternatives." Pp. 60–79 in *Aggregate Data: Analysis and Interpretation*, ed. Edgar F. Borgatta, and David J. Jackson. Beverly Hills, Calif.: Sage.

Bowers, William J. 1984. *Legal Homicide: Death as Punishment in America, 1864–1982.* Cambridge, Mass.: Northeastern University Press.

Braithwaite, John. 1979. *Inequality, Crime, and Public Policy.* London: Routledge & Kegan Paul.

Brenner, M. Harvey. 1978. "Economic Crises and Crime." Pp. 555–572 in *Crime in Society*, ed. Leonard D. Savity and Norman Johnston. New York: John Wiley.

Brindenberg, David, and Louise H. Kidder, eds. 1982. *New Directions for Methodology of Social and Behavioral Science: Forms of Validity in Research.* San Francisco, Calif.: Jossey-Bass.

Bristow, Edward J. 1977. *Vice and Vigilance: Purity Movements in Britain Since 1700.* Totowa, N.J.: Rowman and Littlefield.

Brown, Richard Maxwell. 1979. "The American Vigilante Tradition." Pp. 153–185 in *Violence in America: Historical and Comparative Perspectives*, ed. Hugh Davis Graham and Ted Robert Gurr. Beverly Hills, Calif.: Sage.

Brownmiller, Susan. 1975. *Against Our Will: Men, Women, and Rape.* New York: Simon & Schuster.

Bruce, Dickson D. 1979. *Violence and Culture in the Antebellum South.* Austin: University of Texas Press.

Bureau of Justice Statistics. 1983. *Criminal Victimization in the United States, 1981.* Washington, D.C.: U.S. Department of Justice.

Burgess, Ernest W. 1967. "The Growth of the City: An Introduction to a Research Project." Pp. 47–62 in *The City*, ed. Robert E. Park, Ernest W. Burgess, and Roderick McKenzie. Chicago: University of Chicago Press.

Burkett, Steven R., and Mervin White. 1974. "Hellfire and Delinquency: Another Look." *Journal for the Scientific Study of Religion* 13:455–462.

Bursik, Robert J. 1988. "Social Disorganization and Theories of Crime and Delinquency: Problems and Prospects." *Criminology* 26:519–551.

Burstyn, Varda. 1985. "Political Precedents and Moral Crusades: Women, Sex, and the State." Pp. 4–31 in *Women Against Censorship*, ed. Varda Burstyn. Manchester, N.H.: Salem House.

Burt, Martha R. 1980. "Cultural Myths and Supports for Rape." *Journal of Personality and Social Psychology* 38:217–230.

Byrne, Donn, and Kathryn Kelly. 1984. "Introduction: Pornography and Sex Research." Pp. 1–15 in *Pornography and Sexual Aggression*, ed. Neil M. Malamuth and Edward Donnerstein. Orlando, Fla.: Academic Press.

Campbell, Donald T., and Donald W. Fiske. 1959. "Convergent and Discriminant Validation by the Multitrait-Multimethod Matrix." *Psychological Bulletin* 56:81–105.

Cantor, David, and Lawrence E. Cohen. 1980. "Comparing Measures of Homicide Trends: Methodological and Substantive Differences in the Vital Statistics and Uniform Crime Report Time Series." *Social Science Research* 9:121–145.

Caplan, Gerald. 1964. *Principles of Preventive Psychiatry.* New York: Basic Books.

Carey, James T. 1975. *Sociology and Public Affairs: The Chicago School.* Beverly Hills, Calif.: Sage.

Carr, Edward A. 1987. "Feminism, Pornography, and the First Amendment: An Obscenity-Based Analysis of Proposed Antipornography Laws." *UCLA Law Review* 34:1265–1304.

Chafetz, Janet Saltzman. 1984. *Sex and Advantage: A Comparative Macro-Structural Theory of Sex Stratification.* Totowa, N.J.: Rowman.

Check, James V. P., and Neil M. Malamuth. 1983. "Sex Role Stereotyping and Reactions to Depictions of Stranger Versus Acquaintance Rape." *Journal of Personality and Social Psychology* 45:344–356.

Check, James V. P., and Neil M. Malamuth. 1984. "Can Participation in Pornography Experiments Have Positive Effects?" *Journal of Sex Research* 20:14–31.

Cherry, Frances. 1983. "Gender Roles and Sexual Violence." Pp. 245–260 in *Changing Boundaries: Gender Roles and Sexual Behavior*, ed. Elizabeth Rice Allgeier and Naomi B. McCormick. Palo Alto, Calif.: Mayfield.

Chiricos, Theodore, G. 1987. "Rates of Crime and Unemployment: An Analysis of Aggregate Research Evidence." *Social Problems* 34:187–212.

Clark, L., and D. Lewis. 1977. *Rape: The Price of Coercive Sexuality.* Toronto: Womanpress.

Cohen, Erik. 1984. "The Sociology of Tourism: Approaches, Issues, and Findings." Pp. 373–392 in *Annual Review of Sociology*, ed. Ralph H. Turner and James F. Short, Jr. Palo Alto, Calif.: Annual Reviews.

Cohen, Jacob, and Patricia Cohen. 1983. *Applied Multiple Regression/Correlation Analysis for the Behavioral Sciences.* 2nd ed. Hillsdale, N.J.: Lawrence Erlbaum.

Cohen, Lawrence, James Kluegel, and Kenneth Land. 1981. "Social Inequality and Predatory Criminal Victimization: An Exposition and Test of a Formal Theory." *American Sociological Review* 46:505–524.

Cohen, Stanley, and Laurie Taylor. 1978. *Escape Attempts: The Theory and Practice of Resistance to Everyday Life.* New York: Penguin Books.

Coleman, Diane H., and Murray A. Straus. 1986. "Marital Power, Conflict, and Violence in a Nationally Representative Sample of American Couples." *Violence and Victims* 1:141–157.

Commission on Obscenity and Pornography. 1970. *The Report of the Commission on Obscenity and Pornography.* Washington, D.C.: U.S. Government Printing Office.

Cook, Philip J., and Gary A. Zarkin. 1985. "Crime and the Business Cycle." *Journal of Legal Studies* 14:115–129.

Cook, Thomas D., and Donald T. Campbell. 1979. *Quasi Experimentation: Design and Analysis Issues for Field Settings.* Chicago: Rand McNally.

Court, John H. 1980. *Pornography: A Christian Critique.* Exeter, England: Paternoster Press.

Court, John H. 1984. "Sex and Violence: A Ripple Effect." Pp. 143–172 in *Pornography and Sexual Aggression*, ed. Neil M. Malamuth and Edward Donnerstein. Orlando, Fla.: Academic Press.

Cronbach, Lee J. 1970. *Essentials of Psychological Testing.* 3rd ed. New York: Harper & Row.

Crutchfield, Robert D., Michael R. Geerken, and Walter R. Gove. 1982. "Crime Rate and Social Integration: The Impact of Metropolitan Mobility." *Criminology* 20:467–478.

Curtain, Leslie B. 1982. *Status of Women: A Comparative Analysis of Twenty Developing Countries.* Washington, D.C.: Population Reference Bureau.

Curtis, Lynn A. 1975. *Violence, Race, and Culture.* Lexington, Mass.: Lexington.

Curtis, Lynn A. 1976. "Sexual Combat." *Society* 13:69–72.

Curtis, Lynn A. 1978. "Violence and Youth." House Committee on Science and Technology, Subcommittee on Domestic and International Scientific Planning, Analysis, and Cooperation, Research into Violent Behavior: Sexual Assaults (Hearing, 95th Congress, 2nd Session, January 10–12) Washington, D.C.: U.S. Government Printing Office.

Dallas, Dorothy M. 1982. "The Use of Visual Materials in Sex Education." Pp. 65–79 in *The Influence of Pornography on Behavior,* ed. Maurice Yaffe' and Edward C. Nelson. London: Academic Press.

Daly, Mary. 1973. *Beyond God the Father: Toward a Philosophy of Women's Liberation.* Boston: Beacon Press.

Daly, Mary. 1978. *Gyn/Ecology: Metaethics of Radical Feminism.* Boston: Beacon Press.

Davis, James A. 1985. *The Logic of Causal Order.* Sage University Paper series on Quantitative Applications in the Social Sciences, series no. 07055. Beverly Hills, Calif.: Sage.

Davis, James A., and Tom Smith. 1985. *General Social Surveys, 1972–1984: Cumulative Codebook.* National Opinion Research Center, University of Chicago.

DeFronzo, James. 1983. "Economic Assistance to Impoverished Americans." *Criminology* 21:119–136.

Diamond, Irene. 1980. "Pornography and Repression: A Reconsideration of 'Who' and 'What.'" Pp. 187–203 in *Take Back the Night: Women on Pornography,* ed. Laura Lederer. New York: William Morrow.

Dibble, Ursula, and Murray A. Straus. 1980. "Some Social Structure Determinants of Inconsistency Between Attitudes and Behavior: The Case of Family Violence." *Journal of Marriage and the Family* 42:71–80.

Dietz, Park Elliot, Bruce Harry, and Robert R. Hazelwood. 1986. "Detective Magazines: Pornography for the Sexual Sadist?" *Journal of Forensic Sciences* 31:197–211.

Divale, William, and Marvin Harris. 1976. "Population, Warfare, and the Male Supremacist Complex." *American Anthropologist* 78:521–538.

Dobash, R. Emerson, and Russell Dobash. 1979. *Violence Against Wives.* New York: Free Press.

Donnerstein, Edward, and Leonard Berkowitz. 1981. "Victim Reactions in Aggressive-Erotic Films as a Factor in Violence Against Women." *Journal of Personality and Social Psychology* 41:710–724.

Donnerstein, Edward, Daniel Linz, and Steven Penrod. 1987. *The Question of Pornography.* New York: Free Press.

Dugan, Lisa, Nan Hunter, and Carole S. Vance. 1985. "False Promises: Feminist Antipornography Legislation in the U.S." Pp. 130–151 in *Women Against Censorship*, ed. Varda Burstyn. Vancouver: Douglas and McIntyre.

Duncan, Otis D. 1975. *Introduction to Structural Equation Models.* New York: Academic Press.

Durkheim, Emile. 1964. [1897]. *Suicide.* Glencoe, Ill.: Free Press.

Durkheim, Emile. 1954 [1912]. *The Elementary Forms of Religious Life.* Glencoe, Ill.: Free Press.

Dworkin, Andrea. 1979. *Pornography: Men Possessing Women.* New York: G. P. Putnam's Sons.

Dworkin, Andrea. 1983. *Right-Wing Women.* New York: Pergee.

Dworkin, Andrea. 1985. "Against the Male Flood: Censorship, Pornography, and Equality." *Harvard Women's Law Journal* 8:1–29.

Dworkin, Andrea. 1987. *Intercourse.* New York: Free Press.

Dworkin, Andrea, and Catharine A. MacKinnon. 1988. *Pornography and Civil Rights: A New Day for Women's Equality.* Minneapolis, Minn.: Organizing Against Pornography.

Echols, Alice. 1983. "The New Feminism of Yin and Yang." Pp. 439–459 in *Powers of Desire: The Politics of Sexuality*, ed. Ann Snitow, Christine Stansell, and Sharon Thompson. New York: Monthly Review Press.

Echols, Alice. 1984. "The Taming of the Id: Feminist Sexual Politics, 1968–83." Pp. 50–72 in *Pleasure and Danger: Exploring Female Sexuality*, ed. Carole S. Vance. Boston: Routledge & Kegan Paul.

Ehrlich, Issac. 1975. "The Deterrent Effects of Capital Punishment: A Question of Life and Death." *American Economic Review* 65:397–417.

Einsiedel, Edna F. 1988. "The British, Canadian, and U.S. Pornography Commissions and Their use of Social Science Research." *Journal of Communication* 38:108–121.

Eisenstein, Zillah R. 1984. *Feminism and Sexual Equality: Crisis in Liberal America.* New York: Monthly Review Press.

Elshtain, Jean Bethke. 1976–77. "Review of Susan Brownmiller's Against Our Will." *Telos* 30:237–242.

Elshtain, Jean Bethke. 1982. "The Victim Syndrome: A Troubling Turn in Feminism." *The Progressive* 42:42–47.

Emerson, Thomas I. 1984. "Pornography and the First Amendment: A Reply to Professor MacKinnon." *Yale Law and Policy Review* 3:130–143.

Eron, Leonard D. 1982. "Parent-Child Interaction, Television Violence, and Aggression of Children." *American Psychologist* 37:197–11.

Eysenck, H. J., and D. K. B. Nias. *Sex, Violence and the Media.* London: Sphere Books.

Falwell, Jerry. 1980. *Listen America.* Garden City, N.Y.: Doubleday.

Faris, Robert E. L. 1955. *Social Disorganization.* 2nd ed. New York: Ronald Press.

Faris, Robert E. L., and H. Warren Dunham. 1939. *Mental Disorders in Urban Areas.* Chicago: University of Chicago Press.

Federal Bureau of Investigation. 1968. Uniform Crime Report: *Crime in the United States, 1967.* Washington, D.C.: U.S. Government Printing Office.

Federal Bureau of Investigation. 1981. Uniform Crime Report: *Crime in the United States, 1980.* Washington, D.C.: U.S. Government Printing Office.

Federal Bureau of Investigation. 1983. Uniform Crime Report: *Crime in the United States, 1982.* Washington, D.C.: U.S. Government Printing Office.

Federal Bureau of Investigation. 1988. Uniform Crime Report: *Crime in the United States, 1987.* Washington, D.C.: U.S. Government Printing Office.

Feinberg, Joel. 1985. *Offense to Others: The Moral Limits of the Criminal Law.* New York: Oxford University Press.

Feminist Anti-Censorship Taskforce. 1985. "Feminism and Censorship: Strange Bedfellows? *Changing Men* 15–12.

Field, Hubert S. 1978. "Attitudes Toward Rape: A Comparative Analysis of Police, Rapists, Crisis Counselors, and Citizens." *Journal of Personality and Social Psychology* 36:156–179.

Freeman, Richard B. 1983. "Crime and Unemployment." Pp. 89–106 in *Crime and Public Policy,* ed. James Q. Wilson. San Francisco: ICS Press.

Friday, Paul C. 1983. "Urban Crime." Pp. 1582–1587 in *Encyclopedia of Criminal Justice.* Vol. 4, ed. Sanford H. Kadish. New York: Free Press.

Friedl, Ernestine. 1975. *Women and Men: An Anthropologist's View.* New York: Holt, Rinehart & Winston.

Friedan, Betty. 1963. *The Feminine Mystique.* New York: W. W. Norton.

Gagnon, John H. 1977. *Human Sexualities.* Glenview, Ill.: Scott, Foresman.

Gagnon, John H., and William Simon. 1973. *Sexual Conduct: The Sources of Sexuality.* Chicago: Aldine.

Gallagher, Neil. 1981. *The Porno Plague.* Minneapolis: Bethany House.

Garfinkel, Harold. 1967. *Studies in Ethnomethodology.* Englewood Cliffs, N.J.: Prentice-Hall.

Garofalo, James, and Michael J. Hindelang. 1977. *An Introduction to the National Crime Survey.* Law Enforcement Assistance Administration (L.E.A.A.). National Criminal Justice Information and Statistics Service. Washington, D.C.: U.S. Government Printing Office.

Gastil, Raymond D. 1971. "Homicide and a Regional Culture of Violence." *American Sociological Review* 36:412–427.

Gastil, Raymond D. 1975. *Cultural Regions of the United States.* Seattle: University of Washington Press.

Gastil, Raymond D. 1978. "Comments." *Criminology* 16:60–65.

Geertz, Clifford. 1973. *The Interpretation of Cultures.* New York. Basic Books.

Geis, Gilbert. 1977. "Forcible Rape: An Introduction." Pp. 1–44 in *Forcible Rape: The Crime, the Victim and the Offender,* ed. Duncan Chappell, Robley Geis, and Gilbert Geis. New York: Columbia University Press.

Gelles, Richard J., and Murray A. Straus. 1979. "Determinants of Violence in the Family: Toward a Theoretical Integration." Pp. 549–581 in *Contemporary Theories*

About the Family. Vol. 1, ed. Wesley R. Burr, Rueben Hill, F. Ivan Nye, and Ira Reiss. New York: Free Press.

Gibbs, J. P. 1968. "Crime, Punishment, and Deterrence." *Social Science Quarterly* 48:515–530.

Gillan, Patricia. 1978. "Therapeutic Use of Obscenity." Pp. 127–147 in *Censorship and Obscenity*, ed. Rajeev Dhavan and Christie Davies. London: Martin Robertson.

Goetting, Ann. 1981. "Divorce Outcome Research: Issues and Perspectives." *Journal of Family Issues* 2:350–378.

Goffman, Erving. 1979. *Gender Advertisements*. New York: Harper & Row.

Gongla, Patricia A., and Edward H. Thompson, Jr. 1987. "Single-Parent Families." Pp. 397–418 in *Handbook of Marriage and the Family*, ed. Marvin B. Sussman and Suzanne K. Steinmetz. New York: Plenum Press.

Gordon, Margaret T., and Stephanie Riger. 1989. *The Female Fear*. New York: Free Press.

Gould, Louis. 1977. "Pornography for Women." Pp. 185–293 in *Sexuality in Today's World*, ed. John H. Gagnon. Boston: Little Brown.

Gove, Walter. 1979. "Sex Differences in the Epidemiology of Mental Disorder: Evidence and Explanations." Pp. 23–68 in *Gender and Disordered Behavior: Sex Differences in Psychopathology*, ed. Edith S. Gomberg and Violete Franks. New York: Brunner-Mazel.

Gove, Walter, and Michael Hughes. 1980. "Reexamining the Ecological Fallacy: A Study in Which Aggregate Data Are Critical in Investigating the Pathological Effects of Living Alone." *Social Forces* 58:1157–1177.

Gove, Walter R., Michael Hughes, and Michael Geerken. 1985. "Are Uniform Crime Reports a Valid Indicator of the Index Crimes? An Affirmative Answer with Minor Qualifications." *Criminology* 23:451–491.

Gove, Walter and Jeanette F. Tudor. 1973. "Adult Sex Roles and Mental Illness." *American Journal of Sociology* 78:812–835.

Gray, Susan H. 1982. "Exposure to Pornography and Aggression Toward Women: The Case of the Angry Male." *Social Problems* 29:387–398.

Greenblat, Cathy S. 1983. "A Hit is a Hit is a Hit . . . Or is it? Approval and Tolerance of the Use of Physical Force by Spouses." Pp. 235–260 in *The Dark Side of Families: Current Family Violence Research*, ed. David Finkelhor, Richard J. Gelles, Gerald T. Hotaling, and Murray A. Straus. Beverly Hills, Calif.: Sage.

Greer, Germaine. 1973. "Seduction is a Four-Letter Word." *Playboy* 20:80–82, 164, 178, 224–228.

Griffin, Susan. 1971. "The All-American Crime." *Ramparts* (September):26–35.

Groth, Nicholas A. 1979. *Men Who Rape: The Psychology of the Offender*. New York: Plenum Press.

Gusfield, Joseph R. 1963. *Symbolic Crusade: Status Politics and the American Temperance Movement*. Urbana: University of Illinois Press.

Hackney, Sheldon. 1969. "Southern Violence." *American Historical Review* 74:906–925.

Hagood, Margaret J., and Daniel O. Price. 1952. *Statistics for Sociologists.* New York: Holt.

Harries, Keith D. 1973. *The Geography of Crime and Justice.* New York: McGraw-Hill.

Harries, Keith D. 1980. *Crime and the Environment.* Springfield, Ill.: Charles C. Thomas.

Hayner, Norman. 1929. "Hotel Life and Personality." Pp. 108–120 in *Personality and the Social Group*, ed. Ernest W. Burgess. Chicago: University of Chicago Press.

Heise, David R. 1969. "Problems in Path Analysis and Causal Inference." Pp. 38–73 in *Sociological Methodology*, ed. E. F. Borgatta and G. W. Bohrnstedt. San Francisco: Jossey-Bass.

Henry, Andrew F., and James F. Short, Jr. 1954. *Suicide and Homicide.* New York: Free Press.

Hetherington, E. Mavis, Martha Cox, and Roger Cox. 1978. "The Aftermath of Divorce." Pp. 146–176 in *Mother-Child, Father-Child Relations*, ed. J. H. Stevens, Jr., and M. Matthews. Washington, D.C.: National Association for the Education of Young Children.

Hicks, Alexander, Roger Friedland, and Edwin Johnson. 1978. "Class, Power and State Policy: The Case of Large Business Corporation, Labor Unions and Governmental Redistribution in the American States." *American Sociological Review* 43:302–315.

Hindelang, Michael J. 1974. "The Uniform Crime Reports Revisited." *Journal of Criminal Justice* 2:1–17.

Hindelang, Michael J., and Bruce J. Davis. 1977. "Forcible Rape in the United States: A Statistical Profile." Pp. 87–114 in *Forcible Rape: The Crime, the Victim, and the Offender*, ed. Duncan Chappell, Robley Geis, and Gilbert Geis. New York: Columbia University Press.

Hirschi, Travis. 1969. *The Causes of Delinquency.* Berkeley: University of California Press.

Hirschi, Travis, and Michael Gottfredson. 1983. "Age and the Explanation of Crime." *American Journal of Sociology* 89:552–584.

Hirschi, Travis, and Hanan C. Selvin. 1967. *Principles of Survey Analysis.* New York: Free Press.

Hirschi, Travis, and Rodney Stark. 1969. "Hellfire and Delinquency." *Social Problems* 17:202–213.

Holmes, Thomas H., and Richard H. Rahe. 1967. "The Social Readjustment Rating Scale." *Journal of Psychosomatic Research* 11:213–218.

Hommes, R. 1978. "The Status of Women." In *Demographic Aspects of the Changing Status of Women in Europe*, ed. Marry Niphuis-Nell. Boston: Martin Dyboff.

Huber, Joan. 1986. "Trends in Gender Stratification, 1970–1985." *Sociological Forum* 1:476–495.

Huesmann, L. Rowell. 1982. "Television Violence and Aggressive Behavior." In *Television and Behavior: Ten Years of Scientific Progress and Implications for the 80s*, ed. David Pearl, Lorraine Bouthilet, and Joyce B. Lazar. Washington, D.C.: U.S. Government Printing Office.

Huff-Corzine, Lin, Jay Corzine, and David C. Moore. 1986. "Southern Exposure: Deciphering the South's Influence on Homicide Rates." *Social Forces* 64:906–924.

Huggins, Martha D., and Murray A. Straus. 1980. "Violence and the Social Structure as Reflected in Childrens Books From 1850 to 1970." Pp. 51–67 in *The Social Causes of Husband-Wife Violence*, ed. Murray A. Straus and Gerald T. Hotaling. Minneapolis: University of Minnesota Press.

Jacobs, David, and David Britt. 1979. "Inequality and Police Use of Deadly Force: An Empirical Assessment of a Conflict Hypothesis." *Social Problems* 26:403–412.

Jaffee, David, and Murray A. Straus. 1987. "Sexual Climate and Reported Rape: A State-Level Analysis." *Archives of Sexual Behavior* 16:107–123.

Jelen, Ted G. 1986. "Fundamentalism, Feminism, and Attitudes Toward Pornography." *Review of Religious Research* 28:97–103.

Jensen, Eric L., and Rodney K. Baxter. 1985. "The Vietnam War and Domestic Homicide Rates: The Legitimation of Violence." Paper presented at the annual meeting of the American Society of Criminology, San Diego, Calif.

Johnston, Dennis F. 1985. "The Development of Social Statistics and Indicators on the Status of Women." *Social Indicators Research* 16:233–261.

Kalmuss, Debra S., and Murray A. Straus. 1983. "Feminist, Political, and Economic Determinants of Wife Abuse Services in American States." Pp. 363–376 in *The Dark Side of Families: Current Family Violence Research*, ed. David Finkelhor, Richard J. Gelles, Gerald T. Hotaling, and Murray A. Straus. Beverly Hills, Calif.: Sage.

Katz, Sedelle, and Mary Ann Mazur. 1979. *Understanding the Rape Victim: A Synthesis of Research Findings*. New York: John Wiley.

Kendrick, Walter. 1987. *The Secret Museum: Pornography in Modern Culture*. New York: Viking.

Kessler, Marc, and Albee, George W. 1975. "Primary Prevention." *Annual Review of Psychology* 26:557–591.

Kirk, Jerry R. 1985. *The Mind Polluters*. Nashville: Thomas Nelson.

Kirkpatrick, R. George, and Louis A. Zurcher. 1984. "Women Against Pornography: Feminist Anti-Pornography Crusades in American Society." *International Journal of Sociology and Social Policy* 3:1–30.

Kobrin, Frances E., and Gerry E. Hendershot. 1977. "Do Family Ties Reduce Mortality? Evidence From the United States 1966–68." *Journal of Marriage and the Family* 33:373–377.

Kornhauser, Ruth. 1978. *Social Sources of Delinquency*. Chicago: University of Chicago Press.

Kristol, Irving. 1971. "Pornography, Obscenity, and the Case for Censorship." *New York Times Magazine* (March 28).

Krohn, Marvin D. 1976. "Inequality, Unemployment and Crime: A Cross-National Analysis." *Sociological Quarterly* 17:303–313.

Kutchinsky, Berl. 1983. "Obscenity and Pornography: Behavioral Aspects. Pp. 1077–1086 in *Encyclopedia of Criminal Justice*. Vol. 3, ed. Sanford H. Kadish. New York: Free Press.

Kutchinsky, Berl. 1988. "Pornography and Sexual Violence: The Criminological Evidence From Aggregate Data in Several Countries." Paper presented at the 14th International Congress on Law and Mental Health, Montreal, Canada.

Lab, Steven P. 1987. "Pornography and Aggression: A Response to the U.S. Attorney General's Commission." *Criminal Justice Abstracts* 19:301–321.

Lambert, William W., Leigh Minturn Triandis, and Margery Wolf. 1959. "Some Correlates of Beliefs in the Malevolence and Benevolence of Supernatural Beings: A Cross-Societal Study." *Journal of Abnormal and Social Psychology* 58:162–169.

Lavrakas, Paul J. 1985. "Citizen Self-Help and Neighborhood Crime Prevention Policy." Pp. 87–115 in *American Violence and Public Policy*, ed. Lynn A. Curtis. New Haven, Conn.: Yale University Press.

Lederer, Laura, ed. 1980. *Take Back the Night: Women on Pornography*. New York: William Morrow.

LaFree, Gary D. 1982. "Male Power and Female Victimization: Toward a Theory of Interracial Rape." *American Journal of Sociology* 88:311–328.

Leiter, Kenneth. 1980. *A Primer on Ethnomethodology*. New York: Oxford University Press.

Lerman, Lisa G., and Fanci Livingston. 1983. "State Legislation on Domestic Violence." *Response to Violence in the Family and Sexual Assault* 6:1–28.

LeVine, Robert A. 1977. "Gusii Sex Offenses: A Study in Social Control." Pp. 189–226 in *Forcible Rape: The Crime, the Victim, and the Offender*, ed. Duncan Chappell, Robley Geis, and Gilbert Geis. New York: Columbia University Press.

Levitan, Sar A., and Richard S. Belous. 1981. *What's Happening to the American Family?* Baltimore: Johns Hopkins University Press.

Linz, Daniel, Edward Donnerstein, Michael Bross, and Margo Chapin. 1986. "Mitigating the Influence of Violence on Television and Sexual Violence in the Media." Pp. 165–194 in *Advances in the Study of Aggression*. Vol. 2, ed. Robert J. Blanchard and D. Caroline Blanchard. New York: Academic Press.

Linz, Daniel, Edward Donnerstein, and Steven Penrod. 1984. "The Effects of Multiple Exposure to Filmed Violence Against Women." *Journal of Communication* 34:130–147.

Linz, Daniel, Edward Donnerstein, and Steven Penrod. 1987. "The Findings and Recommendations of the Attorney General's Commission on Pornography: Do the Psychological Facts Fit the Political Fury?" *American Psychologist* 42:946–952.

Loftin, Colin. 1980. "Alternative Estimates of the Impact of Certainty and Severity of Punishment on Levels of Homicide in American states." Pp. 75–81 in *Indicators of Crime and Criminal Justice: Quantitative Studies*, ed. Stephen E. Fienberg and Albert J. Reiss, Jr. Washington, D.C.: U.S. Government Printing Office.

Loftin, Colin, and Robert H. Hill. 1974. "Regional Subculture and Homicide: An Examination of the Gastil–Hackney Thesis." *American Sociological Review* 39:714–724.

Long, Sharon K., and Ann D. Witte. 1981. "Current Economic Trends: Implications for Crime and Justice." Pp. 69–143 in *Crime and Criminal Justice in a Declining Economy*. ed. Kevin N. Wright, Cambridge, Mass.: Oelgeschlager, Gunn and Hain.

Long, Susan B. 1979. "The Continuing Debate Over the Use of Ratio Variables: Facts and Fiction." Pp. 3–6 in *Sociological Methodology*, ed. Karl F. Schuessler. San Francisco: Jossey-Bass.

Longino, Helen E. 1980. "Pornography, Oppression, and Freedom: A Closer Look." Pp. 26–41 in *Take Back the Night, Women on Pornography*, ed. Laura Lederer. New York: William Morrow.

Lynn, Barry W. 1986a. *Polluting the Censorship Debate: A Summary and Critique of the Final Report of the Attorney General's Commission on Pornography*. Washington, D.C.: American Civil Liberties Union.

Lynn, Barry W. 1986b. "'Civil Rights' Ordinances and the Attorney General's Commission: New Developments in Pornography Regulation." *Harvard Civil Rights–Civil Liberties Law Review* 21:27–125.

McCarthy, John D., Omar R. Galle, and William Zimmerman. 1975. "Population Density, Social Structure, and Interpersonal Violence: An Intermetropolitan Test of Competing Models." *American Behavioral Scientist* 18:771–791.

McCarthy, Sarah J. 1980. "Pornography, Rape, and the Cult of Macho." *The Humanist* (September/October):11–20.

McConahay, Shirley A., and John B. McConahay. 1977. "Sexual Permissiveness, Sex-Role Rigidity, and Violence Across Cultures." *Journal of Social Issues* 33:134–143.

MacDonald, John M. 1971. *Rape Offenders and their Victims*. Springfield, Ill.: Charles C. Thomas.

MacKinnon, Catharine A. 1982. "Feminism, Marxism, Method and the State: An Agenda for Theory." *Signs* 7:515–544.

MacKinnon, Catharine A. 1984. "Not a Moral Issue." *Yale Law and Policy Review* 2:321–345.

MacKinnon, Catharine A. 1985. "Pornography, Civil Rights, and Speech." *Harvard Civil Rights–Civil Liberties Law Review* 20:1–70.

MacKinnon, Catharine A., and Andrea Dworkin. 1983. "An Ordinance of the City of Minneapolis." Minneapolis, Minn.

MacNamara, Donald E. J., and Edward Sagarin. 1977. *Sex, Crime, and the Law*. New York: Free Press.

Madge, John. 1962. *The Origins of Scientific Sociology*. Glencoe, Ill.: Free Press.

Malamuth, Neil M., and James V. P. Check. 1984. "Debriefing Effectiveness Following Exposure to Pornographic Rape Depictions." *Journal of Sex Research* 20:1–13.

Malamuth, Neil M., and Edward Donnerstein. 1982. "The Effects of Aggressive Erotic Stimuli." Pp. 104–136 in *Advances in Experimental Social Psychology*. Vol. 15, ed. Leonard Berkowitz. New York: Academic Press.

Malamuth, Neil M., and B. Spinner. 1980. "A Longitudinal Content Analysis of Sexual Violence in Best-Selling Erotic Magazines." *Journal of Sex Research* 3:226–237.

Marcus, Steven. 1974. *The Other Victorians: A Study of Sexuality and Pornography in Mid-Nineteenth-Century England*. 2nd ed. New York: New American Library.

Martin, Patricia Yancey, Kenneth Wilson, and Caroline Dillman. 1986. "Southern-Style Gender: Trends in Relations Between Men and Women." Unpublished.

Martindale, Don. 1957. "Social Disorganization: The Conflict of Normative and Empirical Approaches." Pp. 340–367 in *Modern Sociological Theory in Continuity and Change*, ed. Howard Becker and Alvin Boskoff. New York: Rinehart & Winston.

Mason, Karen Oppenheim. 1986. "The Status of Women: Conceptual and Methodological Issues in Demographic Studies." *Sociological Forum* 1:284–300.

Math, Mara. 1985–86. "Andrea Dworkin Talks about Feminism and Pornography." *Gay Community News* 13, 24.

Medea, Andra, and Kathleen Thompson. 1974. *Against Rape*. New York: Farrar, Straus & Giroux.

Menzel, Herbert. 1950. "Comments on Robinson's Ecological Correlations and the Behavior of Individuals." *American Sociological Review* 15:674.

Messner, Steven F. 1980. "Football and Homicide: Search for the Subculture of Violence." Paper presented at the First Annual Meeting of the North American Society for the Sociology of Sport, Denver, Colorado, Oct. 16–19.

Messner, Steven F. 1982. "Poverty, Inequality, and the Urban Homicide Rate." *Criminology* 20:103–114.

Messner, Steven F. 1983. "Regional and Racial Effects on the Urban Homicide Rate: The Subculture of Violence Revisited." *American Journal of Sociology* 88:997–1007.

Messner, Steven F. 1986. "Television Violence and Violent Crime: An Aggregate Analysis." *Social Problems* 33:218–235.

Messner, Steven F., and Judith R. Blau. 1987. "Routine Leisure Activities and Rates of Crime: A Macro-Level Analysis. *Social Forces* 65:1035–1052.

Miller v. California, 413 U.S. 15 (1973).

Moore, Jamie M. 1985. "Civil Rights Pornography Ordinances: A Status Report." *Response to the Victimization of Women and Children* 8:28.

Morgan, Robin. 1980. "Theory and Practice: Pornography and Rape." Pp. 134–140 in *Take Back the Night: Women on Pornography*, ed. Laura Lederer. New York: William Morrow.

Morgan, Robin. 1982. *The Anatomy of Freedom: Feminism, Physics, and Global Politics*. Garden City, N.Y.: Anchor Press/Doubleday.

Mosher, Donald L., and Ronald D. Anderson. 1986. "Macho Personality, Sexual Aggression, and Reactions to Guided Imagery of Realistic Rape." *Journal of Research in Personality* 20:77–94.

Mower, Ernest R. 1941. "Methodological Problems in Social Disorganization." *American Sociological Review* 6:639–849.

National Center for the Prevention and Control of Rape. 1981. *National Directory: Rape Prevention and Treatment and Resources*. Rockville, Md.: National Institute of Mental Health, DHHS Publication No. (ADM) 81–10008.

National Coalition on Television Violence. 1981. "Research Review." *NCTV News* (January):1–8.

Nettler, Gwynn. 1984. *Explaining Crime.* 3rd edition. New York: McGraw-Hill.

Nicholls, Leland L. 1976. "Tourism and Crime." *Annals of Tourism Research* 3:176–182.

Nie, Norman H., C. Hadlai Hull, Mark N. Franklin, Jean G. Jenkins, Keith J. Sours, Marija J. Norusis, and Viann Beadle. 1980. *SCSS: A User's Guide to the SCSS Conversational System.* New York: McGraw-Hill.

Nie, Norman H., C. Hadlai Hull, Jean G. Jenkins, Karin Steinbrenner, and Dale H. Bent. 1975. *SPSS: Statistical Package for the Social Sciences.* 2nd ed. New York: McGraw-Hill.

Nobile, Philip, and Eric Nadler. 1986. *United States of America vs. Sex: How the Meese Commission Lied About Pornography.* New York: Minotaur Press.

Nunnally, Jim C. 1978. *Psychometric Theory.* 2nd ed. New York: McGraw-Hill.

O'Brien, Robert M. 1983. "Metropolitan Structure and Violent Crime: Which Measure of Crime?" *American Sociological Review* 48:434–437.

O'Brien, Robert M. 1987. "The Interracial Nature of Violent Crimes: A Reexamination." *American Journal of Sociology* 92:817–835.

Ogburn, William Fielding. 1922. *Social Change with Respect to Culture and Original Nature.* New York: B. W. Huebsch.

Orsagh, Thomas. 1980. "Unemployment and Crime: An Objection to Professor Brenner's View." *Journal of Criminal Law & Criminology* 71:181–183.

Oxford English Dictionary. Vol. VII. 1970. Oxford: Clarendon Press.

Park, Robert E., and Ernest W. Burgess. 1921. *Introduction to the Science of Sociology.* Chicago: University of Chicago Press.

Park, Robert E., Ernest W. Burgess, and Roderick D. McKenzie. 1967. *The City.* Chicago: University of Chicago Press.

Parke, R. D., L. Berkowitz, J. P. Leyens, S. G. West, and R. J. Sebastian. 1979. "Some Effects of Violent and Nonviolent Movies on the Behavior of Juvenile Delinquents." In *Advances in Experimental Social Psychology.* Vol. 10, ed. Leonard Berkowitz. New York: Academic Press.

Parker, Robert, and M. Dwayne Smith. 1979. "Deterrence, Poverty, and Type of Homicide." *American Journal of Sociology* 85:614–624.

Parsons, Talcott. 1947. "Certain Primary Sources and Patterns of Aggression in the Social Structure of the Western World." *Psychiatry* 10:167–181.

Pearce, Diana, and Harriette McAdoo. 1981. *Women and Children: Alone and in Poverty.* Washington, D.C.: National Advisory Council on Economic Opportunity.

Pearce, Philip L. 1982. *The Social Psychology of Tourist Behavior.* New York: Pergamon Press.

Peckham, Morse. 1971. *Art and Pornography.* New York: Basic Books.

Pedhazur, Elazar J. 1982. *Multiple Regression in Behavioral Research.* 2nd ed. New York: Holt, Rinehart & Winston.

Pfohl, Stephen J. 1985. *Images of Deviance and Social Control.* New York: McGraw-Hill.

Phillips, David P. 1983. "The Impact of Mass Media Violence on U.S. Homicides." *American Sociological Review* 48:560–568.

Powers, Mary G. 1983. "Existing Data Systems as Sources for Indicators of the Situation of Women." Social Statistics Section Proceeding of the American Statistics Association.

Quinn, Naomi. 1977. "Anthropological Studies on Women's Status." *Annual Review of Anthropology* 6:181–225.

Rabkin, Judith Godwin. 1979. "The Epidemiology of Forcible Rape." *American Journal of Orthopsychiatry* 49:634–647.

Ratterman, Debbie. 1982. "Pornography: The Spectrum of Harm." *Aegis* (Autumn): 42–52.

Reckless, Walter C. 1973. *The Crime Problem.* 5th ed. Englewood Cliffs, N.J.: Prentice-Hall.

Reed, John Shelton. 1977. "Below the Smith and Wesson Line: Reflections on Southern Violence." Presented at the Second Annual Hugo L. Black Symposium, University of Alabama in Birmingham, April 21.

Reiss, Ira L. 1986. *Journey into Sexuality: An Exploratory Voyage.* Englewood Cliffs, N.J.: Prentice-Hall.

Report of the Special Committee on Pornography and Prostitution. 1985. *Pornography and Prostitution in Canada.* Ottawa, Canada: Canadian Government Publishing Centre.

Rhodes, Albert Lewis, and Albert J. Reiss, Jr. 1970. "The 'Religious Factor' and Delinquent Behavior." *Journal of Research in Crime and Delinquency* 7:83–98.

Riger, Stephanie, and Margaret T. Gordon. 1981. "The Fear of Rape: A Study in Social Control." *Journal of Social Issues* 37 (4):71–92.

Robinson, W. S. 1950. "Ecological Correlations and the Behavior of Individuals." *American Sociological Review* 15:351–357.

Roncek, Dennis W. 1975. "Density and Crime." *American Behavioral Scientist* 18:843–860.

Rooney, John F., Jr. 1975. "Sport From a Geographic Perspective." Pp. 51–115 in *Sport and Social Order: Contributions to the Sociology of Sport,* ed. Donald Ball and John Loy. Reading, Mass.: Addison-Wesley.

Roos, Patricia A. 1983. "Marriage and Women's Occupational Attainment." *American Sociological Review* 48:852–863.

Rosen, Raymond C., and Francis J. Keefe. 1978. "The Measurement of Human Penile Tumescence." *Psychophysiology* 15:366–376.

Rosenfeld, Richard. 1986. "Urban Crime Rates: Effects of Inequality, Welfare Dependency, Region, and Race." Pp. 116–130 in *The Social Ecology of Crime.* ed. James M. Byrne and Robert J. Sampson. New York: Springer-Verlag.

Ross, Susan Keller, and Ann Barcher. 1983. *The Rights of Women—The Basic ACLU Guide to a Woman's Rights.* New York: Bantam Books.

Russ, Joanna. 1985. *Magic Mommas, Trembling Sisters, Puritans & Perverts.* New York: Crosing Press.

Russell, Diana E. H. 1975. *The Politics of Rape: The Victim's Perspective.* New York: Stein and Day.

Russell, Diana E. H. 1977. "On Pornography." *Chrysalis* 4:11–15.

Russell, Diana E. H. 1980. "Pornography and Violence: What Does the New Research Say?" Pp. 218–238 in *Take Back the Night: Women on Pornography*, ed. Laura Lederer. New York: William Morrow.

Russell, Diana E. H. 1982. *Rape in Marriage.* New York: Macmillan.

Russell, Diana E. H. 1983. "The Prevalence and Incidence of Forcible Rape and Attempted Rape of Females." *Victimology* 7:61–93.

Russell, Diana E. H. 1984. *Sexual Exploitation: Rape, Child Sexual Abuse, and Workplace Harassment.* Beverly Hills, Calif.: Sage.

Russell, Diana E. H. 1988. "Pornography and Rape: A Casual Model." *Political Psychology* 9:41–73.

Sacks, Karen. 1974. "Engels Revisited: Women, the Organization of Production and Private Property. Pp. 207–222 in *Woman, Culture and Society*, ed. M. Z. Rosaldo and L. Lamphere. Stanford, Calif.: Stanford University Press.

Sampson, Robert J. 1987. "Communities and Crime." Pp. 91–114 in *Positive Criminology*, ed. Michael Gottfredson and Travis Hirschi. Beverly Hills, Calif.: Sage.

Sanday, Peggy Reeves. 1981. "The Socio-Cultural Context of Rape: A Cross-Cultural Study." *Journal of Social Issues* 37:5–27.

Sapiro, Virginia. 1983. *The Political Integration of Women: Roles, Socialization, and Politics.* Urbana: University of Illinois Press.

Savitz, Leonard D. 1978. "Official Police Statistics and Their Limitations." Pp. 69–81 in *Crime in Society*, ed. Leonard D. Savitz. New York: John Wiley.

Schiff, Arthur F. 1973. "Rape in Foreign Countries." *Medical Trial Technique Quarterly* 20:66–74.

Schafly, Phyllis. 1984. "New Weapons in the Battle Against Pornography." *Phyllis Schafly Report* (June):1–6.

Schechter, Susan. 1982. *Women and Male Violence.* Boston: South End Press.

Schorr, Alvin, and Phyllis Moen. 1979. "The Single-Parent and Social Policy." *Social Policy* (March/April):15–21.

Schwed, John A., and Murray A. Straus. 1979. "The Military Environment and Child Abuse." Mimeographed paper, Family Research Lab, University of New Hampshire, Durham.

Schwendinger, Julia R., and Herman Schwendinger. 1983. *Rape and Inequality.* Beverly Hills, Calif.: Sage.

Scott, Joseph E. 1985. "Violence and Erotic Material: The Relationship Between Adult Entertainment and Rape?" Paper presented at the American Association for the Advancement of Science Annual Meeting, Los Angeles, Calif., May 26–31.

Scott, Joseph E., and Steven J. Cuvelier. 1987. "Sexual Violence in Playboy Magazine: A Longitudinal Content Analysis." *Journal of Sex Research* 23:534–539.

Scully, Diana, and Joseph Marolla. 1985. "'Riding the Bull at Gilley's': Convicted Rapists Describe the Rewards of Rape." *Social Problems* 32:251–263.

Sharkansky, Ira. 1970. *Regionalism in American Politics.* New York: Bobbs-Merrill.

Shaw, Clifford R., and Henry D. McKay. 1931. *Report on the Causes of Crime*, Vol. 12, no. 13. Washington, D.C. National Commission on Law Observance and Enforcement.

Shaw, Clifford R., and Henry D. McKay. 1942. *Juvenile Delinquency and Urban Areas.* Chicago: University of Chicago Press.

Shaw, Clifford R., and Henry D. McKay. 1969. *Juvenile Delinquency and Urban Areas.* Rev. ed. Chicago: University of Chicago Press.

Shortridge, Kathleen. 1984. "Poverty is a Woman's Problem." Pp. 492–501 in *Women: A Feminist Perspective.* 3rd ed., ed. Jo Freeman. Palo Alto, Calif.: Mayfield.

Shorter, Edward. 1977. "On Writing the History of Rape." *Signs: Journal of Women in Culture and Society,* 3:471–482.

Simpson, Miles E. 1985. "Violent Crime, Income Inequality, and Regional Culture: Another Look." *Sociological Focus* 18:199–208.

Skogan, Wesley. 1986. "Fear of Crime and Neighborhood Change." Pp. 203–229 in *Communities and Crime,* ed. Albert J. Reiss, Jr., and Michael Tonry. Chicago: University of Chicago Press.

Small, Fred. 1985. "Pornography and Censorship." *Changing Men* 15:7–8, 43–45.

Smith, David M. 1973. *The Geography of Social Well-Being.* New York: McGraw-Hill.

Smith, Douglas A., and G. Roger Jarjoura. 1988. "Social Strucuture and Criminal Victimization." *Journal of Research in Crime and Delinquency* 25:27–52.

Smith, M. Dwayne, and Nathan Bennett. 1985. "Poverty, Inequality, and Theories of Forcible Rape." *Crime and Delinquency* 31:295–305.

Smith, M. Dwayne, and Robert Nash Parker. 1980. "Type of Homicide and Variation in Regional Rates." *Social Forces* 59:136–147.

Smith, Tom W. 1987. "The Use of Public Opinion Data by the Attorney General's Commission on Pornography." *Public Opinion Quarterly* 51:249–267.

Snitow, Ann. 1985. "Retrenchment versus Transformation: The Politics of the Antipornography Movement." Pp. 107–120 in *Women Against Censorship,* ed. Varda Burstyn. Manchester, N.H.: Salem House.

Soble, Alan. 1986. *Pornography: Marxism, Feminism, and the Future of Sexuality.* New Haven: Yale University Press.

Sommers, Paul M. 1982. "Deterrence and Gun Control: A Reply." *Atlantic Economic Journal* 10:54–57.

Stack, Steven. 1980. "The Effects of Marital Dissolution on Suicide." *Journal of Marriage and the Family* 42:83–92.

Stack, Steven. 1982. "Suicide: A Decade Review of the Sociological Literature." *Deviant Behavior* 4:41–66.

Stack, Steven, and Mary Jeanne Kanavy. 1983. "The Effect of Religion on Forcible Rape: A Structural Analysis." *Journal for the Scientific Study of Religion* 22:67–74.

Stanko, Elizabeth A. 1981. "Judicial Intervention and Domestic Violence: Does the Solution Fit the Problem?" Paper presented at the American Society of Criminology Annual Meetings, Washington, D.C., November.

Stark, Rodney. 1987. "Deviant Places: A Theory of the Ecology of Crime." *Criminology* 25:893–909.

Stark, Rodney, Daniel P. Doyle, and Lori Kent. 1980. "Rediscovering Moral Com-
   munities: Church Membership and Crime." Pp. 43–52 in *Understanding Crime:
   Current Theory and Research*, ed. Travis Hirschi and Michael Gottfredson. Beverly
   Hills, Calif.: Sage.

Stark, Rodney, Lori Kent, and Daniel P. Doyle. 1982. "Religion and Delinquency:
   The Ecology of a 'Lost' Relationship." *Journal of Research in Crime and Delinquency*
   19:4–24.

Stark, Rodney, William Sims Bainbridge, Robert D. Crutchfiled, Daniel P. Doyle, and
   Roger Finke. 1983. "Crime and Delinquency in the Roaring Twenties." *Journal of
   Research in Crime and Delinquency* 20:4–23.

Steele, Lisa. 1985. "A Capital Idea: Gendering in the Mass Media." Pp. 58–78 in
   Women Against Censorship, ed. Varda Burstyn. Manchester, N.H.: Salem House.

Steinem, Gloria. 1980. "Erotica and Pornography: A Clear and Present Difference."
   Pp. 35–39 in *Take Back the Night: Women on Pornography*, ed. Laura Lederer. New
   York: William Morrow.

Stoller, Robert J. 1976. "Sexual Excitement." *Archives of General Psychiatry* 33:899–
   909.

Stone, Geoffrey R. 1986. "Anti-Pornography Legislation as Viewpoint-Discrimina-
   tion." *Harvard Journal of Law & Public Policy* 9:461–480.

Straus, Murray A. 1964. "Measuring Families." Pp. 335–400 in *Handbook of Marriage
   and the Family*, ed. H. T. Christensen. Chicago: Rand.

Straus, Murray A. 1973. "A General Systems Theory Approach to a Theory of
   Violence Between Family Members." *Social Science Information* 12:105–125.

Straus, Murray A. 1974. "Leveling, Civility and Violence in the Family." *Journal of
   Marriage and the Family* 36:13–29.

Straus, Murray A. 1980. "Indexing and Scaling for Social Science Research with
   SPSS." Unpublished manuscript, University of New Hampshire, Durham,
   N.H.

Straus, Murray A. 1985. "The Validity of U.S. States as Units for Sociological Research." Paper presented at the 1985 meeting of the American Sociological
   Association.

Straus, Murray A., and Bruce W. Brown. 1978. *Family Measurement Techniques Abstracts of Published Instruments, 1935–1974*. Rev. ed. Minneapolis: University of
   Minnesota Press.

Straus, Murray A., Richard J. Gelles, and Suzanne K. Steinmetz. 1980. *Behind Closed
   Doors: Violence in the American Family*. New York: Doubleday/Anchor.

Sugarman, David B., and Murray A. Straus 1988. "Indicators of Gender Equality for
   American States and Regions." *Social Indicators Research* 20:229–270.

Svalastoga, Kaare. 1962. "Rape and Social Structure." *Pacific Sociological Review*
   5:48–53.

Theodorson, George A., and Achilles G. Theodorson. 1969. *A Modern Dictionary of
   Sociology*. New York: Thomas Y. Crowell.

Thomas, William I., and Florian Znaniecki. 1927. *The Polish Peasant in Europe and
   America*. Vols. I and II. New York: Knopf.

Thrasher, Frederick M. 1927. *The Gang: A Study of 1,313 Gangs in Chicago.* Chicago: University of Chicago Press.

Tigue, Randall D. B. 1985. "Civil Rights and Censorship—Incompatible Bedfellows." *William Mitchell Law Review* 11:81–125.

Tiryakian, Edward A. 1981. "Sexual Anomie, Social Structure, Societal Change." *Social Forces* 59:1025–1053.

Toby, Jackson. 1957. "Social Disorganization and Stake in Conformity: Complementary Factors in the Predatory Behavior of Hoodlums." *Journal of Criminal Law, Criminology, and Police Science* 64:90–98.

Toby, Jackson. 1966. "Violence and the Masculine Ideal: Some Quantitative Data." *Annals of the American Academy of Political and Social Science* 364:20–27.

Treiman, Donald J., and Patricia A. Roos. 1983. "Sex and Earnings in Industrial Society: A Nine-Nation Comparison." *American Journal of Sociology* 89:612–650.

U.S. Bureau of the Census. 1980. *Social Indicators III: Selected Data on Social Conditions and Trends in the United States.* Washington, D.C.: U.S. Department of Commerce, Bureau of the Census.

U.S. Department of Commerce. 1984. *State Personal Income: Estimates for 1929 to 1982 and a Statement of Sources and Methods.* Washington, D.C.: U.S. Government Printing Office.

Valverde, Mariana, and Lorna Weir. 1985. "Thrills, Chills and the 'Lesbian Threat' or, The Media, the State and Women's Sexuality." Pp. 99–106 in *Women Against Censorship*, ed. Varda Burstyn. Manchester, N.H.: Salem House.

van den Haag, Ernest. 1970. "The Case for Pornography is the Case for Censorship and Vice Versa." Pp. 122–130 in *Perspectives on Pornography*. New York: St. Martin's Press.

Vance, Carole S., ed. 1984. *Pleasure and Danger: Exploring Female Sexuality.* Boston: Routledge & Kegan Paul.

Vance, Carole S. 1986. "The Meese Commission on the Road." *Nation* (August):75–82.

Von Hentig, H. 1951. "The Sex Ratio." *Social Forces* 30:443–449.

Walkowitz, Judith. 1980. *Prostitution and Victorian Society: Women, Class, and the State.* Cambridge: Cambridge University Press.

Wallace, Walter L. 1983. *Principles of Scientific Sociology.* New York: Aldine.

Wallerstein, Judith S., and Joan Berlin Kelly. 1980. *Surviving the Breakup.* New York: Basic Books.

Warr, Mark. 1985. "Fear of Rape Among Urban Women." *Social Problems* 32:238–250.

Webb, Eugene T., Donald T. Campbell, Richard D. Schwartz, Lee Sechrist, and Janet Belew Grove. 1981. *Nonreactive Measures in the Social Sciences.* Boston: Houghton Mifflin.

Webster's Third New International Dictionary, Unabridged. 1976. New York: G. C. Merrian.

Weis, Joseph G. 1983. "Reporting Systems and Methods." Pp. 378–391 in *Encyclopedia of Crime and Justice.* Vol. 1, ed. Sanford H. Kadish. New York: Free Press.

Weis, Kurt, and Sandra S. Borges. 1977. "Victimology and Rape: The Case of the Legitimate Victim." Pp. 35–75 in *The Rape Victim*, ed. Deanna R. Nass. Dubuque, Iowa: Kendall/Hunt.

Weiss, Robert. 1976. "The Emotional Impact of Separation." *Journal of Social Issues* 32:135–145.

West, Robin. 1987. "The Feminist-Conservative Anti-Pornography Alliance and the 1986 Attorney General's Commission on Pornography Report." *American Bar Foundation Research Journal* 12:681–711.

Whyte, Martin K. 1978. *The Status of Women in Preindustrial Societies*. Princeton: Princeton University Press.

Wildmon, Donald E. 1986. *The Case Against Pornography*. Wheaton, Ill.: Victor Books.

Williams, Bernard. 1979. *Report of the Committee on Obscenity and Film Censorship*. London: Her Majesty's Stationery Office. Command 7772.

Williams, Kirk R. 1984. "Economic Sources of Homicide: Reestimating the Effects of Poverty and Inequality." *American Sociological Review* 49:283–289.

Williams, Linda M. 1982. "Rape Laws and Social Structure: A Cross-National Survey." Paper presented at the 1982 meeting of American Society of Criminology, Toronto, Ontario.

Williams, Robin M. Jr. 1970. *American Society: A Sociological Interpretation*. 3rd ed. New York: Alfred A. Knopf.

Williamson, Jeffrey G. 1965. *Regional Inequality and the Process of National Development*. Chicago: University of Chicago Press.

Wilson, James Q., and Richard Hernstein. 1985. *Crime and Human Nature*. New York: Simon and Schuster.

Wilson, W. Cody. 1973. "Pornography: The Emergence of a Social Issue and the Beginning of Psychological Study." *Journal of Social Issues* 29:7–18.

Winick, Charles. 1985. "A Content Analysis of Sexually Explicit Magazines Sold in an Adult Bookstore." *Journal of Sex Research* 21:206–210.

Wirth, Louis. 1940. "Ideological Aspects of Social Disorganization." *American Sociological Review* 5:472–482.

Wolgang, Marvin E. 1978. "Overview of Research into Violent Behavior." House Committee on Science and Technology, Subcommittee on Domestic and International Scientific Planning, Analysis, and Cooperation, Research into Violent Behavior: Sexual Assaults (Hearing, 95th Congress, 2nd Session, January 10–12). Washington, D.C.: Government Printing Office.

Wolfgang, Marvin E., and Franco Ferracuti. 1967. *The Subculture of Violence: Towards an Integrated Theory of Criminology*. London: Tavistock.

Women Against Pornography. 1982. "Slide Show Script." Women Against Pornography, New York, N.Y.

Yaffé, Maurice. 1982. "Therapeutic Uses of Sexually Explicit Material." Pp. 119–150 in *The Influence of Pornography on Behavior*, ed. Maurice Yaffé and Edward C. Nelson. London: Academic Press.

Yeamans, Robin. 1980. "A Political-Legal Analysis of Pornography." Pp. 248–251 in

Take Back the Night: Women on Pornography, ed. Laura Lederer. New York: William Morrow.

Yllo, Kersti, and Murray A. Straus. 1984. "Patriarchy and Violence Against Wives: The Impact of Structural and Normative Factors." *Journal of International and Comparative Social Welfare* 1:16–29.

Zillmann, Dolf, and Jennings Bryant. 1982. "Pornography, Sexual Callousness, and the Trivialization of Rape." *Journal of Communication* 32:10–21.

Zillmann, Dolf, and Jennings Bryant. 1984. "Effects of Massive Exposure to Pornography." Pp. 115–138 in Neil M. Malamuth and Edward Donnerstein, eds. *Pornography and Sexual Aggression*. Orlando, Fla.: Academic Press.

Zuckerman, Marvin. 1971. "Physiological Measures of Sexual Arousal in the Human." *Psychological Bulletin* 75:297–328.

Zurcher, Louis A., and R. George Kirkpatrick. 1976. *Citizens for Decency: Antipornography Crusades as Status Defense*. Austin: University of Texas Press.

INDEX

age standardization, 28
age structure of population, 3, 10, 36, 54–55, 173
aggregation, 22–23
Alaska, 4, 22, 35, 41, 54, 55, 120
alcohol deaths, 134
American Booksellers, Inc. v. Hudnut, 102
Amir, Menachem, 147–48
anomie, 125*n*
anticensorship feminists. *See* censorship; pornography
antipornography groups, 7, 189. *See also* feminist movement; pornography
Archer, Dane, 22, 30
arousal: definitions of, 115
Attorney General's Commission on Pornography, 7–8, 102, 190
Audit Bureau of Circulation, 152

battered women shelters, 18, 203
Berkowitz, Leonard, 192
bivariate correlations, 169
blacks. *See* racial factor in rape
Blalock, Hubert M., 14
Bolen, Kenneth A., 38
Borges, Sandra S., 6
Bowers, William J., 159
British Committee on Obscenity and Film Censorship, 8
Britt, David, 20, 64
Brown, Richard Maxwell, 158
Brownmiller, Susan, 7
Bryant, Jennings, 177
Burger, Warren, 111
Burgess, Ernest W., 125, 128
Burkett, Steven R., 135
Burstyn, Varda, 98–99

Burt, Martha R., 6
Buss shock apparatus, 8

California, 4
capital: access to, 69
capital punishment, 150, 158–59, 166; race and, 159–60
Caplan, Gerald, 193
Carey, James T., 126–27
catharsis theory of media violence, 151
causal inference, 34–35
causal order, 35–36
cause and effect, 34
censorship, 97*n*, 98–99, 189; problems with, 190–92. *See also* pornography
Census Bureau, 32, 33
Check, James V., 192
Chic magazine, 116, 124
Chirocos, Theodore, 55
Christian theology, 95
cities as research units, 21
civil rights, 100–01, 123–24, 190. *See also* censorship; pornography
Clark, L., 61
Club magazine, 116, 124
"collective representations" concept, 149
concentric zone theory of urban growth, 128
Connecticut, 68, 75
Contagious Diseases Acts, 98
control theory, 127–28
corporal punishment, 150
Corporal Punishment Permission Index, 157–58
County and City Data Book, 23
Cox, Martha, 133
Cox, Roger, 133
Crutchfield, Robert D., 132
cultural norms and values, 3, 4*n*

cultural spillover theory, 9, 16, 147–48, 168, 175
cultural support for violence, 5, 9–10, 48; rape and, 166–69, 175, 176–77. *See also* legitimate violence
Curtis, Lynn A., 188

Davis, James A., 34
death sentence. *See* capital punishment
degradation of women, 110, 111, 124
Delaware, 74
delinquency, 128
depression, 64
determinants: defined, 38
District of Columbia, 25–26
Divale, William, 176
divorce, 20, 23, 133, 145
Donnerstein, Edward, 192
Dugan, Lisa, 101
Dunham, H. Warren, 125
Durkheim, Emile, 149, 176
Dworkin, Andrea, 15, 123–24; antipornography legislation, 96–97, 99, 100–01

Easy Rider magazine, 253
ecological fallacy, 12
Economic Equality Index, 71, 73, 85; reliability analysis of, 72T
economic equality/inequality, 3, 5, 10, 23, 36, 92; rape and, 53–54, 64, 173, 182–83, 188, 194, 195; indicators for, 66T, 67–71. *See also* poverty; regional grouping of states; states as research units
employment, 66, 69
English, Diedre, 96
Equal Rights Amendment, 193–94
erotica, feminist, 97n
Evans, Sara, 102
explain: use of term, 37–38

Family Violence Research Program, 3
Faris, Robert E. L., 125, 137
Federal Bureau of Investigation, 3, 4, 27
Feinberg, Joel, 186n
female-headed households, 134–35, 145

"feminine mystique," 63
Feminist Anti-Censorship Taskforce, 97n, 101
feminist movement, 96; working with right-wing groups, 97, 98–99; criticism of antipornography legislation, 101–02
feminist scholarship, 3, 6–7
feminist theories of rape, 5–9. *See also* censorship; patriarchal societies; pornography
Ferracuti, Franco, 175
First Amendment, 97n, 102
Florida, 54
football, 150, 156
Forum magazine, 117n
Fraser, Donald, 100n
Frazer Committee on Pornography and Prostitution (Canada), 8
Friedland, Roger, 20
Furman decision, 159

Gallery magazine, 116, 124
Gartner, Rosemary, 22, 30
Geerkin, Michael R., 132
gender attainment, 61, 62–64
Gender Equality Index, 7, 64–65, 86–87; reliability analysis of, 88, 89T; rape and, 91–92, 93–94
gender equality/inequality, 15, 61, 62–64, 181n; interrelationship of indexes, 84–85; sociodemographic characteristics and, 88–90; social-psychological characteristics and, 90–91; rape and, 92–94, 176–77, 185. *See also* economic equality/inequality; legal equality; political equality; regional grouping of states; states as research units
gender gap, 194
General Social Survey, 90, 165, 168
Genesis magazine, 116, 124
Gibbs, J. P., 20
Gini Index of income inequality, 53–54, 91, 178, 184
Gove, Walter R., 31, 132
governmental use of violence, 150
gun permits, 166
Guns and Ammo magazine, 153

hard-core pornography, 116
Harris, Marvin, 176
Hawaii, 41, 66, 71, 74
Hayner, Norman, 132
Heavy Metal magazine, 153
Hendershot, Gerry E., 134
Hetherington, E. Mavis, 133
Hicks, Alexander, 20
Hill, Robert H., 20, 21
Hindelang, Michael J., 26, 30, 31
Hirschi, Travis, 34, 135
Hollibaugh, Amber, 96
Holmes, Thomas H., 133
homicide, 23, 32, 194
Hunter, Nan, 101
hunting licenses, 150, 157
Hustler magazine, 116, 119, 124

immigration, 10
income inequality. *See* economic
    equality/inequality
independent/dependent variables, 34, 35–
    36
indicators. *See individual theories of rape*
individual-level research, 11–12
industrialization, 10
intent of producer. *See* pornography
Iowa, 4

Jacobs, David, 20, 64
Johnson, Edwin, 20
Johnston, Dennis F., 63*n*, 65*n*

Kansas, 120
Kobrin, Frances E., 134
Kornhauser, Ruth, 125*n*, 127, 136

laboratory research, 8, 186, 190, 192; on
    pornography, 8–9, 115*n*
Lambert, William W., 147
law enforcement, 18, 201–02
LeFree, Gary D., 54*n*
legal equality, 80*T*, 81. *See also* regional
    grouping of states; states as research units
Legal Equality Index, 81, 85; reliability
    analysis of, 85*T*

legitimate violence, 146–48; rape and, 161,
    164, 181–82*n*, 187. *See also* regional
    grouping of states; states as research units
Legitimate Violence Index, 10, 16, 91, 92,
    148–49, 162*T*; indicators for, 150–54,
    156–60; reliability analysis of, 161*T*; rape
    and, 166–67, 168–69
Lerman, Lisa G., 80
lesbian sex magazines, 99*n*
lesbians, 99
LeVine, Robert A., 9
Lewis, D., 61
Livingston, Franci, 80
Loftin, Colin, 20, 21
Long, S. B., 38
lynchings, 158

McConahay, John B., 6
McConahay, Shirley A., 6
macho culture pattern, 186
McKay, Henry D., 125, 128, 131
MacKinnon, Catharine, 15, 123–24; anti-
    pornography legislation, 97, 99, 100–01
macrolevel analyses, 11–12
macrosociological analyses, 4, 11–12, 23, 62
macrosociological control theory, 127–28
magazines. *See* sex magazine circulation; Vi-
    olent Magazine Circulation Index
Maine, 4
Malamuth, Neil M., 192
male domination, 96. *See also* gender
    equality/inequality
males living alone, 134, 145
marital status, 10, 55. *See also* divorce
masculinity: norms of, 61
Mason, Karen Openheim, 62, 88
mass media indicators, 150
media violence: mitigating effects of, 191–
    92
Menzel, Herbert, 11
Messner, Steven, 20, 21, 151, 156
methodological analyses, 184–85, 200–07
Michigan, 75
militarism, 166
militaristic societies, 176
military magazines, 153
Miller v. California, 111, 112

Mississippi, 23, 120
Montana, 157
Morgan, Robin, 96
movie violence, 191
Ms. magazine, 204
multimethod triangulation, 25
multiple regression, 16, 34–39

National Coalition on Television Violence,
   151
National Collegiate Athletic Association,
   156
National Crime Survey, 29, 39, 40
National Guard, 150, 156, 167
National Organization for Women (NOW),
   90, 203–04
Nebraska, 79*T*
Nevada, 4, 18
New Right moralists, 97
New York, 156, 159
Nicholls, Leland, 132
Nielson Index, 151
Nontraditional Sex Roles Attitude Index,
   90*n*
norms of community, 111
North Carolina, 68, 71
North Dakota, 4, 14, 18, 54
Not a Love Story (documentary), 113, 114

objectification of women, 96
O'Brien, Robert M., 26
obscenity, 111, 112
obscenity law, 100, 102–03
O'Connor, Sandra Day, 74
Ogburn, William F., 125
Oui magazine, 116, 124
outliers, 79*n*, 197, 200–01

Park, Robert, 125
Parker, Robert, 20
path analysis, 173–74, 180
patriarchal societies, 61; rape and, 5–7
patriarchy: defined, 63
Pearce, P. L., 132
Penthouse magazine, 116, 117*n*, 124
Playboy magazine, 116, 119, 124, 183
Playgirl magazine, 186

police, 28, 29; violence by, 20; police striking male citizen, 166
Polish Peasant in Europe and America
   (Thomas and Znaniecki), 126
political equality, 73, 74*T*, 75. *See also*
   regional grouping of states; states as research units
Political Equality Index, 79, 85; reliability
   analysis of, 78*T*
Population Reference Bureau, 62
population turnover, 131–32, 135, 145
pornography, 12, 48, 123–24; effect on
   rape, 7–9, 175–76, 177, 185–86, 189;
   feminist controversy over, 95–97; power
   of state and, 98–99; victim ideology and,
   99; concept and definitions of, 100, 102–
   03, 104–10*T*, 111–12; MacKin-
   non/Dworkin legislation against, 100–02;
   intent of producer, 112, 113–14, 115;
   context dimensions, 114–15; state and
   regional differences in, 118–22; violence
   and, 190–91. *See also* Sex Magazine Circulation Index
poverty, 5, 23, 53, 194; feminization of, 69,
   135
predictors: defined, 38
primary prevention of rape: concept of,
   193–95
prostitution, 98

racial factor in rape, 10, 21–22, 23, 34*T*,
   54, 128
racism, 127; capital punishment and, 159–
   60
Rahe, Richard H., 133
rape, 3–4; as instrument of social control,
   6–7, 61; single-cause model, 13; integrated theory of, 16; UCR definition,
   40*n;* theoretical model for, 173, 174*F;*
   integration of theories, 175–77; test of
   model, 177–78, 179*T;* direct effects on,
   180–81, 182*F;* indirect effects on, 183–
   84; social origins of, 185–88; pornography-rape linkage, 188, 189–92; social
   policy and, 188–89; media violence and,
   190, 191–92; primary prevention of, 193–
   95. *See also* cultural support for violence;

gender equality/inequality; pornography; social disorganization

rape crisis centers, 202–03

rape myths, 6, 146, 186, 192

ratio variables, 38–39

regional grouping of states, 43, 44F, 45, 205–06; statistics, 31, 32–33, 34T; economic equality in, 70T, 71; political equality in, 76, 77T; legal equality in, 81, 84T; ranking by gender equality, 87T; sex magazine circulation in, 120T; social disorganization in, 142T; legitimate violence in, 155T, 160–61, 164F

Reiss, Albert J., Jr., 135

Reiss, Ira L., 176

reliability analyses. See individual indexes

religious affiliation, 135–36, 145

reporting rape, 3–4, 19–20, 40, 202–05; underreporting, 27–28, 30–31

research techniques, 13–16; macrolevel analysis, 11–12; theoretical models and multiple regression, 34–39; values and outliers, 79n; path analysis, 173–74; standard errors, 178; unstandardized regression coefficients, 178, 179T; path coefficients, 180, 183; methodological analyses, 184–85, 200–07; standardizing indexes, 197–98. See also regional grouping of states; states as research units

Rhode Island, 68, 157

Rhodes, Albert Lewis, 135

right wing morality, 97, 98, 102, 189

Robinson, W. S., 11

Rooney, John F., Jr., 156

Rubin, Gayle, 96

rural patterns in rape, 45, 46T, 47T

Russell, Diana, 7, 61

Sanday, Peggy Reeves, 6, 147, 176

Scandinavian countries, 194

Schlafly, Phyllis, 97

Scholar and Feminist IX Conference, 96

secular morality and pornography, 95

Selvin, Hanan C., 34

sex education programs, 192

sex magazine circulation, 12, 35, 36, 116T, 117–22; effect on rape, 123–24, 183–84.

See also regional grouping of states; states as research units

Sex Magazine Circulation Index, 9, 15, 91, 92, 95, 116, 122F, 124; reliability analysis, 117T

sex ratio of population, 5, 10, 55

sex roles, 6, 61, 173, 194; nontraditional attitudes, 90–91

sexual equality. See gender equality/inequality

Sexual Liberalism Index, 90n, 204–05

sexual minorities, 99

Shaw, Clifford R., 125, 128, 131

Shooting Times magazine, 153

significance tests, 35

Small, Fred, 190

Smith, D. M., 136–37n

Smith, M. Dwayne, 20

social disorganization, 3–4n, 5, 10, 15–16, 125; concept of, 126–27; constructive effects of, 127, 184, 187; as macrosociological control theory, 127–28; causal model, 136–37, 138F; effect on rape, 144–45, 175–76, 182–83, 195. See also regional grouping of states; states as research units

Social Disorganization (Faris), 137

Social Disorganization Index, 10, 91, 126, 129, 130T, 142, 143T, 144F, 145; reliability analysis, 130T; indicators for, 131–36

social organization variables, 48, 49T, 50T, 51T

social problems: distinguished from social disorganization, 137

social structure, 3–4n

sociodemographic variables, 88, 89T, 90

sociopsychological variables, 90–92

soft-core pornography, 116

specification error, 37

Stack, Steven, 20

Standard Metropolitan Statistical Areas (SMASAs), 21, 22, 23, 51, 52T. See also urban patterns in rape

Stanko, Elizabeth A., 80

Stark, Rodney, 132, 135, 136

states as research units, 14, 17–20; disadvantages of, 20–25; incidence of rape in,

states as research units (*continued*)
40–41, 42*T;* rural and urban patterns of
rape in, 45–47; social organizational variables, 48–49, 51, 53–56; economic
equality in, 66, 67*T,* 68*T;* political equality in, 75*T,* 76*T;* legal equality in, 81, 82–
83*T;* rank in gender equality, 86*T;* sex
magazine circulation in, 118*T,* 119*T,*
121*T;* social disorganization in, 139,
140*T,* 141*T;* legitimate violence in, 152*T,*
153*T,* 154*T,* 160–61, 163*T*
Statistical Package for the Social Sciences
(SPSS), 71
status attainment, 93
status equality, 93
status of women, 28, 36, 61, 62–64, 176–
77, 184. *See also* gender
equality/inequality
Steele, Lisa, 191
Straus, Murray A., 14, 23
structural analysis, 3*n*
subculture of violence theory, 146
suicide, 20, 134, 176
Supreme Court, 102, 112, 158, 159

television violence, 150–51
testing models, 37
Texas, 156
Thomas, W. I., 125, 126–27
Thrasher, Frederick M., 125
time series studies, 186, 190
Tiryakian, Edward A., 175, 183
tourism and crime, 132–33, 145
Triandis, Leigh Minturn, 147
tribal societies, 6, 9, 63, 147, 176, 184

unemployment, 10, 12, 55–56, 182–83,
188. *See also* economic equality/inequality
Uniform Crime Reports (UCR), 14, 17, 19,
39, 43*T;* data on rape, 26–32; criticisms
of, 30–32
uniformity in United States, 17–18, 21–22
urban patterns in rape, 45, 46*T,* 47*T*

urbanization, 10, 36, 48, 173, 182–83, 188,
194–95

values, 65*n,* 79*n*
Valverde, Mariana, 99
Vance, Carole, 101
victim ideology, 99, 100
violence, 3–4, 7, 124, 195; pornography
and, 8, 110; violent attitudes, 91; against
women, 100, 101–02; nonsexual, 123;
defined, 148*n;* socially approved violent
activities, 150; punching male strangers,
166; rape and, 191–92. *See also* cultural
spillover theory; cultural support for violence; legitimate violence
Violence Approval Index, 16, 165–69, 186,
187
Violent Magazine Circulation Index, 152–
54, 157
Violent Television Viewing Index, 151

Walkowitz, Judith, 98
Ward, Sally, 38
Weir, Lorna, 99
Weis, Kurt, 6
West Virginia, 66, 71
White, Mervin, 135
Whyte, Martin K., 88
Williams, L. M., 80
Williams, Robin, 3*n*
Willis, Ellen, 96
Wisconsin, 79*n*
Wolf, Margery, 147
Wolfgang, Marvin E., 175
women. *See* status of women *and individual
theories of rape*
Women Against Pornography Slide Show,
113
Wyoming, 71

Zillmann, Dolf, 177
Znaniecki, Florian, 125, 126–27